A Study of *Time* in Indian Philosophy

A Study of *Time* in Indian Philosophy

Anindita Niyogi Balslev

SINCE 1903

MOTILAL BANARSIDASS
PUBLISHING HOUSE • DELHI
Email: naraina@mlbd.in • Website: www.mlbd.in
@mlbdofficial
+91 89 2999 9000

4th Reprint: Delhi, ***2022***
Third edition with a new preface and an appendix, 2009
First published by Otto Harrassowitz, Wiesbaden, 1983

ISBN: 978-93-5760-493-2 (Hardcover)
ISBN: 978-93-90064-08-3 (Paperback)

Printed & Published by
Rajendra P Jain *for*
Motilal Banarsidass Publishing House
A-44, Naraina Industrial Area, Phase I,
New Delhi–110 028 (INDIA)
Email: naraina@mlbd.in Website: www.mlbd.in
Tel.: (+91-11)4751 1592
Showroom:
4637/20, F-2, Hari Sadan, First Floor, Ansari Road, Daryaganj
Delhi–110 002 (Opp. Fire Station) ***Tel.*** : (+91-11)4559 7999

This work is dedicated with profound respect to the memory of my beloved father Saradindu K. Niyogi

Contents

Preface to the third edition

It is a pleasure for me that a third edition of *A Study of Time in Indian Philosophy* is now ready to go to press. It is indeed a remarkable fact that although time is often depicted as an enigma, it nevertheless retains a place of central interest in multiple academic disciplines, be that in the domaine of humanities, science or religious studies. Indeed, the theme remains a subject of continued intellectual scrutiny and concerned readers keep exploring the range of views held on this topic.

Since the second edition of this book, published by Munshiram Manoharlal Publishers, New Delhi, was sold out in 2006, there has been many enquiries about it. The Indian publisher Motilal Banarsidass deserves my thanks for bringing out this new edition and for making it again available to students and scholars interested in the areas of Indian and comparative philosophy, culture-studies, religious studies as well as in science-religion dialogue.

Based on original sanskrit sources, this book seems to have succeeded in showing that the treatment of time in Indian thought is not exclusively a matter of interest for indologists but for anyone who is curious to learn about this topic from the history of ideas in the global context. Apart from referring to and analyzing the impact of a wide variety of views on time that are documented in the highly articulate traditions of ancient India - the importance of which, unforunately, was previously underplayed in philosophical renditions as well as in culture studies dealing with the Indian conceptual world - this study has also demonstrated in a separate section how one can gradually construe a common frame of enquiry by bringing in ideas from the European philosophical literature on time. This has led to a deeper appreciation of the cognitive approaches associated with secular as well as religious traditions of thought cutting across cultures. In that process, the book has drawn attention to the abuses of metaphorical designations of conceptual interpretations of time as cyclic and linear. In the preface to the second edition, included here, I have discussed briefly the issue of how these misleading metaphorical designations cause havoc in cross-cultural settings and in the context of encounter of world religions.

Some of my readings and observations made in this book have in the course of years led to many discussions since it was first published by Otto Harrassowitz, Wiesbaden, Germany (1983). Consequently, I conceived and co-edited a volume entitled, *Religion and Time* (1993, E. J. Brill, The Netherlands). This collection of essays was particularly deemed to be fruitful as a preparation for an authentic encounter of world religions. The paper that I contributed to this volume viz.

'Time and the Hindu Experience' is reprinted here in the appendix with permission from the aforesaid publisher.

Given that disciplinary boundaries are generally recognized in academic endeavors, it is important to recall that the roots of conceptual preoccupation with the question of time can be traced back, both within the frame of Indian and Western thought, to a period when a clear-cut disciplinary boundary between scientific, philosophical and religious thinking was yet to be drawn. A perusal of the global history of ideas shows the differences in the interpretations of time-experience in the theory-making effort. These differences, as expressed in diverse traditions, call for a careful examination especially because the theme of time is vital not only for the study of nature but also for that of cultures. It is specially noteworthy that, as history of Indian philosophy amply demonstrates, the concern for time has played an important role not in the context of nature entailing physical processes but also as well in the attempts to explore a range of issues including the large theme of consciousness. It is therefore crucial to make an accurate assessment of the metaphors of cyclicity and linearity that have been utilized in natural and human sciences as well as in the discourses of religious traditions so that their significance is properly grasped.

To summarise, it may be observed that the complexities of time-experience need to be appreciated in physical, cosmological as well as in metaphysical and soteriological contexts. In the long run, it seems to me, that attempts to achieve a conceptual transparency through open discussions regarding the multiple dimensions of this complex theme form part of the ultimate striving for obtaining deeper insights into our own time-bound existence.

Preface to the second edition

I write this new preface for my book, entitled *A Study of Time in Indian Philosophy*, with a deep sense of satisfaction that is derived from engaging in a work that does not end with the writing of a single monograph. My endeavor to uncover the distinctly different views on time in the Indian philosophical traditions has led me to appreciate the rich, multiple dimensions of this large theme that are manifested in the network of ideas constituting the core of philosophical, religious and scientific thinking across cultures.

This monograph was first published, now fifteen years ago, by the German publisher Otto Harrassowitz, Wiesbaden in 1983. Since then, the book has been much reviewed and discussed. However, it has been now quite sometime—since the first edition was sold out—the book has not been available in the market. Although many have enquired about a new edition, especially an Indian edition, I have been unable to attend to that task due to various other commitments that kept me busy. I am indeed pleased that the Indian publisher Munshiram Manoharlal Publishers, New Delhi, has taken the initiative to bring out this new edition.

Time, being a multi-dimensional issue, is of interest to a wide range of disciplines belonging to both humanistic and natural sciences. Since the first publication of this study, I have continued my research work concerning this large theme and have become more aware of its multi-disciplinary and intercultural dimensions. Consequently, I feel that my intellectual involvement with this topic has only increased over the years. Moreover, I have been invited to deliver a number of talks in international forums and in this process have not only gained deeper appreciation of the bearing that philosophical thinking on time has for the Indian culture as a whole but have also learnt more about this multi-faceted problem from scholars who work in fields that are different from mine. In this connection, mention may be made that my further contributions concerning time and related issues have been published in various journals and are available in print.[1]

These days when attempts are being made to initiate a conversation among science, philosophy and religion, I am very pleased that this book has been looked upon by scholars to be useful in that context. The major streams of Indian philosophical thought have flown through a vast territory and have given rise to an opulent diversity in the interpretations of time-experience. These reflections form a significant part of the philosophico-religious as well as scientific narratives that

1 For references cf. n 1 of my paper entitled 'Time and the Hindu experience' in *Religion and Time*, edited by Anindita N. Balslev and J.N. Mohanty, E.J. Brill, Leiden, 1995.

have encircled the global history of ideas. As author, I am indeed grateful that my work has not been considered to be of interest only and exclusively for the indologists.

During the years preceding the actual writing of this book I struggled strenuously in order to obtain a broad, comprehensive view of the Indian philosophical scene that forms the necessary background for a study of the various conceptual models of time. As I scanned through primary and secondary sources with the goal of discerning the overt and subtle implications of this diversity in interpreting time-experience, it gradually became clear to me how time as a theme plays a crucial role in the making of distinct cultural traditions. Myths and symbols, philosophical views and religious ideas concerning time endow a distinctive flavor to a cultural traditions as a whole which is singularly of its own.

It seems to me that one of the outstanding characteristics of the conceptual world of India, which has been consequential to the thought traditions outside of her geo-political boundary as well, stems from the varied expressions of her profound time-consciousness. This is exemplified not only in philosophical texts but also in cosmology and mythology as well. Indeed amazing is the manner in which the ramifications of such ideas about time are incorporated into the Puranic narratives. The philosophical schools are of course fully aware of the implications of the diverse views about time. The network of ideas woven by specific schools of philosophy not only combines distinctly different views of time with various contending notions of creation and annihilation, being and becoming, space and causality, etc., but also puts forward notions concerning timelessness and eternity. It is a philosophical vista that inspires awe and demands that it is comprehended in its complexity. Indeed, I am tempted to remark that a careful study of this important theme in the context of Indian traditions augments one's sense for philosophical acuity, as one notices the conceptual strategies that lie embedded in the diverse attempts to explore time-experience along different lines. We begin to perceive more and more poignantly why the Brahmanical tradition, for example, for which the idea of Ātman is of pivotal concern cannot but reject a position for which the distinction between time and being [more precisely, the moment and the momentary] is seen merely as a linguistic convention. Thus, it is a kind of an intellectual adventure to investigate why—despite the fact that the Brahmanical tradition has given rise to a wide variety of conceptual models regarding time—a conceptual space is maintained by all the Brahmanical systems for an ontological category that remains outside the influence of time [***kālaprabhāva-mukta***]. Such an investigation unveils primarily the Brahmanical philosophical conviction that the Ātman or self cannot be sublated and discloses the argumentations supporting that claim. However variously conceived by the different schools within that tradition, attempts are made to demonstrate why time can by no means negate the immutability of the Ātman or the self and in which sense the latter as a category retains its foundational character. Thus, the theme of time can be seen as vital not only for a study of nature i.e., for analyzing matter, space, causality etc. but also for a number of issues connected with the idea of self and consciousness. These

Preface to the first edition

"There is no cognition in this world where time is not manifest"[1]—thus goes the famous saying. It seems evident that any attempt at a philosophical interpretation of human existence—be it ultimately religious or secular in import—will eventually have to face the problem of time. Being a central issue, the multi-faceted problem of time can be explored in various directions. Thus it is found to be a proper subject for an inter-disciplinary study. In recent years efforts have already been made towards this.[2] Again, the intercultural perspective of a study of the problem of time is by no means insignificant as it provides a common theme which is central to philosophical investigations, viewed globally. Moreover, for the question of the encounter of religions, it is highly important that the theological considerations which operate behind the various doctrines of creation are brought into full focus with their implications for the problem of time as well as their understanding of the transcendent as timeless. The impact of the study of time in this direction is not merely of historical interest. It has its bearing on the present day meeting of cultures as well. It is pointed out that a principal clue for understanding a culture-pattern lies in a proper grasping of its theological foundations. It is even said that ideologies which claim to break away from the theological framework of a given culture yet may be found to bear characteristics of the same. In all cases, however, a philosophy of time remains an indispensable and an integral part of a coherent picture of human existence.

The spectrum of views about time that has emerged in the philosophies of India, is thus of interest also for an appraisal of Indian religions as well as for an understanding of Indian culture in general.

I take this opportunity to record my thanks due to B.B. Bhattacharya, Reader, Sanskrit Department, Jadavpur University, for the fruitful discussions pertaining to the analysis of the relevant Sanskrit texts used for this work. I would also like to thank the Danish Research Council for the Humanities for providing support for this project during the years 1977 and 1978 as well as for a grant covering a substantial part of the printing cost. This support has enabled me to carry out the research both in Denmark and in India, utilising the library facilities at Statsbiblioteket, Aarhus, and the National Library, Calcutta. Finally I want to thank Lissi Daber for her excellent work in typing the manuscript.

1 *Na so'sti pratyaya loke yatra kālo na bhāsate*—ascribed to the school of Mīmāṃsā, source unidentified.

2 *The Study of Time*, vols. 1–4 [102].

Indian philosophers is a matter that can keep a scholar engaged for many years. This book contains some of these stimulating exchanges.

While sharing the story of the Brahmanical and Buddhist reflections, one also becomes aware of the conceptual space for one more distinct tradition of thought viz. Jainism. It was for the Jaina tradition to take up the challenge and arrive at a position where the idea of an unchanging core of reality could be combined with that of the changing aspects of ourselves and things around us, providing a logic in support of such a position.

In fact, these basic philosophical preferences have deservedly earned the Brahmanical, Buddhist and the Jaina traditions the designations of Ātmavāda, Anātmavāda and Anekāntavāda respectively.

An effort to understand the great variety of views concerning time that have emerged in the history of Indian thought demands that we grasp the significance of these views not simply in isolation but in relation to the other major concepts such as that of being and non-being, space and causality etc. that have emerged in each of these traditions of thought. This is also why comprehending a specific notion of time in depth calls for taking into account both the expository and the polemical aspects that are documented in the relevant literature. All these shed light on the amalgam of observations and reasonings that have gone into the making of specific theories and how such theories are philosophically defended in the face of attack from their adversaries. Through this process of intellection, one deepens one's understanding regarding the central role that the theme of time plays in a given conceptual system and what makes it impossible to substitute one view by another in a given network of ideas without damaging the identity and distinctness of that specific schools of thought. The reader will come across adequate examples that support these observations.

It seems obvious that in any appraisal of the Indian conceptual experience of time, all these details needs to be considered. Unfortunately, what has been in vogue in an intercultural context can be described not only as an oversimplified picture of the Indian philosophical scenario but a projection of an entirely distorted one. It is commonplace to come across opinions that ascribe a 'cyclic' view of time to the Indian culture. I have brought this misleading metaphorical designation of 'cyclic time' to the attention of the reader in the last chapter of this book. I have also repeated this tirelessly, with more detailed arguments, on many occasions. I believe that I have succeeded in uprooting this distorted view in certain circles and hope that a wider distribution of this book will promote that cause.

At this point, it is amusing to share with my readers the circumstances that led me to examine the theme of time-metaphors and how that eventually has inspired me to take up 'cross-cultural conversation[4] as an indispensable program of studies. During the years when I was looking into the Sanskritic philosophical tradition in order to make a study of the principal conceptual models of time that developed in the course of history of Indian thought, the question that was most

4. Cf. *Cross Cultural Conversation* edited by Anindita N. Balslev, Cultural Criticism series, AAR, Scholars Press, 1996.

frequently posed by my interlocutors was why the Indian conceptual world projects a 'cyclic' view of time. At first I took that as a populistic query but I was intrigued by the question and wanted to search for the reasons why this was assumed to be a dominant feature of the Indian conceptual world. As I began enquiring how this idea has received so wide a publicity, I was amazed to come across in the writings of culture-historians (such as Arnold Toynbee and others) and theologians (such as Paul Tillich and others) as well as of some anthropologists, all claiming that the Indo-Hellenic time is 'cyclic' as opposed to the Judaeo-Christian understanding of 'linear' time.

As I have discussed these issues elsewhere, I will not recapitulate the arguments here.[5] However, let me restate briefly that this unwarranted use of time-metaphors has created serious obstacles for cross-cultural understanding and has blocked interreligious exchanges What is even more disturbing in the context of these improper metaphorical designations of cultural experience of time, is to note how the expressions 'linear' and 'cyclic' have gradually ceased to be simple time-metaphors and have come to be associated with such concepts as that of history, that of progress and even that of salvation. What is needed is a creative conversation, which by consciously avoiding these age-old clichés can make room for fresh exchanges enabling the participants to appreciate the inner dynamism of alternative modes of thinking about this multi-faceted problem.

Finally, let me observe that if no major culture is monolithic, no major philosophical tradition—as the global history of ideas bears witness to—cherishes an unanimous view about time. This should be evident not only from a careful perusal of the philosophical accounts in the Indian context, but also from a study of time in western philosophy. Just as in the history of Indian thought one comes across a variety of views, similarly western thought discloses a spectrum of views about this fundamental topic, such as the notion of absolute time, time as a relational concept, time as process and so on and so forth. Thus, seen in a cross-cultural context, this wide range of interpretations of time-experience expose to our critical gaze the various strata of complexities pertaining to cosmological, metaphysical, epistemological and soteriological enquiries.

What is also of great importance in this connection is to note, that the early formulations of philosophers and theologians are not merely of antiquarian interest, these are still forces to reckon with as these have strongly shaped the contemporary conceptual worlds in which we are participating and struggling to comprehend the *raison d'être* of plurality of traditions.

Given that human reflections on the theme of time has a very long history—perhaps longer than most other themes—taking place already in a period when there was no well-drawn line demarcating the areas between philosophy and science, it has been very unfortunate that the major philosophical and theological traditions have often been set up against each other because of their supposedly distinct cultural experience of time.

5 See my paper entitled 'Reflections on Time in Indian Philosophy: with Comments on So-called Cyclic Time' in *The Study of Time V*, edited by Fraser et al., University of Massachusetts Press, Amherst, 1986.

The project to understand and appreciate traditions of thought in and through their respective time-models is a fascinating enterprise. The diversity of views is to be noted and registered not only while distinguishing one tradition from another but must be recognized within the frame of a given major tradition that splits itself into various schools and sub-schools. As one becomes keenly aware of the internal differences that are there with regard to time, it also enables us to detect where lies the basic thrust of a specific tradition despite its internal variations.

I am persuaded to think, as I have repeatedly said on many occasions, that more involvement with these issues, both inside and outside the academia, can considerably improve the present state of crisis in interreligious communication. A repetition of clichés only vitiates the possibility of exploring the overall messages of traditions of thought. If this book—restrained to a modest size—can be seen as a contribution in that direction, I will consider all the pains that I have taken to sort out from the vast material that I had collected to be worthwhile.

Preface to the first edition

"There is no cognition in this world where time is not manifest"[1]—thus goes the famous saying. It seems evident that any attempt at a philosophical interpretation of human existence—be it ultimately religious or secular in import—will eventually have to face the problem of time. Being a central issue, the multi-faceted problem of time can be explored in various directions. Thus it is found to be a proper subject for an inter-disciplinary study. In recent years efforts have already been made towards this.[2] Again, the intercultural perspective of a study of the problem of time is by no means insignificant as it provides a common theme which is central to philosophical investigations, viewed globally. Moreover, for the question of the encounter of religions, it is highly important that the theological considerations which operate behind the various doctrines of creation are brought into full focus with their implications for the problem of time as well as their understanding of the transcendent as timeless. The impact of the study of time in this direction is not merely of historical interest. It has its bearing on the present day meeting of cultures as well. It is pointed out that a principal clue for understanding a culture-pattern lies in a proper grasping of its theological foundations. It is even said that ideologies which claim to break away from the theological framework of a given culture yet may be found to bear characteristics of the same. In all cases, however, a philosophy of time remains an indispensable and an integral part of a coherent picture of human existence.

The spectrum of views about time that has emerged in the philosophies of India, is thus of interest also for an appraisal of Indian religions as well as for an understanding of Indian culture in general.

I take this opportunity to record my thanks due to B.B. Bhattacharya, Reader, Sanskrit Department, Jadavpur University, for the fruitful discussions pertaining to the analysis of the relevant Sanskrit texts used for this work. I would also like to thank the Danish Research Council for the Humanities for providing support for this project during the years 1977 and 1978 as well as for a grant covering a substantial part of the printing cost. This support has enabled me to carry out the research both in Denmark and in India, utilising the library facilities at Statsbiblioteket, Aarhus, and the National Library, Calcutta. Finally I want to thank Lissi Daber for her excellent work in typing the manuscript.

1 *Na so'sti pratyaya loke yatra kālo na bhāsate*—ascribed to the school of Mīmāṃsā, source unidentified.

2 *The Study of Time*, vols. 1–4 [102].

Introduction

The concept of time presents a challenge to a wide variety of disciplines, which fall within the domain of the humanistic as well as the natural sciences. Accordingly, many different methods and lines of approach have been followed in the investigation and treatment of this fundamental problem.

History of ideas bears witness to the central role, that is played by the problem of time in the philosophical and theological traditions across the cultural boundaries. Moreover, the endeavours to interpret the enigmatic character of the time-experience have given rise to a multiplicity of views within each tradition. An attempt at a global view, focusing on certain aspects of the wide variety of conceptual models of time, is made in the last chapter of this work. This intercultural perspective not only provides an interesting background scene for the study of time in Indian philosophy, but also brings into focus some of the similar features that the universal struggle of the philosophical intellect with this problem has given rise to. Thus, for example, one finds controversies in the different cultures regarding such central issues as whether time is real or unreal, whether it is a conceptual constrution or is an objective category, etc.

The study of time in Indian philosophy is rewarding in many ways. It makes one aware of the rich and varied philosophical speculations about the problem from the earliest phase of its history.

Going through the forest of the early sources of the Indian tradition, one comes across a host of ideas touching upon different aspects of the problem of time scattered in the form of myths and allegories. These ideas are rich in suggestion and might even be said to anticipate some later theories but were not themselves fullfledged views about time. Mention should be made of such popular ideas as are contained in the *Purāṇas*, the epic *Mahābhārata* and the *Atharva Veda*.

The *Atharva Veda* contains hymns dedicated to time.[1] Here time is described as that which is in contact with all that there is, as that which regulates and controls all. Some lines describe time to be the cause of the origin, maintenance

1 cf. 3/2/6/3/8, 19/6/53/7/3-10 and 19/6/53/8/1-5 of *Atharvaveda Saṃhitā* with the commentary of Sāyanācārya [1].

and destruction of the universe. Some ascribe to time the status of God, hailing it to be the ultimate, the all-powerful principle.

The idea of time as power of the Absolute is ancient and can be seen worked out in the integral philosophy of Kashmir Saivism.[2]

In the *Purāṇas* one finds the idea of the four *yugas*[3]*-satya, tretā, dvāpara* and kali-along with that of the world-cycles, which provide a vision of vast expanse of time in astronomical terms. Thus the *Brahmāṇda Purāṇa* dramatically describes the four *yugas* as the four faces of time which are said to create and destroy all beings. Again, the idea that the solar motion is the basis for time-divisions is found in the *Agni Purāṇa* (chapter 122).

In the *Mahābhārata* one comes across the well-known simile where time is described as the wire-holder (*sūtradhāra*)[4] of the universe, permitting events and preventing them from taking place. Time is thus responsible for the order and sequence of events.

The *Śvetāśvatara Upaniṣad* (1/2) refers to the view which held time to be the cause of everything.[5]

Examples can be multiplied. But before we go deeper into the matter, let us note the significance of the word *kāla* which in Sanskrit stands for time. The etymological root of the term *kāla* is √*kal* which means to count (cf. Latin *calculo*).[6] Thus according to some the word *kāla* signifies that which can count up the age of all.

The root √*kal* also signifies 'to devour', which leads to the ascription of the destructive power to time. Thus, *kāla* also refers to death.

The different nuances of the word *kāla* can be seen in the *Bhagavad-Gītā* in the various utterances of Lord Kṛṣṇa.

Thus, in *Bhagavadgītā* X/30:

– *kālaḥ kalayatām aham* –
'Of calculators I am Time'.

Again in the same work, XI 32

Kālo'smi, lokakṣayakṛt –
'Time am I world-destroying'.

2 cf. *kāla* as *kañcuka* in the Pratyabhijñā philosophy.

3 world ages.

4 i.e. stage-manager.

5 *Kālakāraṇavāda*.

6 *Sanskrit-English dictionary* by Monier Williams [104].

Here the supreme spirit as the destroyer of the universe is seen as a personification of the destructive principle, which is identified with time.

The idea of time as the Supreme Principle or Lord, found in the *Atharva Veda* and in *Viṣṇu Purāṇa*, can also be found in the *Bhagavadgītā* X/33:

– *aham evā'kṣayaḥ kālo* –
'I also am imperishable time'.[7]

Bhartṛhari, the great grammarian philosopher, also focuses on the etymological meaning of *kāla* through illuminating imageries and metaphors. Thus, we read in his *Vākyapadīya* (3/9/14) –

»By means of activities similar to the turning of the water-wheel the eternal and all-pervasive Time turns out (*kalayati*) all the fragments (*kalāh* = objects) and thus acquires the name of *kāla* (time)« [75]. So much for the etymological meaning of the word *kāla*.

In this work, however, we have selected for our study the well-formulated views about time that have emerged in the history of Indian philosophy. An attempt is made, first and foremost, to give a systematic presentation of the distinct conceptual models concerning time, which allow for a philosophical scrutiny and appraisal.

A careful perusal of the philosophies of India, as this study amply bears witness to, discloses a spectrum of views about time. The philosophical contrasts of ideas involved in the different theories are indeed fascinating. On the one hand, there is the view which emphasises the reality of time mentioning its ontological properties e.g. all-pervasiveness, etc.; on the other hand, there is the view which dialectically rejects the ontological reality of time pointing to its phenomenal character. Again, we find the view of time as indivisible, ubiquitous and unitary, as opposed to the theory which vehemently holds time to be essentially discrete, all ideas of time-continuum being merely a conceptual construction. Moreover, the differences even amongst the various theories of time as discrete disclose a variety of philosophical patterns. As an example of such observations based on the present investigation, we refer to the section VII (ii), 'A Comparative Note on the Concept of Instant'.

More significant, as this study points to, is to note the drastic consequence of a specific view of time on a given philosophical scheme which aims at interconnecting the major concepts in a systematic, harmonious whole. Thus, the impact of a specific view about time on such major issues as those of being, non-being, creation and causality are noted in different sections of this work.

7 The translations of quotations from *Bhagavadgītā* are from Radhakrishan [2].

To give a major example of how through a radical formulation of time as instant one arrives at a novel conception of being, reference could be made to the Buddhist doctrine of 'being as instantaneous'. Again, the impact of this doctrine as destructive of Brahmanical metaphysics is evident and accounts for the wholesale attack on this idea by all Brahmanical schools of thought. For comments on this subject see section VII (iv) on 'Being and Time'.

Based on the original Sanskrit texts as well as important secondary literature, an effort is made to expose the principal contending views about time, which can be detected in the conceptual structures that have have emerged in Brahmanism, Buddhism, and Jainism. For the purpose of focusing on the major as well as subtle differences of the views and their implications for other important philosophical issues, the historical documents of the polemics between the schools have been collected and used when necessary and relevant. In the case of certain important schools, where preoccupation with time does not take the form of a direct treatment of a distinct philosophical problem, it is nevertheless found to be implicit in the general structure of their metaphysical thinking. An attempt is then made to see the significance of their stand regarding time within the compass of the entire framework of the system or on the basis of the record of their rejection of an opponent's position.

Observations and comments are made in separate sub-sections of the earlier expository chapters of the book. The last two chapters are, however, more exclusively devoted to an overall view within the panorama of Indian philosophy as well as to a global view of the problem with an inter-cultural perspective. Chapter VII contains reflections resulting from our study. It is emphasised that the problem of time is central and decisive in the history of the development of philosophical thought in India. Chapter VIII contains an outline of some of the major philosophical interpretations of time found in the history of Western philosophy and theology. An attempt has been made to throw light on the notion of the so-called cyclic time in the context of Greek and Indian philosophy. Finally, the problem of time is seen as a bridge for an encounter between different theological structures.

General background

A survey of philosophical and theological thinking, pertaining to the problem of time, reveals a continued search for greater clarification and understanding, involving different approaches and methods, and consequently resulting in widely divergent philosophical formulations.

It is evident that a study of such a fundamental problem as that of time cannot be isolated and disconnected from other major philosophical issues of a specific system in a given tradition. It is interrelated and interwoven with such basic concepts as those of being and becoming, change and causality, creation and annihilation.

The present endeavour to study the problem of time in Indian philosophy emphasises the fact that the significance of the different views on time, that have emerged in the course of its history, can be grasped only in the framework of the general scheme of thought – in all its metaphysical, logical and epistemological aspects – of each particular philosophical school.

This calls for an understanding of the general conceptual structures of the principal schools of Indian philosophy as a context for our specific study. As the investigation proceeds, it will be clear to what extent the basic metaphysical intuitions of the different schools, supported by their epistemology and logic, provide for alternative conceptual models which shape their respective views regarding the problem of time.

We shall, therefore, attempt to give a broad outline of the major streams of the Indian philosophical tradition, of which the principal ones are Brahmanism and Buddhism and the relatively minor one is Jainism. The historical perspective of the study is meant to take account of the fundamental conceptual patterns of each of these philosophico-religious traditions and is not intended for a chronological record of ideas.

The predominating source of speculative ideas in pre-Buddhistic India is the Brahmanical tradition. It has its roots in the *Vedas* and the *Upanisads.* The fundamental intuitions contained in these scriptures – which are considered by the tradition as revealed – form the very basis on which is built the whole edifice of Brahmanism. We shall leave aside here the fascinating transition from the early Vedic to Upaniṣadic thought and the development of ideas that took place in the process of intense philosophical quest of the Upaniṣadic seers. However, let us take note of the most important idea, emerging from the *Upaniṣads*, which pervades the entire Brahmanical philosophy, viz. that of the identical, immutable reality underlying all change and becoming. This is the core of the *ātma*-doctrine of the *Upaniṣads*, which sets the pattern of all subsequent philosophisations on the part of those who carried on this tradition historically down the centuries, long after the Vedic period.

For the purpose of the present investigation we shall focus our attention exclusively on the stages of philosophical thinking crystallised into well-formulated schools of philosophy. The six principal schools that developed in the Brahmanical tradition are Sāṅkhya, Yoga, Nyāya, Vaiśeṣika, Pūrva-Mīmāṃsā and Uttara-Mīmāṃsā. Remaining faithful to the basic intuition of the *Upaniṣads* – the reality of the immutable Ātman – they venture to formulate and explain the phenomenon of change in diverse ways. In their effort to interpret and systematise the Upaniṣadic ideas these schools developed different metaphysical structures.

Historically the oldest school, Sāṅkhya is also from the philosophical point of view a system, with reference to which other systems could be fruitfully studied. It sets up a dualistic metaphysics, tracing the whole course of the universe to an interplay of two ultimate principles – Puruṣa and Prakṛti. Puruṣa is the unchanging principle of consciousness, Prakṛti being the ever-changing principle of matter. The Yoga system shares the Sāṅkhya metaphysical attitude, but whereas the latter is atheistic, the former is theistic. The inherent tension present in the Sāṅkhya metaphysical idea of two reals led eventually to the rise of the pluralistic metaphysics of the Nyāya-Vaiśeṣika schools on the one hand and to the development of the philosophy of non-dualism via the monistic metaphysics of the Uttara-Mīmāṃsā on the other. In opposition to the *ātmavāda* of the *Upaniṣads* emerges the *anātmavāda* of Buddhism, the second principal philosophico-religious tradition of India. Buddhism, unlike Brahmanism, does not owe its origin to any sacred, revealed scripture. The tradition owes its inspiration entirely to the experience and teaching of Gotama, the Buddha,[1] the enlightened one.

The Buddhist tradition stands out as a denial of the *ātmavāda* tradition, which expressed the nature of the ultimate real as unchanging and unchangeable. It is the negation of the *ātmavāda*, i.e. the substance-view of reality, which forms the very basis of Buddhist philosophy. Accordingly, the tradition is termed *anātmavāda*. It sets up an altoghether different metaphysics, where the ultimate principle is conceived as dynamic. Everything is in a state of flux. There is absolutely nothing which remains identical and immutable. Change is total. Thus, at the very point of departure it is clear, that the substance-view (*ātmavāda*) and the

1 The birth of Buddha is generally accepted to be around 560 B.C.

modal view (*anātmavāda*) are entirely opposed to one another in their approaches. One has a static view, the other a dynamic view – one champions the doctrine of soul, the other stands out for its no-soul doctrine. Brahmanism and Buddhism, thus set apart by their respective metaphysical standpoints, developed in harmony with their original intuitions in the course of centuries, giving rise to many schools and sub-schools.

We have mentioned briefly the six chief schools of the Brahmanical tradition. The entire history of Indian Buddhism, as it is known to us, can be broadly divided into three periods,[2] which are known as »the three swingings of the wheel of law« (*dharmacakrapravarttana*).[3] The first period is characterised by its pluralistic and realistic trend. The no-soul, no-substance theories dominate early Buddhism. As in the external world, so in consciousness, no stable, immutable element is to be found. But an important idea which emerges here is, that this process of perpetual becoming is not just haphazard, accidental, but governed by the law of »dependent origination« (*pratītya-samutpāda*). This doctrine is of such enormous significance, that some scholars go so far as to say that the entire history of Buddhism can be said to be nothing but an attempt to understand this doctrine of *pratītya-samutpāda* – the Buddhist theory of causality, which is intimately connected with the doctrine of momentariness. The early period is known as Hināyana Buddhism, the most important schools being Theravāda, Vaibhāṣika and Sautrāntika. The second phase of Buddhism saw the rise of the Mādhyamika school. In contrast with the first period, which denied the substance but accepted the reality of elements, this phase denies also the elements (*dharma-nairātmya*). The doctrine of *pratītya-samutpāda* is interpreted in new light – interdependence shows the unreality of the elements. The emergence of the idea of two truths (*saṁvṛti-satya* and *paramārtha-satya* i.e. empirical and ultimate) is characteristic of the period. The last phase of Buddhism is embodied in the idealistic philosophy of the Vijñānavāda school. It maintains the absolute reality of consciousness as against the Mādhyamika thesis, that consciousness and object are relative to each other and therefore both are unreal. The Buddhist idea of time will be carefully studied in and through a critical exposition of the doctrine of momentariness in its various versions, as it appeared in the three phases of the history of Indian Buddhism.

A study of the development of the Brahmanical and Buddhist schools discloses a fascinating history of philosophical exchanges which shaped and stimulated their growth. They reacted against and were influenced by each other while

2 cf. Stcherbatsky [63] p. 3-13; according to this author, the three periods are, roughly speaking, of a duration of 500 years each, beginning 500 B.C.

3 cf. Bu-Ston [58] vol 2, p. 51-56.

steadfastly holding on to their original intuitions. The tension between Brahmanism and Buddhism, created by their opposite points of departure, resulted in a fascinating and fruitful philosophical development. The Nyāya-Buddhist disputes, for example, which went on for centuries, contributed immensely to the growth of logic. The profound influence, that Vedānta and late Buddhism exerted on one another, is also evident.

In contrast to the *ātmavāda* and *anātmavāda*, Jainism seeks to set up a yet different conceptual structure, namely *anekāntavāda* i.e. the many-sided view of reality. We shall refer to this metaphysical approach and follow up the Jaina treatment of the problem of time in sections IV (i) and (ii).

Creation, causality, and time

Each of the well-formulated systems of the different schools of Indian philosophy has its distinct theory of causality in support of and in accordance with its specific metaphysical structure. As we shall see on the following pages, it is within these conceptual schemes that one has to search for their respective views regarding the problem of time and detect also the philosophical motivation which makes these specific views necessary and indispensable for the alternative structures of metaphysics. However, before we venture to expose and analyse the critique of causality – which is a central problem of Indian philosophy and a key for the present investigation regarding the contending conceptual models of time-let us note the philosophical development of this idea in the earliest speculations about the creation of the universe.

The philosophical wondering about the origin of the universe is found universally, across the cultural boundaries. The consequent reflections, however, have given rise to ideas and views which have parallels and oppositions within as well as outside of a given tradition. As we focus our attention on the Indian scene, we find a variety of speculations attempting to account for the origin of the world. We pass aside the wealth of myths of the *Purāṇas* and select only those which have definite content for a philosophical analysis, leading to the discernment of a principle which is characteristic of the entire Brahmanical tradition.

A number of views termed as *ākasmikavāda* – sudden occurrence, *yadṛcchāvāda* – haphazard happening, *svabhāvavāda* – naturalism, attributed to the materialists, must have been current at a very early date. Whatever subtle differences the views may have from one another, what they all seem to advocate in common is, that the occurrence of an event is without any invariable cause (*niyata kāraṇa*), that the happening has no necessary dependence on anything else. These theories of spontaneous, indeterminable origination were obviously challenges offered by the sceptics against any explanation of the universe through the idea of causal operation. They claim that the occurrence of the event is not due to any cause but it is in the nature (*svabhāva*) of the event that it at all happens. These views, to which we find references in the *Upaniṣads*,[1] are treated by the Brahmanical philosophers as views of the opponent, and they have at-

1 *Kālah svabhāvo niyatiryadṛcchā – Śvetāśvatara* 1/2 and *Suśruta saṃhitā, Śarīrasthāna* 1/11/3

tempted to expose the fallacies, that are inherent in them. To give an example, Udayanācārya[2] – an exponent of the Nyāya-Vaiśeṣika school – elaborately discusses the question, indicating why the idea of causality cannot be dispensed with. He argues to prove his thesis, that events cannot be said to occur haphazardly, by showing the absurdities that are involved in the opponent's position. The fact, that an event occurs only at a particular time and neither always nor at any other time, can be accounted for only on the premise that there is a necessary, antecedent cause to it. If the cause is absent, the event in question cannot take place. The events of the universe are tied to such a chain of causal operation, which accounts for rule and order in every case of occurrence and happening. The sudden occurrence as well as dissolution of an effect or why a particular effect does not occur all the time cannot be accounted for without the idea of causation. The above, in brief, points to why the opponents' views are not acceptable. It is, however, also important to note that the Cārvāka materialists did raise significant objections against the idea of necessary relation between the antecedent and consequent as the basis of the idea of causality. They point out that there is no ontological or logical connection between them. It is merely imagined to be there as a habit of thought. The details – which we omit – of Udayanācārya's[3] answers, demonstrating the objective validity of causal operation, make the notion of contingency (*kādacitkatva*) clear. He points out that if the occurrence is held to be without a cause, it will lead to one of the absurd conclusions, viz. it is to be accepted as ever-present or never-present. Its contingency – that it is sometimes there and not always – cannot be accounted for. Thus, it has to be accepted that the contingent must have a cause. In other words, the question of causality arises only in relation to what is contingent. The eternal (ever-present), the fictitious (never-present) can be regarded as uncaused.

This view – that the contingent is always caused – is supported both by the Sāṅkhya[4] and the Vedānta systems. It is equally shared by the Buddhist[5] philosophers, in whose metaphysical structure, as we shall see, there is no room for any uncaused category of existent at all. Again Brahmanical philosophers, as they direct their enquiry towards discerning whether cause could be of the nature of non-being, unanimously deny the position. The view – termed *asatkāraṇavāda* – that being can come out of nothing – is held to be the opponents' view and every system rejects it. The view, which is referred to in the *Upaniṣads*

2 *Nyāyakusumāñjali* 1/5 [24]
Hetubhutiniṣedho na svānupākhyavidhirna' ca svabhāvarṇanā naivamavadherniyatatvatah

3 *Nyāyakusumāñjali* 1/4 [24].

4 Vācaspati Miśra's commentary on *Sāṅkhya-Kārikā* 9 and 10 [11].

5 *Pramāṇavārttika* 3/34 by Dharmakīrti [53], *nityaṃ sattvam asattvam vā'hetor anyānapekṣaṇāt apekṣāto hi bhāvānāṃ kādācitkatvasaṃbhavaḥ*.

and repudiated by all subsequent Brahmanical philosophers, is of interest as it gives the logic behind their cosmological speculations. We shall allude to some of the representative discussions from each system to indicate the philosophical argumentation for the unanimous repudiation of this idea by the Brahmanical tradition.

This question is discussed at length in the Nyāya texts – such as the *Nyāya Sūtra* 4/1/14 – 4/1/18 [15]. If it is held that the principal cause of this world is non-being but the world is a positive entity (*bhāva-vastu*), the position is unacceptable on the ground that the effect has to be of the same essence as the cause.

The Sāṅkhya argument as put forward by Vācaspati Miśra in his *Sāṅkhyatattvakaumudī* – commenting on the 9th kārikā of *Sāṅkhya-Kārikā* – is that if a positive entity can be said to come out of nothing, »it would involve the absurd contingency of all things being produced at all places and at all times« [11]. In *Nyāyavārttikatātparyaṭīkā* [21] 4/1/14-15, a work of the same author, the discussion has been taken up from the Nyāya standpoint. One of the significant arguments there is directed to show that nothingness, being devoid of any difference within itself, cannot give rise to any difference in effects. Moreover, an effect being in principle of the same essence as cause, it would remain inconceivable how nothing could give rise to being.

Advaita Vedānta also refutes the position. Śaṅkara, in his commentary on *Brahma Sūtra* 2/12/26 [39], puts the question as to how to distinguish the non-being, which is taken to be the cause of different effects. If one admits of different kinds of non-being, non-being ceases to be non-being and becomes indistinguishable from being. Moreover, no account for rule and order in the causal operation can be given. Nothing could give rise to just about anything, in that case.

The Brahmanical tradition, thus, repudiates the two positions, viz. that the contingent can be without a cause and that nothing can give rise to being. We shall note that in all philosophical and theological formulations the principle of *ex nihilo nihil fit* is never transgressed. This basic tenet of the entire Brahmanical tradition is expressed in the *Bhagavad-Gītā* II, 16 (see p. 130).

If this brings us to a central point of agreement in the pattern of philosophisation of this tradition, this is also a point of departure from where we can begin to trace the differences of the divergent metaphysical structures, with their distinct understanding of creation, supported by different formulations of the conception of causality. Let us only briefly mention here, that *ārambhavāda* of Nyāya-Vaiśeṣika is supported by their theory of causality, termed *asatkāryavāda; abhivyaktivāda* of Sāṅkhya goes hand in hand with its theory of causality, termed *satkāryavāda; vivartavāda* of Advaita Vedānta goes with its distinct formula tion, termed *satkāraṇa* or *sat-vivartavāda*. The meaning of the terms will be clarified shortly. The different positions will be stated here only in brief, as in the subsequent chapters we shall expose in detail the structure of each system and try to discern, how the philosophical treatment of the problem of time is harmonised in each system with its total vision of reality. Let us take note of the different formulations about creation in the above mentioned systems.

For Sāṅkhya, all that is manifest could not have come out of nothing and must necessarily be caused. Moreover, all that is manifest was potentially existing in the cause prior to its actualisation. This manner of conceiving the causal operation is the basis of the Saṅkhya theory of causality, termed *satkāryavāda*. Creation is manifestation, actualisation (*abhivyakti*) of that which is unmanifest (*avyakta*). A philosophical enquiry leads the Sāṅkhya philosophers to postulate two ultimate principles: matter, which is dynamic, and consciousness, which is ever-constant. Sāṅkhya gives reasons for the postulation of these two principles, as we shall see later on. Here our task would be to focus on, what is – in this dualistic metaphysical structure – the philosophical account of the time-experience. In this connection we shall go deeper into the specific understanding of the Sāṅkhya theory of causality and note, how Sāṅkhya could do without a conception of time as an objective category of existence. The significant contribution of Yoga philosophy to the understanding of the problem of time will also be discussed.

If *satkāryavāda* supports the Sāṅkhya metaphysical structure, it is *asatkāryavāda*, the theory of causality of the Nyāya-Vaiśeṣika system, which goes along with its doctrine of creation – *ārambhavāda* – and its pluralistic metaphysics. Here, the causal operation is conceived not as a mere actualisation of what was pre-existent in the cause – as in Sāṅkhya – but as the cause giving rise to the effect which was non-existent (*asat*). In the *ārambhavāda* the effect is a beginning (*ārambha*) of that, which was not, before the causal operation. The system sets up a metaphysical pluralism and lists the ultimate metaphysical entities, in which figures time. To the Nyāya-Vaiśeṣika philosophers it is only with reference to time as a category of existence, that one could at all talk about causal operation. In this system one comes across a mode of conceiving creation in time, and time is granted an ontological status.

In the school of Advaita Vedānta there is to be found yet another conceptual pattern. Its philosophy of non-dualism goes with its understanding of causality, which is to be distinguished not only from the Nyāya-Vaiśeṣika theory of *asatkāryavāda*, but also from the *satkāryavāda* of the Sāṅkhya-Yoga schools. In the metaphysical scheme of Advaita-Vedānta there is no room for plurality and movement. This is expressed in the doctrine – termed as *satkāraṇavāda* – where the cause alone is conceived as real, the effect has only an epistemic status. The problem of creation, along with the problem of time, are reduced here to problems of appearance.

Thus, as this broad outline of the Brahmanical tradition with its three principal and distinct conceptual structures points to, the conception of time propounded in each system is motivated by and connected with their respective ideas of being, causality, etc.

An analytical exposition of the different views of time, to be taken up system by system in subsequent chapters of this work, is intended to bring out the interdependence of philosophical concepts as the different schools formulate their distinct stands.

This becomes more accentuated, when we come to consider the Buddhist philosophical stand, which formulates its theory of causality in a pattern, which is destructive of the Brahmanical metaphysical structures, leaving no room for any uncaused category. In the Buddhist conceptual structure there emerges a novel conception of being and time. It offers a bold challenge to the *ātmavāda* tradition, which is taken up by the adherents of the latter tradition – giving rise to lively philosophical exchanges.

With this brief introduction as a guideline to the enormous wealth of ideas found in Indian philosophy, we shall now launch into a study of the problem of time in all its philosophical variations as found in the history of Indian thought. Speculations regarding this fundamental problem – a problem which has drawn wide attention of philosophers across cultures – know, as we shall see, of an enormous divergence from school to school, tradition to tradition.

I

(i) On the reality of absolute time – the Nyāya-Vaiśeṣika view

A study of the problem of time in Indian philosophy is of special interest in connection with the Nyāya and Vaiśeṣika schools of thought. It is here that one comes across a bold realistic view of time. These schools, advocating a pluralistic metaphysics, focus on the reality of time as vital to their entire conceptual framework. Their philosophical stand regarding the problem of time is distinctly different from that of other schools, not only outside of the pale of the Brahmanical tradition but also within it. A specific view on time has a necessary impact on many other issues of basic importance. Therefore, the philosophical challenges offered by the Nyāya-Vaiśeṣika conception of time is taken up by the other Brahmanical schools as well as by the various Buddhist schools as an important subject of controversy.

Let us note that the main difference between the Nyāya and the Vaiśeṣika schools lies in their orientation and emphasis. The Vaiśeṣika deals with metaphysical questions, whereas Nyāya concentrates mostly on logic and epistemology.

As one proceeds, one observes that the Nyāya-Vaiśeṣika philosophers have studied the problem of time in its various aspects.[1] It is significant that a wide variety of questions, that suggest themselves to any investigation of the problem of time, such as what could be the ontological properties of time – granted it is a real per se – how is time known, how does it stand in relation to such basic problems as causality, motion and space, are raised and squarely faced by the philosophers of these schools, in harmony with their general conceptual framework of thinking.

The importance of the problem of time in the context of the Nyāya-Vaiśeṣika metaphysical pluralism comes into focus in all their philosophical assessments,

1 cf. S. Bhaduri [28] p. 183-213.

such as regarding the classification of the whole universe of reals, their conception of causal operation, etc.

It is interesting to observe that their classification of reals in two, as those which are products or perishable (*kṛtakas*) and those which are unproduced or imperishable (*akṛtakas*), eventually has a significant bearing on time and its specific function. In his commentary on the *Nyāya-Sūtra* [16], Vātsyāyana develops the Nyāya position by rejecting two distinct views. First he exposes and refutes the view that claims all is impermanent (4/1/25), since all is subject to production and destruction; secondly he discusses and denounces the view which maintains that all is eternal (4/1/29). Against the first position Vātsyāyana urges, that there is no valid means of knowledge (*pramāṇa),* which can establish that the whole universe of reals is subject to production and destruction. He insists, to mention only a few from the list of entities (*padārtha*) of their system of metaphysical pluralism, that such categories as soul (*ātman*), atoms (*paramāṇu*), ether (*ākāśa*), space (*dik*), and time per se (*kāla*) (4/1/28) are never apprehended by any valid means of knowledge as subject to production and destruction.

It is important to make the observation, in this connection, that although the other Brahmanical schools do not accept the Nyāya-Vaiśeṣika list of plurality of eternal entities, they all agree with them in rejecting the position which denies the category of the eternal, i.e. the unproduced and indestructible, ontological status. The eternality of Ātman lies at the very foundation of the Brahmanical tradition.

Vātsyāyana argues, that all that is liable to production must have a material cause, in which it inheres. The parts of a pot, for example, are its material cause as it is sustained by these constituents. But a substance (*dravya*) which is uncomposite, partless (*niravayava*), must be eternal. In other words, one cannot maintain that a substance is subject to production unless one can indicate its material cause and this is not possible in the case of time. The idea is later taken up in connection with the ontological properties of time.

The above, in other words, amounts to saying that the whole universe of reals cannot be classified as non-eternal, since production and destruction cannot be attributed to all of them. Subsequently, Vātsyāyana attempts the refutation of the second view – in two versions – which claims that all is eternal. According to the upholders of this view – in the first version – since all arises from the ultimate eternal elements (viz. the atoms of fire, earth, water, etc.) their products also have to be characterised equally to be eternal.

In his commentary on *Nyāya-Sūtra* (4/1/30) Vātsyāyana elaborates the objection that is raised against this position. Some entities, like a pot, are clearly apprehended as non-eternal. They are perceived as being subject to production and destruction. To say, that the products share the properties of the ultimate elements (*bhūtalakṣaṇākrānta*), does not entail that the former are not different from the latter. The eternality of the elements cannot be attributed to that which is produced and therefore necessarily non-eternal. Moreover, if the product is not taken as a distinct whole (*pṛthak avayavī*) in contrast to the constituent parts, i.e. atoms, it could not even be perceptible, as the atoms are imperceptible. In other words, to be liable to production and to be composed of parts are indicative of the non-eternal. Thus, in brief, the proposition that all is eternal cannot be accepted.

Again, the commentator exposes and refutes a second version (4/1/31) of the position claiming that all is eternal. The refutation of this view, attributed to the Yoga school, is highly significant as it brings forth the Nyāya philosophical stand in clear perspective and enables us to perceive the importance of the conception of time as a real per se in this system.

In the Yoga analysis of change (*pariṇ*āma) all the characteristics of *abhivyaktivāda*,[2] also shared by Sāṅkhya, are present. Production and destruction are attributed only to the qualities (*dharma*), whereas the ultimate substance (*dharmī*) is conceived as eternal, i.e. beginningless and endless. Moreover, the quality or the attribute (*dharma*) is not granted any independent existence. The Yoga conceptual pattern holds to the idea that the quality (*dharma*) is existent in the substance (*dharmī*) prior to production as well as posterior to its destruction. This is reflected in their theory of causality, *satkāryavāda*.[3] It is, however, necessary to refer to the conception of *lakṣaṇa pariṇāma*,[4] which has direct bearing on the temporal aspect of change. The conventional usages of past, present and future are taken as referring to the sub-latent, actual, and the potential states of a *dharma*. And in so far as the *dharma* has no distinct existence, it is in a relation of identity with the *dharmī*, which is taken as eternal.

The Nyāya philosophers take it up for refutation.[5] The criticism has immediate impact on their interpretation of the time-experience. It is pointed out that existence has its locus in the present time. If, as in the view of the opponent, a *dharma* is to be conceived as existent – prior to its production and posterior to its destruction – the idea and the experience of temporal sequence is violated. It is not possible to attribute past or future to such an entity. In other words, no meaningful reference can be made regarding such an entity in terms of production and destruction. They point to the fact, that production can be meaningfully ascribed to that, which now is (at present) but was previously not (in the past).

2 The technical term for the Sāṅkhya theory of evolution.

3 See section II (i).

4 See section II (ii).

5 *Nyāya-Sūtra* 4/1/25-4/1/33 [15].

Again an entity is non-existent posterior to destruction. If any entity in question is to be conceived as existent prior to its production and even subsequent to its destruction, there would be no account of any temporal order possible. This does not do justice to our experience and cannot, therefore, be accepted.

Thus, both the propositions-viz. the one claiming universal impermanence and the other claiming eternality – are rejected. What experience as well as philosophical analysis testify to is that the universe of reals is to be classified into two: those liable to production and destruction (the non-eternal) and those which are not so (the eternal).

Now, the immediate question that presses for consideration is whether production is possible without any causal operation. This is to be understood in the context of a series of objections brought up against the principle of causality by the sceptics and the materialists. Fully aware of the chaotic situation that would arise if there were no necessary, invariable relation between that which is produced (the effect) and its cause, the philosophers of this school sought to answer these objections that are raised against the idea of causality.

A summary review of these exchanges is found in *Nyāyakusumāñjali* written by Udayanācārya [24].[6] If an event is to be taken as uncaused, it could happen at any time or all the time. The fact that it happens only at a determinate time and not otherwise indicates that there is an antecedent cause for its production. The coming into being of all that is contingent can be explained only on the basis of the assumption of a cause, which alone can account for the cessation of the prior non-existence of the effect. Again, no event can be said to produce itself, as a sceptic would have it. Its occurrence is determined by the cause, which is temporally antecedent. Thus cause and effect are distinct from one another. Lastly, an event or an entity cannot come out of nothing. In that case, it could happen just about any time or at any place.

The Nyāya and the Vaiśeṣika philosophical literature contains detailed discussions on the problem of causality and its implications. Their theory of causality, refuting the other contending theories, discloses a conceptual structure, where the question of time reveals itself to be of vital importance. It is interesting to follow the steps of philosophical argumentation, which lead to the formulation of the idea of absolute time as a necessary presupposition for causal operation.

The distinction between the eternal (*nitya*) and the contingent (*kādācitka*) is clearly formulated. An entity which is ever present or never present cannot be amenable to production or destruction. The contingent is precisely that which is not existent prior to its production and ceases to be after its destruction.

6 1/4-5 and the prose commentaries thereon.

The idea of non-existence, as we shall see in a later section, receives a profound philosophical treatment in these systems, leading eventually to controversies with other schools. It is only in the context of an objective time, that the category of non-existence enables one to put into perspective the idea of the contingent as caused.

An entity like ether (*ākāśa*) is never non-existent, whereas an absolute non-entity like the hare's horn (*śaśaśṛṅga*) is ever non-existent. The idea of cause is applicable only in connection with that whose existence is qualified by a previous non-existence. This prior non-existence is evidently a temporal reference, pointing to the fact that all causal operation is necessarily an event in time. No event is conceivable or possible without time as its receptacle (*ādhāra*).

To deny time an objective reality is to confront a static universe, where there is no room for any change or movement. As time is indispensable for all that can be classified as contingent, it is characterised as the instrumental cause for the latter.[7] Again, contingency and causality imply each other. But for the idea of causal operation, entities are conceivable either as ever-existent or never-existent.

The Nyāya-Vaiśeṣika philosophers advocate *asatkāryavāda* as their theory of causality. The theory is so called as the effect is conceived as non-existent (*asat*) prior to the causal operation. This is precisely the idea which differentiates this theory from the Sāṅkhya theory of causality, viz. *satkāryavāda,* where the effect is conceived as pre-existent, i.e. as potential in the cause. The metaphysical commitments of Sāṅkhya and the impact of its causal theory on the conception of time are noted in the next chapter.

The Nyāya-Vaiśeṣika rejects the conceptual pattern of *abhivyaktivāda* of Sāṅkhya and advocates a distinct doctrine of creation – viz. *ārambhavāda.* The doctrine puts in relief – which is supported by their theory of causality – that the effect is a new beginning (*ārambha*) of that which was nonexistent (*asat*).

In the *Nyāya-Sūtra* [15], 4/1/15-4/1/24 and its commentary several views, attributed to the opponents, are reviewed and rejected in order to bring to light the logical and the philosophical advantages of the theory of causal operation that *asatkāryavāda* stands for. The Nyāya and Vaiśeṣika schools devote a considerable study to the problem of causality in its different aspects. The metaphysical, logical and epistemological implications that are drawn from their analysis lead to exchanges and controversies with the views of other schools. The schools of Nyāya and Vaiśeṣika attempt at precise formulations of definitions, classification and the various problems that are connected with it like that of the plurality of causes, etc.

7 cf. *janyānām janakaḥ kālaḥ – Bhāṣa-Pariccheda* by Viśvanātha [22], 45.

Here, however, their conceptual analysis of the problem of causality will be discussed only in so far as it is found to be pertinent to the understanding of their specific conception of time.

The idea of causal operation, in the Nyāya-Vaiśeṣika conceptual framework, presupposes time.[8] Even the very definition of cause is possible only on the premise of the ontological reality of time, with reference to which the idea of sequence of the cause and the effect can be meaningfully understood.

Cause is defined as that which is a necessary and invariable antecedent to an event.[9] Here, the idea of antecedence has an immediate temporal reference. The effect succeeds the cause which evidently involves the idea of time.

There are, however, other aspects to the cause besides its being temporally antecedent. All that precedes the occurrence of the event is not necessarily the cause. Moreover, for the effect to take place what is required is not only a single cause, but the sum-total of all the necessary causal antecedent factors (*sāmagrī*) – an idea which is worked out in their classification of causes. Moreover, their distinct causal theory which denies the Sāṅkhya idea of the effect being nothing but a manifestation of the cause can be viewed and appraised, as will be seen, only in the light of the idea of time as a real per se. The production of the effect is its first conjunction with time. The causal operation does not consist of merely manifesting the potentially existent, as the Sāṅkhya claims, but of creating *de novo* what was non-existent. In other words, the occurrence of the effect is an event-in-time. Note that a necessary implication of the idea of causal operation is the idea of time as an ontological reality.

What can, then, be said of time following the Nyāya-Vaiśeṣika texts?

The ontological properties of time are carefully enumerated in the philosophical literature of both the schools. As no beginning or end of any event or entity is conceivable without reference to time, time itself is classed with the eternal (*nitya*) categories of existence (*padārtha*), i.e. is itself beginningless (*anādi*) and endless (*ananta*). Time in their pluralistic metaphysics occupies a distinct position. It is a real per se. It is a substance (*dravya*), since it has qualities like unity, conjunction, disjunction, etc.

Moreover, it is argued that a substance (like time, space, etc.) which is uncomposite (*niraṁśa*) and does not presuppose any substratum (*anāśrita*) for its existence has to be ascribed eternality. It is an independent real (*svatantra*). Time is further characterised as all-pervading (*vibhū*), as it is in contact with all that is finite[10] and consequently regarded as the receptacle (*ādhāra*) of all that is contin-

8 *Vaiśeṣika Sūtra* 2/2/11 [17] *kāraṇe kālākhyā*.

9 *Ananyathāsiddhaniyatapūrvabhāvitam kāraṇatvam* – *Tarkabhāṣā* of Keśava Miśra [25].

10 *Sarvamūrtasaṁyogānuyogitva* – *Bhāṣā-Paricchеda* [22].

gent (*kādācitka*). The all-pervasive substances are never contained in anything (*ādheya*). It has no form (*amūrta*). Time is uniform and ubiquitous. It has no parts (*niravayava*). As no change in terms of action or modification is conceivable without time as its necessary frame of reference or possible if time were not an objective category of existence, it is itself inactive or unchanging (*niṣkriya*). The argument is that time, being a necessary condition for all movement and change, must itself be free from these attributes.[11] The ontological reality of time is an idea, which the schools vehemently insist on, as opposed to the idea of time as merely a subjective construction (*buddhi-nirmāṇa*).

Again, the schools insist that it is inherently unitary (*eka*) and indivisible (*avibhajya*). The idea of oneness and indivisibility of time leads to controversies. It is asked, if these were ontological properties of time, how should in that case the conventional usages of the plurality of time-divisions be accounted for. The Nyāya-Vaiśeṣika answer will be given shortly.

In this connection let us note that inference is the valid means of knowledge (*pramāṇa*), according to the Nyāya-Vaiśeṣika philosophers, for proving the existence of time. There is controversy amongst the Indian realists regarding the question of how time is known. According to one denomination of the Mīmāṃsā school time is amenable to sense-perception. We refer to the controversy in section I (iii).

The Nyāya-Vaiśeṣika philosophers maintain that time is inferred as the basis of such notions as priority (*paratva*), posteriority (*aparatva*), of simultaneity (*yaugapadya*) and succession (*ayaugapadya*), of quickness (*kṣipratva*) and slowness (*ciratva*). In other words, the above are the grounds (*liṅga*) for the inference of the existence of time.

The Nyāya-Vaiśeṣika philosophers reject the position which proposes solar motion to be the basis of such notions. Their analysis is as follows. When an object is taken as prior in relation to one and posterior to another, they ask, what serves as the basis for the attribution of such qualities to a given object? If it is urged that one is connected with a larger number of solar revolutions than the other, the Nyāya-Vaiśeṣika philosophers raise the problem that there is a direct relation of inherence between the sun and solar motion but not between the object in question and the sun, which are remotely separated from one another. Thus, there must be a common medium which can serve as a link between the two, and which, moreover, is capable of transmitting the quality of one to the other. Through the application of the method of exclusion it is argued, that no

11 The above discussion is based on Śrīdhara's *Nyāyakandalī* [19] as well as Śaṅkara Miśra's *Upaskāra* [17] b) p. 82-85, where detailed enumeration of the ontological properties of time is found.

other substance can perform this specific function, leading to the inference of time.

Thus it is urged, that solar motion can never substitute the function of time. In their analysis of quickness and slowness also the same fact is pointed to. The point of the argument is to focus on the fact, that not only solar motion but no motion whatever can replace time as an objective reality.

To those who insist that solar motion can be the basis for such conventional usages, the question may be posed that in that case, how is one to account for such usages as »the sun is set since long«? The Nyāya-Vaiśeṣika philosophers object to the answer that it is done with reference to other planetary motion, as this would lead to the fallacy of infinite regress. In other words, time as a real per se is to be accepted.

Now, to go back to the question of time as unitary, the philosophers of these schools point out, that all the marks or grounds (*liṅga*), which serve as basis for inferring time, point to it as one and the same objective real. The manyness of time, i.e. the conventional time-divisions, can be explained with the help of limiting adjuncts such as the solar motion etc. on the basis of the postulation of a singular, ubiquitous time. It is the actions which are past, present and future. These do not imply any inherent division or plurality in the time per se.

Now, let us note some aspect of the problems relating to time and space – as it is conceived in these systems.

In the Nyāya-Vaiśeṣika metaphysical pluralism space, as time, is granted a distinct ontological reality. It is to be noted that some of the ontological properties attributed to space are similar to those of time. Space, like time, is classified as a substance (*dravya*), as beginningless and endless, i.e. eternal (*nitya*),[12] as unitary (*eka*).[13] Moreover, the conventional plural usages of space, i.e. the space-divisions – despite that space per se is one – are accounted for as due to its relation to finite bodies, just as the so-called time-divisions are not intrinsic to time but are due to external adjuncts (*upādhi*).

A question that has been raised is whether one cannot conceive of one eternal substance, instead of two, i.e. space and time, in this scheme of pluralistic metaphysics. To this the Nyāya-Vaiśeṣika philosophers answer in the negative. The literature records the position, with an example from common experience, precisely to demonstrate that, despite their similar ontological characteristics, space and time cannot be reduced to one substance. There is no question of substituting one by the other, as their specific functions are absolutely distinct. In this connection, we refer to the *Vaiśeṣika-Sūtra* 2/2/6, where a clear analysis

12 *Vaiśeṣika Sūtra* 2/2/13 [17].

13 *Vaiśeṣika Sūtra* 2/2/14.

of the notions of priority and posteriority focuses on the distinct categories of existences that space and time are. That there is a clear-cut distinction between our awareness of temporal and spatial priority and posteriority is brought out by the example of the old man sitting nearer in point of space than a young man at a remoter distance, with reference to the same observer. The point that the example seeks to make is that the properties of priority and postriority involved in the apprehension of oldness and youth cannot be attributed to space, which leads eventually to the inference of time as their instrumental cause. Space cannot, therefore, be a substitute for time, or vice versa. Their exclusive functions point to their distinct existences.

In the *Praśastapādabhāṣyam* [20] also we find an elaborate discussion on the difference of the priority and posteriority attributed to space (*dikkṛte paratvāparatve*) – as the state of being far or near to a certain given point – from that which is caused by time (*kālakrte paratvāparatve*) – as a happening previous to or later than a certain given event.[14]

The *Nyāyakandalī* too elaborates on the same distinction in order to focus on space and time as ultimate and independent reals. But the philosophical argumentation is more or less alike.

The Nyāya-Vaiśeṣika philosophers are also aware of the inherent distinction between space and time regarding the fact that time has only one form of mensuration. This is to say that the temporal order of events is such that it does not allow for reversibility or inversion (*niyata*), whereas the spatial order makes room for it (*aniyata*).[15] It is also equally pertinent to note how space and time are considered in relation to motion. As the very presupposition of all movement, time and space are held to be without movement (*Vaiśeṣika-Sūtra* 2/2/21). Things are in space and in time in terms of location and duration. Similarly, all motion is conceived as occurring in space and time. Space is taken as a non-inherential cause (*asamavāyi-kāraṇa*) and time as the instrumental cause (*nimitta-kāraṇa*) of all that is non-eternal.

Thus, according to the realists, space and time are characterised as non-composite (*niravayava*), indivisible (*avibhajya*) and ubiquitous (*vibhū*). Things are in space and time (*ādhāra*), but space and time cannot be said to be contained (*ādheya*) in anything. These two categories of existence are conceived as all-pervading (*sarvagata*) and as having no form (*amūrta*). Space and time are classified as substances, since they possess qualities which are enumerated in the *Nyāya-Kandalī* as infinite extension, numerical unity, separateness, conjunction and disjunction.

14 Cf. Faddegon [29].
15 *Upaskāra* (2/2/10) by Śaṅkara Miśra [17].

The conception of time in the Nyāya-Vaiśeṣika schools as single, ubiquitous and all-pervading has been an important subject of controvesy. This idea of absolute time is challenged not only by the Buddhists and the Jaina philosophers, but has also been refuted by the Brahmanical philosophers belonging to Sāṅkhya, Yoga, and the Advaita Vedānta schools of philosophy.

We have referred to these philosophical debates centering on various aspects of the problem of time in different sections of this work. These exchanges between the exponents and opponents of a given view bear witness to the keen philosophical subtleties involved in the analysis of the problem of time.

At the end of this discussion let us note an interesting development, that took place regarding the problem of time in the history of the Nyāya-Vaiśeṣika thought itself.

Raghunātha Śiromaṇi, a reputed philosopher of the Neo-Nyāya (Navya-Nyāya) school – a phase which witnessed remarkable development in the area of logic – questioned the traditional view of absolute time. In his work *Padārthatattvanirupaṇam* [18] he challenged the entire categorical framework that was current in the old Nyāya-Vaiśeṣika pluralistic metaphysics. He criticised the plural categories of existence and questioned their raison d'être. It is in this connection that he also scrutinised the traditional understanding of time and space.

It is to be recalled that the arguments for accepting both space and time, in the Nyāya-Vaiśeṣika philosophy, are analogous. The two substances, accepted as all-pervading and ubiquitous, are inferred as the basis of all temporal and spatial notions and judgements. The time-divisions (*khaṇḍakāla*) – as the old school insisted – could be accounted for only on the presupposition of the universal, indivisible, all-pervasive time (*mahā-kāla*) limited by qualifying adjuncts (*upādhi*). The spatial relations are also similarly explained on the basis of an all-pervasive, singular substance called space (*dik*) with the help of qualifying adjuncts.

Raghunātha Śiromaṇi does not see the necessity for accepting two all-pervasive substances which require anyhow the limiting adjuncts in order to account for spatial and temporal divisions. He does not find enough justification for maintaining two separate categories of existence. Curiously enough, he seeks to reduce the traditional number of the ontological categories of the school by identifying space and time with God, which again is characterised as an all-pervading substance. Thus, although the variety of judgements dependent on qualifying adjuncts limiting an all-pervading substance remain the same in his conceptual system, the number of substances is reduced from three to one. He has also further curtailed the number of categories. But what concerns us, in this present investigation about time, is to note that although Raghunātha gives up the conception of absolute time, he proposes a new category called moment (*kṣaṇa*).

Here it is to be noticed, that he does not approve the manner, in which the old Nyāya-Vaiśeṣika philosophers defined moment with the help of motion. Here we refer to an important Nyāya text, viz. *Siddhāntamuktāvalī* of Visvanātha [22], where it is exemplified how moment is defined with the help of motion with reference to the absolute time as its basis.[16]

Raghunātha Śiromaṇi rejects this procedure as inadequate. Evidently the whole procedure is based on the notion of absolute time. He, therefore, critically demonstrates through a thorough examination of these definitions that the notion of moment cannot be validly accounted for in this manner. He rejects the idea of absolute time as a real per se, but sets up a new category »consisting of individuals which are not motions« ... but »which share the universal, repeatable property of momentariness« [18] p. 75.

But this amendment of Raghunātha Śiromaṇi to abandon the conception of absolute time was not approved by the later adherents of the school. The idea of an absolute time as a real per se is necessitated by and is integral to the metaphysical pluralism of the school which advocated *ārambhavāda* as its doctrine of creation.

Viewing the different philosophical stands regarding time within the Brahmanical tradition,[17] the distinct character of the Nyāya-Vaiśeṣika position is evident. Their philosophical difference from the Sāṅkhya, Yoga and Advaita Vedānta is striking. The Sāṅkhya refusal to accept time as an independent category of existence is wholly untenable to the Nyāya-Vaiśeṣika philosophers. In opposition to Sāṅkhya, they firmly assert that no change, with reference to an entity or

16 A technical analysis is given to account for the four moments of motion. They are:

1) "The motion as limited by the prior absence of disjunction produced by that motion." Suppose an individual x is moving from place y to place z. Then this first moment is the moment when x is just about to leave y. At this moment, the disjunction from y (which will be produced by the motion itself) has not yet come into being, so that there is prior absence of disjunction from y.

2) "(The motion as limited by) the disjunction limited by conjunction with the earlier place." The "earlier place" is place y, and the "later place" z. At this second moment x has not yet left y, but the trope called disjunction has arisen in x with reference to y.

3) "(The motion as limited by) the prior absence of conjunction with the later place, which prior absence is limited by the destruction of conjunction with the earlier place." x has now left y but has not yet arrived at z.

4) "The motion as limited by contact with the later place." x arrives at z.

The old theory, then, was that any one of these four moments, which are motions, may be used to mark off the limits of a temporal span. (Quoted from [18] p. 73).

Note that this text, long after Raghunātha Śiromaṇi, again adopts the procedure of the old Nyāya school.

17 See chapters II and III.

process, is either possible or conceivable without the ontological reality of time as its presupposition. The Sāṅkhya view of the reality of change without time as a distinct, independent real is unacceptable to Nyāya-Vaiśeṣika. All events are events in time, they maintain, and time is to be granted a separate existence. It is only with reference to the ontological background of time, that the reality of change – as production, persistence or destruction – can be conceived.

The atomic view of time, propounded by the Yoga school, is equally unacceptable to the Nyāya-Vaiśeṣika philosophers. The conception of time as ubiquitous and indivisible is no mere construction of thought (*buddhi-nirmāṇa*), as the Yoga school would have it, but an objective reality which is the very condition which makes the conventional time-divisions such as moment etc. possible. In other words, the idea of the reality of time as instant of the Yoga school is rejected by the Nyāya-Vaiśeṣika philosophers, for whom, on the contrary, what is basic to time is its indivisibility, its unity.

To the Advaita Vedānta, on the other hand, the problem of time is a problem of appearance. The issue of the reality of time is just as much detrimental to the Advaita Vedānta metaphysics as it is essential to the Nyāya-Vaiśeṣika. To the Nyāya-Vaiśeṣika philosophers time is an all-pervading, ontological substance (*dravya*) which can by no means be reduced to or characterised as a problem of appearance.

To sum up briefly, in *vivartavāda* time is an appearance, i.e. it has no ontological reality; in *pariṇāmavāda* change is ontological, but time is no independent ontological category, whereas in *ārambhavāda* time is a real per se, the very presupposition of the reality of change.

(ii) An exchange regarding the idea of present time (*vartamāna kāla*)

In the context of the discussion regarding inference as a valid means of knowledge the question of the time-divisions is once more scrutinised. The mark of inference has reference to all the three time-divisions, past, present, and future – which enables one to establish the universal relation (*vyāpti*) between the major and the minor terms.

An opponent – unidentified – raises an objection in which the validity of the three time-determinations is questioned. In the *Nyāya-Sūtra* 2/1/39 and the commentary thereon the opponent's objection is summarised as follows. It is held that there cannot be any present-time, as one could discern with reference to motion and space only a past and a future time determination. The example given in support of this claim is that of a fruit loosened from its stalk falling towards the ground. The space traversed, through which it has fallen (*patitādhvan*), is associated with time-past, and the space which is yet to be traversed before it reaches the ground (*patitavyādhvan*) with the time-future. There is no conceivable in-between these two, which could obtain a time-determination called time-present. Therefore the Nyāya claim, that inference can furnish knowledge of entities of all three times, cannot be accepted.

To this objection the Naiyāyika points out in reply, that if there were no present time, there cannot be past or future time either. The time-denominations of past and future are entirely dependent on the time-present.[18] The objection is based on a false appraisal of time by confounding it with space. Vātsyāyana pointedly brings out, that spatial divisions are not the basis for the three time-distinctions. The different parts of space are co-existent and remain unaffected by the motion – here of the falling fruit – before and after its commencement and cannot therefore be taken as indicating time. It is action (*kriyā*) which reveals it.[19] The three time-distinctions are to be understood with reference to action. The past and the future actions of an entity – the fruit – are absent and they can be discerned only as relative to the action which is present. Action is, then, the basis for the conventional time-divisions. Its previous absence (*prāgabhāva*) is its future, and subsequent absence (*dhvaṁsābhāva*) is its past. The present is precisely the temporal denomination, when the action is actually apprehended, perceived; without this the future and past would be inconceivable. It is clear from this analysis, that the so-called temporal divisions do not pertain to the time per se, but it is only with reference to action that these can be meaningfully understood. Moreover, as Vātsyāyana argues,[20] the past and the future of an action can never be understood except in relation to the present. Thus, the time-present is to be accepted. Moreover, he points out that not only action but the very existence of a thing manifests the reality of the present time. Any talk of existence of whatsoever would be meaningless without its locus as present time. Again, in the next section,[21] he launches an important argument in support of the objectivity of present as a time-determination. If time as present were not an objective fact, the very possibility of knowledge would be at stake. Perception, for example, presupposes sense-object contact (*pratyakṣam indriyārthasannikarṣajam*), and that is not possible unless the object in question is present, that is,

18 *Nyāya-Sūtra* 2/1/40 [15].
19 *Nyāya-Bhāṣya* 2/1/40 [16].
20 *Nyāya-Bhāṣya* 2/1/41.
21 *Nyāya-Sūtra* and *Nyāya-Bhāṣya* 2/1/42 [15,16].

has for its locus the present time.[22] Again, a denial of the present time would not only lead to the impossibility of perception but as a consequence would rule out the possibility of even inferential (*anumāṇa*) and verbal (*śabda*) knowledge which have their eventual basis on perception itself. This is, in brief, a significant point regarding the question as to why all the three time-determinations are to be acknowledged as objectively real. A further analysis again discloses that the time-divisions are external to time per se, the usages being made possible with the help of other qualifying factors (*upādhi*). The purpose of the entire philosophical argumentation is to disclose that no knowledge of any kind is possible without relating it with time. If perception reveals an object, the object by its very presence points to its temporal locus, which again leads to the inference of time per se as a category of existence

The Nyāya-Vaiśeṣika literature abounds in such exchanges where over and over again the reality of time is demonstrated through a refutation of different kinds of objections brought up against the position by its opponents.[23] Thus Vātsyāyana argues for the objective reality of the present time in two distinct modes, through an analysis pertaining to action as well as to the very existence of an entity in question. He goes into further details regarding the conventional linguistic usages. The very existence of a substance bears witness to its presentness – a fact necessarily referring to the present time. Thus, even when the qualities can be expressed in past and future terms, e.g. the jar was black, it is yet to be red, the substance does not cease to be present – as the conventional linguistic usage itself points to.

He has also given an illuminating analysis of such conventional usages, where the verb is used in present tense even when referring to events of near future or past, e.g. instead of 'I came' – 'I come shortly', instead of 'I will come', 'I am coming'. These legitimate grammatical uses are the subsidiary (*gauṇa*) uses of the present tense which presuppose that there is a principal (*mukhya*) use bearing witness to the actual objective time-determination as present.

22 An interesting discussion is documented by P.B. Tarkavagis in *Nyāyadarśana* (in bengali) [30]. Vātsyāyana points out that a sense-object contact is the basis of ordinary perception (*laukikapratyakṣa*), and such a contact is not possible with a past or a future object, but only with that which has its locus in the present time. But the question may be raised here, that in the case of such extraordinary perception (*alaukikapratyakṣa*) – accepted by the Nyāya-Vaiśeṣika school – as that of the Yogi, the future and the past object is also claimed to be perceived. In that case the former argument, that perceptibility points to the reality of present time, cannot be accepted as valid. Some of the Nyāya philosophers like Uddyotakara in reply to this admit the point contained in this objection, but nevertheless support the reality of the present as time-determination on the basis of the fact, that all cases of perception, so far as designated as an event (*kārya*), have the present time as the locus, regardless of the temporal status of the perceived object.

23 e.g. in *Nyāyalīlāvatī* by Vallabhācārya [26] and in *Nyāyakandalī* by Śrīdhara [19].

(iii) Is time perceived or inferred? – a debate amongst the Indian realists

An interesting subject for a philosophical debate amongst philosophers, who otherwise fully agree about the reality of time as an objective category of existence, center on the question as to how time is known. The adversaries in the controversy belonged to the Mīmāṃsā and the Nyāya-Vaiśeṣika schools. To be more precise, one denomination of the Mīmāṃsā school, the Bhāṭṭas, held that time is perceived, whereas the other denomination of the same school, the Prabhākaras,[24] joined the Nyāya-Vaiśeṣika philosophers in maintaining inference to be the valid means for knowing time.

We find a discussion on the perceptibility of time in the work *Śāstradīpikā* of Pārthasārathi Miśra.[25] The Bhāṭṭa Mīmāṃsaka stand, as is brought out here, points to the fact that all perceptual cognitions include as well the time of the perception. Miśra takes recource to such common experiences expressed in statements such as 'we are perceiving the present pot', or 'we are perceiving it from the morning', as clearly bearing witness to the fact that time is perceived. It would be impossible for us to use such expressions as now, then, in our perceptual cognition if time were not also perceived along with the perception of the object. Just as the referrents of the words pot etc. are accepted as objects of perception, so, he maintains, are the referrents of such words as 'now', 'then' etc. These words refer to nothing other than the time-content of the perception itself. The Bhāṭṭa Mīmāṃsaka point is to focus on the fact, that the temporal dimension of all our perceptions would remain unaccounted for without the contention that time is amenable to perception.

The Nyāya-Vaiśeṣika objection is that time cannot be said to be perceived, as it has no sensible qualities such as colour, form etc. It can only be inferred.

To this the Bhāṭṭa Mīmāṃsaka reply is that the objection is based on a fallacious argument. That, which is amenable to perception, need not necessarily possess such qualities as colour etc., although it is a fact that a coloured object can be perceived. In other words, such sensible qualities are not the criteria of perceptibility.

The Bhāṭṭa Mīmāṃsakas, however, acknowledge that time as such is never an object of perception, but it is perceived always as a qualification of sensible objects. This is to say that time is perceived as a qualifying element (*viśeṣa guṇa*)

24 Prabhākara Mīmāṃsā used the same conceptual model of time as that of Nyāya-Vaiśeṣika. We refer to *Prakaraṇa Pañcikā* by Śālikanatha Miśra, p. 155, [34], see also [36], [37].

25 [33], p. 45, 1/2/5. – *kālapratykṣanirupaṇam.*

and never independently of the sensible object. Thus we perceive events as slow, quick etc., which involve a direct reference to time.

In the opinion of the Nyāya-Vaiśesika philosophers, however, perception can never disclose the ontological properties of time as unlimited, beginningless and endless, indivisible and ubiquitous. A directly perceived time would only point to a limited, divided time, which is not the time per se, but a conventional temporal usage determined by such extraneous factors as the solar motion etc. In other words, time as an ontological real can never be an object of perception; inference is to be admitted as the valid means for knowing it.

The Nyāya-Vaiśeṣika philosophers have worked out a series of inferences towards the establishment of time as an independent, objective category of existence. The grounds (*liṅga*) of the inferences are such notions – indicated in the *Vaiśeṣika-Sūtra* 2/2/6, also in *Nyāya-Kandalī* of Śrīdhara – as priority (*paratva*), posteriority (*aparatva*), simultaneity (*yaugapadya*) and succession (*ayaugapadya*), quickness (*ksipratva*) and slowness (*ciratva*) etc. etc.

Time per se is established through inference as the very basis which makes such notions possible, as mentioned above, and is also considered as a cause for all such entities, to which production and destruction can be attributed.

The issue regarding the perceptibility or inferrability of time as a philosophical debate acquires an interesting flavour, as the opponents basically agree on the objectivity of time as an ontological real in their respective realistic conceptual structures.

The Nyāya-Vaiśeṣika position regarding the issue is challenged by the Bhāṭṭa Mīmāṃsaka Nārāyaṇa. In his *Mānameyodaya*,[26] a notable Mīmāṃsā work, the question is discussed once more. The aim of the discussion is to refute the Nyāya-Vaiśeṣika claim, that time is inferred on the basis of such notions as simultaneity etc. This, the Bhāṭṭa Mīmāṃsaka points out, cannot be accepted as a valid ground for inference. He points to such experiences as, for example, 'Devadatta and Yajñadatta came simultaneously', or 'the son came late' and raises the question whether such awarenesses, obtained by perception, can be denied to have time as their essential component. The point is to bring out that such direct, immediate awarenesses as simultaneity or lateness cannot be ascertained, as in these examples, through anything but sense-perception. 'Devadatta', 'Yajñadatta' or 'son' are related directly to time, and the latter is perceived along with the substantives which it qualifies.

The Bhāṭṭa Mīmāṃsaka points out that time cannot be said to be inferrable, as the Nyāya-Vaiśeṣika philosophers would have it, precisely because nothing, other than time, is the very content of the notion of simultaneity etc. The latter

26 [35], *Kārika* 85.

cannot be again used as the ground (*hetu*) for inferring time. This would lead to the fallacy of self-dependence (*ātmāśraya*). Moreover, they point out that time could not be inferred on the basis of any other ground either.

Briefly, the awareness of simultaneity etc. is produced by sense-organs, which have time for their content. This indicates that time is itself a content of sense-perception, which invalidates the claim of the inferrability of time.

The Bhāṭṭa-Mīmāṃsā insistence on perceptibility of time as corroborated by everyday experience is met by some of the distinguished Nyāya-Vaiśeṣika philosophers, who adopted a novel approach to the question.

Śrīdhara in his *Nyāya-Kandalī* [19][27] takes up the question. Again in Jayanta Bhaṭṭa's *Nyāya-Mañjarī* [27][28] we find reference to this exchange, put in his characteristic brilliant manner.

The Nyāya-Vaiśeṣika philosophers meet the problem by pointing out, that time (as much as space) cannot be established as objects of ordinary perception (*laukikapratyakṣa*). As we find in *Nyāya-Kandalī*, it is their contention that to establish a substance through visual perception, it must have a limited dimension and have colour. But time is unlimited, infinite, and it has no manifest colour or form (*udbhūtarūpavattvam*). The sense of touch can also, according to the Nyāya-Vaiśeṣika philosophers, be said to perceive substances, but that presupposes that they possess manifest tangible quality. Evidently, time cannot be established in this way either.

Therefore, the so-called perception of 'the present pot' is analysed by the Nyāya-Vaiśeṣika philosophers in the following manner. They urge that it is a case of, in Nyāya-Vaiśeṣika terminology, extra-ordinary perception (*alaukika-pratyakṣa*), classified as *jñānalakṣaṇa*.[29] This is the type of perception where the perceived object is presented to the senses through a previous knowledge of the same, as for example in the case of the perceptual judgement 'I see the fragrant sandalwood'. Here, the visual perception of fragrance is accounted for as due to a previous knowledge of it in the past experience. Thus, Śridhara explains the perception of 'the present pot' as being composed of two elements. Firstly, 'the pot' is the object of ordinary perception, whereas the second factor, i.e. the time-element indicated by the word 'present', is being derived from previous knowledge of time resulting in the extraordinary perception of 'the present pot'. In other words, Śrīdhara agrees with the general Nyāya-Vaiśeṣika contention that the knowledge of time is inferential. The sense-perception of time as a qualifying

27 *Kālaprakaraṇam* (p. 155-161).

28 part 1, *pramāṇaprakaraṇam* (p. 123-127).

29 It is defined as *viṣayī yasya tasyaiva vyāpāro jñānalakṣanah* in *Bhāṣā-Paricchcda* by Viśvanātha [22].
The Nyāya-Vaiśeṣika deals elaborately with the problem of perception.

element of the object, as the Bhāṭṭa Mīmāṃsaka would have it, is analysed by him as based on the previous inferential knowledge of time.

Jayanta Bhaṭṭa, the reputed advocate of the school, presents the view of the ontological reality of time as inferrable. The discussion is put in the form of an exchange first with the principal opponent, the Buddhists, who deny the Nyāya-Vaiśeṣika conception of time as an all-pervading, ubiquitous, ontological category of reality.

The Buddhist objection to the inferrability of time is summarised as follows. They point out that it is not possible to establish the universal relation (*vyāpti*) between the major (*sādhya*) and the middle term (*hetu*) in the said inference – that is, between time and such marks as quickness, slowness, simultaneity etc. This is not grounded in any previous perceptual experience.[30]

Moreover, the usages of 'now', 'then' etc. do not point to the existence of an indivisible time as substratum. These can be accounted for as pertaining to a sequence of acts. Again, such planetary movements as solar motion do not indicate any separate existent called time. Moreover, if time is accepted as an indivisible, unitary real per se, the usages of past, present and future will be impossible.

Here Jayanta Bhaṭṭa presents the Bhāṭṭa Mīmāṃsā view, seeking to establish the reality of time by immediate perception. They argue that quickness, slowness, simultaneity are not merely attributes of acts, but that they also indicate a substance as the substratum of these notions. And that is time. Without the ontological reality of time one could not account for the awareness of 'the present pot' in contrast to 'this pot'. The attribute 'present' is indicative – as a perceptual datum – of the existence of time. In other words, the purpose of presenting the Bhāṭṭa Mīmāṃsā view is to refute the Buddhist contention, that the conventional temporal usages do not require the postulation of time as a distinct real.

Now, as the Nyāya-Vaiśeṣika is in full agreement with the Mīmāṃsā in their view regarding time as a distinct category of reality, the dispute centers around the issue of what is the valid means of knowing time. The Nyāya-Vaiśeṣika challenges the Bhāṭṭa Mīmāṃsā view, that the ontological reality of time as ubiquitous, uncomposite, can be established by perception. The arguments on either side presented in this connection are similar to those found in Śrīdhara's *Nyāya-Kandalī*.

The Nyāya-Vaiśeṣika maintains that time as a substance could be established by visual perception, only if form/colour (*rūpa*) could be attributed to it. But

30 This is a requirement for valid inference. In the case of inferential knowledge 'this hill is fiery', 'smoke' is the *liṅga* (mark) which is previously perceived as associated with fire.

since it is not the case, inference is to be acknowledged as the valid means of knowing it.

To this the Mīmāṃsaka retort is, that the atoms (*paramānu*), according to Nyāya-Vaiśeṣika philosophers, have form and yet they are not amenable to perception. This goes to indicate that 'having form' itself is no criterion for perceptibility. In other words, the dictum that only a substance having a sensible form/colour can be visually perceived, as the Nyāya-Vaiśeṣika philosophers would have it, is itself in contradiction with experience and is, therefore, untenable. The judgement 'I see the pot now' would not be possible without contact with the visual organs and does not need any other means of knowledge as its basis. It is however so, the Mīmāṃsaka agrees, that time cannot be perceived independently, but only in its attributive capacity. But that it is perceivable is a fact of experience, and no law can invalidate it.

To this the Nyāya-Vaiśeṣika reply is, that if both the substance and its attribute can be shown to be separately amenable to perception, it could also be maintained that the qualifying element is perceptible along with the substance. But on the strength of being alone an attribute of a substance, not otherwise independently perceivable, it cannot qualify itself as a perceptual datum. Such being the case of the perception of time, always as an attribute – which is itself the Mīmāṃsā contention –, it cannot be established as an independent real by perception alone, but on the basis of inference. Moreover, the existence of time is not in jeopardy because it is not amenable to visual perception, it is conclusively proved through inference.

The so-called perceived time as a qualifying element is, of course, a case of extra-ordinary perception – an idea to which we have already referred. But in all cases, it is only inference that can establish the ubiquitous, unitary, all-pervading time.

II

(i) Time as aspect of concrete becoming – the Sāṅkhya view

The conceptual frameworks of the Sāṅkhya and the Yoga schools have many essential features in common. There are, however, divergences regarding certain philosophical issues, other than the well-known distinction between Sāṅkhya atheism and Yoga theism.

In their treatment of the problem of time – although these schools operate within a basic ontological structure which is common to both – a careful investigation shows certain subtle philosophical differences.

The common point of agreement between the two schools is their denial of the Nyāya-Vaiśeṣika view of a unitary time as an absolute and objective existent, as one among the ultimate real entities constituting a metaphysical pluralism. It is interesting to note in this connection, that time does not figure in the list of the categories of existence (*tattvas*) of either Sāṅkhya or Yoga.

For an understanding of their philosophical formulations regarding the problem of time it is indispensable to have an overall idea of the specific metaphysical frame of the systems, along with their distinct theory of causation, termed *satkāryavāda*. Propounding a metaphysical dualism, these schools operate with two ultimate principles which are conceived as having no beginning or end and as being independent of one another.

The whole course of the universe is attributed to an interplay of these two principles – Puruṣa and Prakṛti, to use Sāṅkhya terminology. The dichotomy of matter and consciousness is expressed in the conceptions of Prakṛti and Puruṣa. Puruṣa, which Sāṅkhya identifies with consciousness, is conceived as uncomposite, without attributes (*guṇas*), free from all movement and change. Prakṛti, on the contrary, is the ever-active, ever-changing principle of matter,[1] constituted of

1 This is often given as the English equivlent of the term Prakrti, some people prefer energy, some nature. In any case, Prakṛti is to be understood as the subtle unmanifest, unconscious, dynamic principle, which is the cause of the manifest, gross experiencable world.

the three attributes (*guṇas*). Both the principles are, however, uncaused and indestructible.

In the *Sāṅkhya-Kārikā* of Īśvarakṛṣṇa along with its lucid commentary by Vācaspati Miśra,[2] the philosophical argumentations for postulating these two principles, their nature and functions are elaborately worked out. These contain illuminating documentation of the Sāṅkhya conceptions regarding the major philosophical issues, in the light of which we have to seek to understand and interpret the Sāṅkhya position regarding time.

We shall therefore, following the Sāṅkhya philosophical literature, note the principal ideas developed in their distinct mode of conceiving these two principles and then attempt to grasp their philosophical implications about the problem of time as such. The clue to the Sāṅkhya position on time is to be found in an understanding of the points of similarities and dissimilarities – which are carefully noted and enumerated in the literature as indicated below – between all that is manifest and Prakṛti as the ultimate, unmanifest principle as well as between Prakṛti and Puruṣa. The structure of the system developed through an elaboration of these concepts offers interesting contrasts with those of other systems of Indian philosophy.

The Sāṅkhya concern for detecting a principle, which lies behind all manifestations whatsoever, leads to the postulation of Prakṛti as an unmanifest i.e. pre-empirical reality, accounting for all experiences inclusive the processes involved in all actualisations from a latent or potential state. This involves the Sāṅkhya conception regarding matter as an independent, objective, dynamic principle and a development of a theory of causality.

The distinction between the manifest and the unmanifest is, therefore, clearly indicated in *Sāṅkhya-Kārikā* 10, where we find that the differences are mentioned thus: the manifest is caused, transitory, limited, whereas the unmanifest Prakṛti is uncaused, eternal and all-pervasive.[3]

The Sāṅkhya philosophers also note the similarity between all that is manifest and the unmanifest Prakṛti, in that they are constituted of the same essence, i.e. of the three guṇas – a conception, which we shall discuss shortly. Sāṅkhya

2 The *Tattvakaumudī*, transl. by G. Jha, [11].

3 *Hetumad anityam avyāpi sakriyam anekam āśritaṃ liṅgam. Sāvayavam paratantraṃ vyaktam, viparītam avyaktam.*

conceives of Prakṛti as a tri-unity of *guṇas*[4] – *sattva*, which is described as the illuminating, *rajas* as the active and *tamas* as the restraining forces, which through their mutual co-operation, subjugation and support give rise to the common objective world. This idea of an independent, objective world is to be contrasted with the view advocated by subjective idealism. Leaving aside the elaborate discussions regarding the nature and function of the *guṇas*, we shall turn to the basic question as to why Sāṅkhya comes to postulate Prakṛti as the ultimate, uncaused, unmanifest, eternal principle supporting the entire course of evolution. Prakṛti is dynamic, matter which evolves incessantly. It is the material, formal and instrumental cause of the universe.

It is here that one comes across the Sāṅkhya views about such basic philosophical issues as the conception of causality, involving distinct conceptual models for understanding change, origination and destruction. To retrace the principal philosophical steps, which finally lead to the postulation of Prakṛti, one has to turn to the Sāṅkhya theory of causality, termed as *satkāryavāda*. This theory is of central importance to the system. All that is manifest, Sāṅkhya argues, is dependent (*paratantra*) on a cause. This is what underlies the constitution of all that is contingent, that its origin indicates a causal dependence. To be without a cause would imply – as Vācaspati Miśra points out in his commentary – that the entity in question is either eternal or fictitious. The understanding of the manifest as caused, in Sāṅkhya, leads finally to the postulation of Prakṛti as the unmanifest, uncaused principle.

It is important to note, that the Sāṅkhya understanding of time as an aspect of concrete becoming and why time does not figure as a category of existence (*tattva*) in this system are questions, to which answers have to be sought in this entire metaphysical frame of the system along with the specific theory of causality which it advocates. The ground for rejecting the Nyāya-Vaiśeṣika conception of absolute time as an independent, objective reality can also be better comprehended, when one takes into consideration the entire Sāṅkhya perspective.

It is to be noted that the idea of concrete becoming (*pariṇāma*) is central for all questions regarding temporal sequence in Sāṅkhya. In order to understand the

4 The term guṇa as found in the Sāṅkhya literature is not easily translatable in English. The three meanings of the word *guṇa* in sanskrit are i) quality, ii) subordinate or inferior and iii) string, rope. The difficulty in rendering the term as quality in the Sāṅkhya context is that it tends to distort the Sāṅkhya view if Prakṛti is held to be a substance with these three qualities. G. Jha [11] translates it as attribute, S. Das Gupta in *Yoga Philosophy* [14], p. 70 calls them the ultimate reals. Vācaspati Miśra [10], commenting on the term, points out that they are so-called literally subsidiary or secondary (*gauṇa*), as they exist for the sake of others (*parārtha*) i.e. for the Puruṣas. It may also be interpreted, following the meaning of the term as string, as the guṇas bind the Puruṣa to the transitory object.

Sāṅkhya view, that the principle of change is ultimate and cannot be reduced to or derived from any static, unchanging principle, it is necessary to refer to the Sāṅkhya conception of homogeneous manifestations (*sadṛśa-pariṇāma*) of Prakṛti.

To Sāṅkhya, the movement in Prakṛti, which brings forth the heterogenous categories of creation with all its multi-form, presupposes a primordial movement which persists even when the heterogenous manifestations cease, i.e. the state of cosmic dissolution. This primal movement that is unceasingly present in Prakṛti is due to the inherent restless nature of the *guṇas*. Vācaspati Miśra in his commentary on the *Sāṅkhya-Kārikā* 16 emphasises this ever-changing character of Prakṛti- the three *guṇas* do not abandon their intrinsic nature and continue their homogeneous modification even in the state of cosmic dissolution (*pratisargāvasthā*). No distinct evolute emerges from this homogeneous modification as the *guṇas* do not combine. Yet the process of self-reproduction (*sattva* giving rise to *sattva*, etc.) goes on. Dynamicity being the very nature of *guṇas*, they can never remain unmodified, even for a moment.[5] The creative movement of Prakṛti, on the other hand, brings forth heterogeneity (*visadṛśapariṇāma*).

This intrinsic dynamic nature of Prakṛti, disclosed in the conception of *sadṛśa-pariṇāma*, is evidently pertaining to the transcendental aspect of the ever-active Prakṛti. In other words, the persistently active character of Prakṛti – when the *guṇas* modify incessantly without combining and therefore being unable to bring forth heterogeneous evolutes – does not involve any idea of empirical time-phases. Some scholars, for this reason, have characterised Prakṛti as the very personification of time.[6] To put it differently, the principle of change embedded in Prakṛti, as the tri-unity of *guṇas* in a state of homogeneous modification, is a conception of time in its transcendental aspect. This is an attempt to conceptualise the incessant movement of Prakṛti in its pre-empirical state.

The analysis, at this point, leads to the question, which is of great interest here, whether the process of objective movement is enough to account for time-experience. It is indeed important to emphasise again, that to Sāṅkhya the ever-changing Prakṛti can never know itself as changing. On the other hand Puruṣa, which knows change, is itself free from all movement and change. It is conceived as ever-constant (*kūṭastha*). If Prakṛti is rightly characterised as a personification of time, Puruṣa is the timeless principle. Both remain, however, according to Sāṅkhya, beginningless and endless. This is an important issue which will be taken up later on in section VII (i) entitled 'time and consciousness'.

5 *pariṇāmasvabhāvā hi guṇā nāpariṇamyya kṣaṇamapyavatisthante*.

6 e.g. Mādhavāchārya in his commentry on *Parāśara-Saṁhitā*, cf. [5].

To sum up, Sāṅkhya does not postulate any conception of time as independent of change. Change, on the other hand, is not conceived in abstraction, but as a concrete becoming. This again is further analysed, as we have noted, into homogeneous, being the basic and fundamental, and heterogeneous – involving the idea of a blending and combination of *guṇas*. The notions of temporal sequence, as past, present and future, are to be understood in the perspective of the heterogeneous manifestations of Prakṛti. The Sāṅkhya finds it superfluous to postulate an empty time as a real per se.

Vācaspati Miśra, in his commentary on *Sāṅkhya-Kārikā* 33, observes that in order to account for the temporal usages, if one has to first postulate an indivisible unitary time as a real per se and then adjuncts like action, solar motion, etc. (as the Vaiśeṣika philosophers do), it would simplify the matter, if the conventional time-divisions are accounted for with the qualifying adjuncts alone. In other words, it is unnecessary to admit of a separate category called time.[7]

A direct reference to the problem of time is scarce in Sāṅkhya literature where, however, the problem of becoming undergoes minute philosophical scrutiny. The reason is clear, Sāṅkhya understands the temporal phases with reference to the creative movement of Prakṛti. There is no time apart from this concrete movement. The idea of temporal sequence is intermingled with the idea of objective succession in Prakṛti. The primordial movement in Prakṛti does not involve any idea of heterogeneity, with reference to which empirical time-phases can be meaningfully understood. Thus, in the pre-empirical aspect – described as the state of cosmic dissolution – Prakṛti is to be taken not only as a principle of unconscious matter but as the principle of time itself in its transcendental aspect. In the conception of the dynamic Prakṛti, Sāṅkhya combines time and matter in the same principle.

(ii) Time as instant – the Yoga view

Contrary to the Sāṅkhya school, where involvement with the problem of time is implicit and therefore open to a certain extent to interpretation and construction,

7 Again, Vijñānabhikṣu, a notable Sāṅkhya commentator, advances a slightly different argument for the Sāṅkhya refusal to accept time as a real per se. He says, in his *Sāṃkhyapravacana Bhāṣya* [12] 2/12, that time is nothing apart from the ubiquitous *ākāśa* or ether, which is an evolute of Prakṛti. The same qualifying adjuncts, which are said to account for time-divisions, can do so with reference to *ākaśa*, making it unnecessary to postulate a separate ubiquitous substance called time.

we find in the *Yoga Sūtra* of Patañjali and in the subsequent philosophical works of the commentators profound, pertinent discussions which have direct bearing on the problem of time.

The basic ontological structure of the Yoga school of philosophy is akin to that of Sāṅkhya. The system occupies itself with the question of time and develops its specific stand on the reality of the instant (*kṣaṇa*) and the merely subjective construction of sequence (*krama*). These ideas, which are pronounced and explicitly worked out in the system, support the Sāṅkhya denial of the Nyāya-Vaiśeṣika conception of an indivisible, unitary time as an independent category of existence.

The distinct philosophical features of the conceptual model for understanding time in the Yoga school provide a striking contrast with the Nyāya-Vaiśeṣika view, emerging in the Brahmanical tradition, but also offers points of subtle difference with the Buddhist view. Separate sections are devoted to such studies and observations.[8]

As in Sāṅkhya, so in Yoga the treatment of the problem of time is closely related to their specific conception of becoming (*pariṇāma*). The problem of becoming, both for Sāṅkhya and Yoga, is a metaphysical problem which cannot, by any means, be reduced to a problem of appearance – as in the system of Advaita Vedānta. The Yoga literature – specifically the *Yoga Sūtra* of Patañjali [10] (III, 13-15) and all the important commentaries and subcommentaries thereon – devotes considerable attention exactly to the diverse aspects of this problem. The analytical exposition of their conception of becoming, as we shall see, clearly indicates why in the Yoga metaphysical structure there is no necessity for admitting time as an objective category of existence – a position held and defended by the Nyāya-Vaiśeṣika school – and also brings out its difference from the Buddhist understanding of the universal instantaneous character of being. The conventional usages of the three times are accounted for in accordance with the idea of change inherent in the heterogeneous becoming of Prakṛti, which is an essential feature of the Yoga metaphysical structure.

The *Yoga Sūtra* III, 13 focuses on the three modes of immanent change, which in Yoga terminology are termed as the *dharma-*, *lakṣaṇa-* and *avasthā-pariṇāma.*

Change is incessant in the ever-active *Prakṛti* – the ultimate substance (*dharmin*). When the change is perceptible as a change of quality in a substance it is called *dharma-pariṇāma.*

Lakṣaṇa-pariṇāma refers to the changes involved in the different stages of the mutation of the entity in question in terms of its temporal phases, past, present, and future. The potential state is designated as future, the manifested is the

8 See sections VII (ii), (iii).

present and when it is back in its sublatent state, it is the past phase of the thing. For the purpose of the present undertaking the most significant is this conception of *lakṣaṇa-pariṇāma*, which directly involves the notion of temporal phases. The Yoga conception of instant (*kṣaṇa*), as we shall see shortly, is to be grasped in the context of this analysis.

That aspect of change is *avasthā-pariṇāma*, which involves the notion of new and old, i.e. pointing to the mutations affecting the constitution of the entity in question. Let us take the example of the earth as the substance (*dharmin*), which can be gradually transformed into a jug. The change of quality through the different stages of the mutation of the earth constitutes its *dharma-pariṇāma*. When the temporal aspect of the change is emphasised as in the statement that the earth which is at present a jug was in its past phase a lump, it is *lakṣaṇa-pariṇāma*. Again, when the changes in the same jug lead to its characterization as new or old, it is called *avasthā-pariṇāma*. It is to be noted that the earth as the substance (*dharmin*) remains in and through its various mutations.

The above classification of the three *pariṇāmas* or changes gives the Yoga understanding of the problem a distinct pattern, which stands out in contrast to the Buddhist formulation of the problem, as will be seen later.

Let us observe that the formulation of the problem of change here is in perfect consistency with the Sāṅkhya-Yoga metaphysical stand and its theory of causality, viz. *satkāryavāda*. Emergence or birth does not entail for Sāṅkhya-Yoga the coming into existence of the non-existent, just as death or destruction does not imply the annihilation or passing into non-existence of the existent. The understanding of change or becoming is in full conformity with the dictum of *ex nihilo nihil fit*. The Yoga conceptual model becomes explicit in *Yoga Sūtra* III, 14, which states in unambiguous terms that the substance (*dharmin*) remains and persists through all the three stages, past, present and future, characterised as the quiescent, the uprisen and the indeterminable.[9] Thus, it is to be noted that temporal phases are attributed to the external aspects, i.e. qualities (*dharma*) of the substance, which is itself conceived as persistent through all these phases.

Let us now note the conception of instant in this system. The *Yoga-Bhāṣya*, the important commentary on *Yoga-Sūtra* by Vyāsa [10] contains the remark that the whole universe undergoes change in a single moment.[10] In other words, the contention is that "the collocation of atoms at any moment is different from what it was at the previous moment".[11]

9 *Śāntoditāvyapadeśyadharmānupātī dharmī.*

10 *Tenaikena kṣaṇena kṛtsno lokaḥ pariṇāmam anubhavati* (III,52).

11 *A History of Indian Philosophy* by S. N. Das Gupta, [7], vol. I, p. 256.

What, then, is a moment to Yoga? The *Yoga Sūtra* III, 52 deals directly with the ideas of *kṣaṇa* and *krama*, i.e. moment/instant and sequence. We read in the commentary on the same *Sūtra* that "just as the atom is the minimal limit of matter, so the moment is the minimal duration taken by an atom to change its position" [10 b] p. 28.

It is important to focus on the conception of *lakṣaṇa-pariṇāma* in order to grasp fully why to the Yoga perspective the moment is real and why it designates all ideas about sequence or objective temporal series as nothing but a conceptual construction.

As we have noted, the past and the future are explained in this system as inherent in the mutations. Vyāsa, in his commentary on the *Yoga Sūtra* IV, 12 goes deeper into the problem and points out that amongst the three time-forms, "one time-form is present, the other two time-forms are of course inherent in the substance. Future is that, the phenomenalisation of which is yet to come, the past is that, the (individual) phenomenalised (form) of which has been experienced. The present is that which has entered into its functional activity" [10 b] p. 315.

Let us observe that the idea of a succession of moments as an "absolutely existing continuum"[12] is, as the Yoga analysis shows, a subjective, conceptual construction. The moment is real, it is the basis for the idea of sequence, but whereas the former is objective, the latter is merely subjective.

It is clear that the Yoga is advocating a discrete view of time. The idea of time as a collection of moments does not correspond to anything objectively real (*vastu*). It is a mental structuring. The very idea of sequence would not be possible if two moments existed simultaneously. The real fact is that two moments cannot and do not occur other than successively. There is only the present moment, the earlier (past) and the later (future) moments have no objectivity.

The Yoga school is pronounced and clear in advocating its specific stand about the problem of time. Vyāsa's commentary on the *Yoga Sūtra* III,52 (10a) clearly says that the moment is real,[13] whereas the idea of an unitary objective time either as a collection of moments or as an objective series is a subjective representation, devoid of reality.[14] No two moments can exist simultaneously.[15]

It is evident that the idea of the reality of the instant is to be traced only in the present time-form, where the phenomenalising function is actual. It is the present moment which alone is causally efficient and objective and therefore is to be

12 Das Gupta – *Yoga Philosophy*, [14], p. 215.

13 *Kṣaṇastu vastupatitaḥ kramāvalambī.*

14 *Sa khalvayam kālo vastuśunyo buddhinirmāṇaḥ śabdajñānānupāti.*

15 *Na ca dvau kṣaṇau saha bhavataḥ.*

distinguished from the past and the future moments, which are merely subjective.

As we review the Sāṅkhya and the Yoga positions regarding their understanding of time, certain points of distinction strike a critical reader.

In Sāṅkhya, Prakṛti as time personified is a conception of time as eternal, i.e. beginningless and endless, tending more towards time as unitary than as discrete. In that case, the instant – following this interpretation – is only an abstraction. The analysis of time in Yoga philosophy explicitly advocates a discrete view of time. Therefore, before we conclude our discussion of the Sāṅkhya-Yoga views about the problem of time, let us further investigate into the question.

For both Sāṅkhya and Yoga the problem of becoming is to be grasped in and through an analysis of the causal operation of Prakṛti, which is held as an independent (*svatantra*) and objective principle. They both reject the coneption of time as advocated by the Nyāya-Vaiśeṣika schools.

It is important to understand why in spite of their common basic metaphysical structure, the treatment of the problem of time is not akin in Sāṅkhya and Yoga. We have seen that direct reference to the question of time is explicit and clearly pronounced in the Yoga literature, whereas the Sāṅkhya view despite certain clear indications of disapproval of a conception of an empty, absolute time is open to interpretation.

A search for understanding this disparity, which is overlooked in general, finds illuminating expression in the writings of K.C. Bhattacharya. Fully aware of this difference in their views of time, he traces its source in the subtle distinction in the views of causality of these two schools. Despite the similar conceptual structures of the schools, their emphasis on the formulations regarding the problem of becoming has a certain difference which emerges in their views of time. The philosophical significance cannot be overlooked.

Bhattacharya presents it in the following manner:

"Neither system admits time as a separate *tattva*: time is to both concrete becoming or *pariṇāma*, which is not conceived as an event in time. *Pariṇāma* may be understood as the cause turning up its own limitation or as the limited effect having got manifested. In the former conception, the real objective fact is the act of the cause, its act of turning up or the production, the succession of cause and effect being only a retrospective construction as in the Bergsonian view. In the latter conception, the real fact is the antecendence of the cause to the effect, the prior becoming of the effect, but the causal act as the initial moment of this becoming is but an abstraction. Hence to Yoga, which presents the former conception, time is real as the causal act, the initiation or the initial moment of becoming (*kṣaṇa*) ... To the latter or Sāṅkhya conception of becoming, the effect being pre-existent in the cause is never turned up, so that the time-relation of sequence alone – the prior process of manifestation constitutive of the manifestness of the effect – is real time".[16]

The philosophical involvement of the Yoga school in the problem of time – indicating the reality of instant and the mere mental construction of the sequence – is motivated by the ultimate goal that the system sets before itself, i.e. the discrimination between Puruṣa and Prakṛti, which constitutes the salvatory knowledge. This, the Yoga school claims, demands the one-pointed (*ekāgra*) concentration, which is a mental state to be distinguished from the dispersive, distracted states. The *Yoga Sūtra* provides a technical classification of these mental states, describing their subtle differences from one another. It is important to note that it is precisely in this context that the Yoga conceptual pattern for understanding change – with reference to the substratum which remains selfsame amid its mutations – is discussed.

It is with reference to the same mind (*citta*) that its different states – inimical or conducive to yogic concentration (*samādhi*) – are explained. The philosophical analysis of the past, present and future time-phases is made in connection with the passing-away, the uprising, and the coming forth of the states of the same mind. Consequently, the ideas concerning the mental structuring of the temporal sequence and the reality of the instant as referring to the minutest mutation that is constantly present in all the evolutes of the ever-changing Prakṛti, also gradually take shape.

(iii) Sāṅkhya and Vaiśeṣika on time – a comparative note

It is now possible to note the philosophical bridge, that connects the views of time found in these schools with their respective conceptions of causality. The status of the effect is evidently assessed differently by these schools in accordance with their different causal theories, which in turn have significant bearing on their treatment of the problem of time.

As we have noted, in the *ārambhavāda* framework of Vaiśeṣika the theory of causality viz. *asatkāryavāda* focuses on the effect as a new emergence, as a beginning (*ārambha*) of something which was not before. The effect was nonexistent (*asat*, hence the theory is called *asatkāryavāda*) as opposed to the Sāṅkhya theory, where the effect is existent (*sat*, hence the theory is termed *satkāryavāda*) previous to the causal operation. This philosophical difference in the

16 K.C. Bhattacharya, *Studies in Philosophy* [101], Vol. 1, p. 234-5.

interpretation of the causal operation implies important differences in their views of time.

The Nyāya-Vaiśeṣika philosophers found it necessary to hold a view of time as an all-pervasive, unitary real per se, with reference to which alone contingency is conceivable. The effect is not merely an actualisation of that which was potentially present in the cause – as the Sāṅkhya philosophers would have it – but a beginning of a phenomenon which did not exist before. This prior absence (*prāgabhāva*) of the effect is conceived within a metaphysical structure, where time is attributed a beginningless, endless reality. This is the absolute background for all that is contingent. Time is, therefore, characterised, as has been noted, as substratum of all that has a beginning and/or end, but to which no beginning and end can be attributed. It is classed as an independent substance in support of the Nyāya-Vaiśeṣika pluralistic metaphysics.

This notion of absolute, real, objective time, let us note, is not required as a frame of reference for a theory of causality where the effect is conceived – unlike by the Vaiśeṣika philosophers – not as non-existent but as pre-existent in the cause prior to the causal operation. This is why in the conceptual framework (*abhivyaktivāda*) of the Sāṅkhya-Yoga schools the specific theory of causality (*satkāryavāda*) which is advocated, could go hand in hand with their denial of the Nyāya-Vaiśeṣika view of time as an absolute, unitary, independent existent.

The theories of causality, fully worked out in each system, have significant implications for the problem of time. The philosophical exchange between the schools regarding the status of the effect, whether it is non-existent or pre-existent in the cause prior to the causal operation, is therefore of interest as they neccessitate different views of time. The Sāṅkhya answers to the objection raised by the Nyāya-Vaiśeṣika – as to why the effect cannot be regarded as non-existent – by pointing out that no systematic account of a definite causal relation between the non-existent effect and the existent cause would be established. In that case, a cause could give rise to any effect without any restriction whatsoever.[17] Evidently, experience does not testify to that. The specific effect emerges as it is already latent in the specific cause.

Thus, in the Sāṅkhya formulation, the effect is not viewed as a new beginning, marked by prior absence, but as a manifestation, an actualisation of that which was present in the cause. This theory, therefore, can do away with the notion of an empty time as a category of existence. It is not required as a necessary reference for any understanding of causal operation which, however, is the case in the Nyāya-Vaiśeṣika metaphysical scheme with its specific view of causality.

17 *Sarvasambhavābhāvāt*, *Sāṅkhya Kārikā* 8 [11].

For Sāṅkhya time is nothing independent of the concrete becoming of Prakṛti. This is why the Sāṅkhya philosophers urge, that the usages of past, present and future do not indicate the existence of or call for a postulation of time as a unitary substance, but that such usages can be accounted for »... as being the modes of the constitution of the things in its different manifesting stages of evolution (*adhvan*) ...«.[18]

The Nyāya-Vaiśeṣika philosophers, however, insist that the conventional usages of past, present, future not only indicate but are made possible by the very existence of an all-pervading, partless, uniform time. This is the basis for all such conventions, which, however, do not introduce any division in the unitary time but are measures by such actions as the solar motion. The contingent is in time. The indivisible time is a reality per se.

A search through the available Sāṅkhya literature shows that a direct reference to the problem of time is scarce, which is, again, a contrast to the Vaiśeṣika literature, where ample material concerning the problem of time is to be found. This is understandable, as the philosophical perspective in each case differs and along with it their involvement with the problem. It is causality which is the key problem for understanding change, becoming, in Sāṅkhya. To Vaiśeṣika philosophers even the very problem of causality presupposes the existence of the absolute time as a feature of reality. Their philosophical concern for the problem of time is, therefore, of a different dimension.

A reference to the problem of time, however, arises in the context of the Sāṅkhya account of the subdivision of organs as external and internal. The author of *Sāṅkhya Kārikā* mentions in Kārikā 33 that an important point of difference between them is that the former – the sense organs – act at the present time whereas the latter act at all three times, making inferential knowledge about past, present and future happenings possible. It is while commenting on this Kārikā that Vācaspati Miśra in his *Tattvakaumudī* points out in unambiguous terms the difference of the Sāṅkhya position regarding time from that of the Vaiśeṣikas. His comment is that even the Vaiśeṣika philosophers according to whom time is one, indivisible, attribute the conventional usages of time-divisions as past, present and future to certain qualifying adjuncts (*upādhi-bheda*) – like the solar motion. The Sāṅkhya teachers maintain that these qualifying adjuncts can in that case account for such usages and they, therefore, do not admit of time as a separate category of existence. In other words, the postulation of an indivisible time-substance (*kāladravya*) is held to be unnecessary.

Thus the philosophical perspective of Sāṅkhya offers an interesting contrast to that of Vaiśeṣika – both systems arising within the Brahmanical tradition. The

18 Das Gupta [7], Vol. 1, p. 310.

Sāṅkhya position can be seen as a challenge to the very conception of vacant time as a separate, independent category of existence (*tattva*), a position held by the Nyāya-Vaiśeṣika philosophers. This assumption appears superfluous and untenable to the Sāṅkhya analysis of experience, adopting a different metaphysical structure. There is no room for an event-in-time conception in this system.

III

(i) On time as appearance – the Advaita Vedānta appraisal

The most significant ideas in the system of Advaita Vedānta, that are to be noted in the context of our present undertaking, center primarily on the conception of being as timeless, involving the notion of time as appearance.

The continuing philosophical march of Advaita Vedānta, covering historically a long period, has witnessed the emergence and growth of a bewildering mass of literature of great philosophical depth and logical subtleties. The masterpieces of Śaṅkara, as well as the significant formulations of his predecessors – of whom Gauḍapāda is notable – and the post-Śaṅkara contribution in defence of the school against its opponents, have all without exception focused on the ontological conception based on the Upaniṣadic expression of the reality as "the-one-without-a-second" (*ekamevādvitiyam*).[1]

The conceptual framework of this system has a unique character of its own, having its stamp on all the different aspects – epistemological, logical, metaphysical –, worked out in consistency with its fundamental philosophy of being.

Advaita Vedānta, considered as representing the culmination of the Brahmanical tradition, rejects the pluralistic metaphysics of Nyāya-Vaiśeṣika as well as the dualism of Sāṅkhya-Yoga. As the very term *advaita* signifies, a systematic effort is made to construct a metaphysical structure on the basis of the idea that the real is non-dual.

This understanding, which the Advaita Vedānta maintains to be the final goal of all the teachings of the revealed texts of the *Upaniṣads*, has led to a rigorous formulation of the conception of the non-dual real – Brahman – as timeless, which reduces on the other hand all duality i.e. difference to a problem of 'appearance'.

It is, therefore, indispensable to have a brief summary of the philosophical tenets of the school, their implications and consequences, in order to bring out

1 *Chāndogya Upaniṣad* – 6/2/1 [3].

its subtle differences from the conceptual models present in the other Brahmanical schools.

We have already noted the metaphysical structures along with the respective theories of causality of the dualistic Sāṅkhya-Yoga and the pluralistic Nyāya-Vaiśeṣika. The *pariṇāmavāda* of the former has *satkāryavāda* as its supporting theory of causality, whereas the *ārambhavāda* of the latter has its theoretical basis for causal operation in the *asatkāryavāda*. The Advaita Vedānta metaphysical conception, which is more rightly termed as non-dualistic than monistic, requires a corresponding development in its understanding of causal operation, which is formulated in its *vivartavāda*. The specific Advaita stand can be made clearer in the light of these other systems, as the controversies between the two theories philosophically paved the way for the emergence of a full-fledged causal theory, which is peculiar to this system. A global assessment of these theories brings into clear perspective the differences in the respective conceptual structures with their eventual implications pertinent to the problem of time.

In the dualistic structure of Sāṅkhya, besides the principle of Puruṣa – a conception modelled closely after the Upaniṣadic pattern of the real as unchanging and unchangeable – there is the conception of Prakṛti, the principle of concrete becoming. Both are granted ontological status. The *pariṇāmavāda* of Sāṅkhya interprets causal operation as involving a real transformation of the cause into the effect.

In Advaita Vedānta, however, there is no room for two reals. The corresponding principle of multiplicity and change that Prakṛti stands for in the Sāṅkhya system is replaced by a still more complex conception of *avidyā* to which no ontological status is granted. The quest for the ontological real as non-dual and immutable cannot admit of either the Sāṅkhya metaphysical structure nor its theory of causality.

In this connection, let us recall the implications of the problem of time in the *pariṇāmavāda* framework. The Sāṅkhya theory of causality does not advocate the effect to be non-existent prior to its production. The causal theory maintaining the prior non-existence (*prāgabhāva*) of the effect has a meaningful temporal reference in the Nyāya-Vaiśeṣika which operates with the event-in-time conception. The Sāṅkhya does not hold time as a separate ontological category, as apart from the process of concrete becoming. In the Sāṅkhya formulation of causal operation, in terms of manifestation of the effect from potentiality to actualisation, the conventional temporal usages are accounted for differently.

As we have discussed before, the conventional usages of time can be viewed as an aspect of the heterogeneous evolution of Prakṛti (*visadṛśa-pariṇāma*). The Yoga school holds the empirical time-phases of past, present and future to be equivalent to the sub-latent, actual and potential states of an entity in question.

In other words, the time-phases refer to that aspect of evolution which breaks through the homogeneous process of self-reproduction bringing forth the heterogeneous categories of existence. Emergence as present, dissolution as past and the potential as future can thus account for conventional temporal usages without having to grant time a distinct existence per se, as the Nyāya-Vaiśeṣikas would have it.

We have also noted that time could be, as some Sāṅkhya interpreters maintain, taken as co-eval with Prakṛti itself. Viewed thus, the state of homogeneous modification (*sadṛśapariṇāma*) could be identified with time in its pre-empirical aspect. Here, the intrinsic movement – involving self-reproduction of the three *guṇas* – is, as it were, the temporal throb, which continues. In this state the three *guṇas*, however, do not combine and therefore cannot evolve any novel category of existence with reference to which the three temporal usages of past, present and future can be made possible –, as we gather from the *Yoga-Sūtra*. The significant point, which is relevant for comparing the position with that of Advaita Vedānta, is that the time-aspect of Prakṛti, involved in its nature of constant modification (*pariṇāmī-svabhāva*), is ontological in character. It is to be noted that although the problem of time receives distinctly different philosophical treatment in Sāṅkhya in comparison to Vaiśeṣika, yet the ontological reality that it grants to Prakṛti, as eternal-in-change, makes the position radically different from that of Advaita Vedānta.

The above account of the implication of the problem of change and time in *pariṇāmavāda* is intended, on the one hand, to focus on its philosophical closeness to Advaita Vedānta – and on the other hand to point out its difference from the latter.

Advaita Vedānta agrees with Sāṅkhya in denying a distinct reality to the effect, which – as has been amply demonstrated in the Nyāya-Vaiśeṣika structure – requires the presupposition of the ontological reality of time. Advaita Vedānta refutes this realistic view of time. We take up some examples of the Advaita Vedānta refutation of the reality of time in section III(ii).

It is, however, of basic importance to note where Advaita Vedānta parts company with Sāṅkhya. It is clear as one considers the metaphysical structure as well as the theory of causality found in the Advaita Vedānta philosophical literature.

As we have already noted, the Sāṅkhya and the Vaiśeṣika conceptions of the effect (*kārya*) – as expressed in their respective theories of causality – vary according to their metaphysical commitments.

In the *ārambhavāda* structure of Nyāya-Vaiśeṣika pluralism the effect is viewed as a distinct existent, different (*bheda*) from the cause. In the *pariṇāmavāda* of Sāṅkhya dualism, the effect is conceived as pre-existent in a potential state in the cause and is, therefore, non-different (*abheda*) from the latter.

In the Advaita Vedānta metaphysics of non-dualism, the effect is characterised – in its specific theory, viz. *vivartavāda,* as 'no other' (*ananya*) to the cause. This term *ananya* acquires a technical significance, which not only bears witness to the underlying metaphysical motivation of the system, but also enables one to distinguish its position from both the Sāṅkhya and Vaiśeṣika schools of philosophy.

In his commentary on the *Brahma-Sūtra* 2/1/14 (*ārambhādhikaraṇa*)[2] Śaṅkara brings out the significance of the term clearly. Again, Vācaspati Miśra in his sub-commentary, *Bhāmatī,* on the same *Sūtra* minutely works out the import and the implication of the term. From the above literature we gather that the effect is not to be conceived as having a distinct existence apart (*bheda*) from the cause, as the Vaiśeṣikas would have it. On the other hand, the Sāṅkhya term *abheda* does neither appropriately express the Advaita appraisal of the effect. The term *ananya* is to be understood as the effect being no other to the cause, which is a subtle and significant difference from the Sāṅkhya commitment to regard the effect as of identical status with the cause. This is the core of the *vivartavāda* of Advaita Vedānta. The significance of the term *vivarta* is explained in the *Vedāntaparibhāṣa* [44],[3] an important work on the Advaita-Vedānta glossary of technical terms. The philosophical import of the term *vivarta* is brought out by contrasting it with the term *pariṇāma.* It is said that when the cause and the effect are taken to be realities of the same order, the effect is designated as *pariṇāma* of the cause, e.g. Prakṛti and its evolutes in Sāṅkhya. But if the effect cannot be ascribed the same ontological status as its cause, it is styled *vivarta,* as in the case of the world as effect in relation to its cause, Brahman, in Advaita Vedānta. It is important to note that the idea of the cause in *vivartavāda* is so conceived, that the cause, unlike in *pariṇāmavāda,* is not said to undergo any transformation or modification. It is thus by denying both the *ārambhavāda* and *pariṇāmavāda* that Advaita Vedānta develops its *vivartavāda.* The conception of the effect as indeterminable, i.e. neither a relation of identity (as in Sāṅkhya) nor that of difference (as in Vaiśeṣika), is of great theological consequence. The distinct approach of this philosophical school leads to the formulation of the effect as the 'appearance' of the cause, which is the real.

That the effect cannot be granted an independent status of its own is a recurrent theme in all the commentaries of Śaṇkara. The point is made emphatically that the effect cannot be meaningfully ascribed a separate existence of its own, other than a difference of name (*nāma*) and form (*rūpa*) – just as the earthen pot

2 *tadananyatvamārambhaṇaśabdādibhyaḥ* [39].

3 *pariṇāmo nāmopādāna-samasattāka-kāryāpattiḥ vivarto nāmopadāna-viṣama-sattāka-kāryāpattiḥ* (*pratyakṣa-pariccheda*).

cannot have reality apart from the earth, its material cause (*upādāna-kāraṇa*).[4] The earth, i.e. the cause, does not, on the other hand, undergo any change.

Advaita Vedānta constantly focuses attention on this idea that no change or modification can be ascribed to that which is real. In other words, change can neve. be granted an o-tological status.

In Appaya Dīkṣita's *Kalpataru-Parimala*[5], a sub-commentary on *Bhāmatī*, we find the author again bringing out in bold relief that to deny difference (*bheda*) is not to assert identity between the effect and the cause. This is the precise technical significance of the term *ananya*.

The philosophical consequence of *vivartavāda* is enormous. It brings forth the conception of appearance – a key idea in Advaita Vedānta philosophy and theology. It is motivated to create an awareness of a shifting of standpoint as one confronts the problems of change and becoming, multiplicity and difference. Advaita Vedānta grants to it empirical reality (*vyavahāra*), thus focusing on its causal dependence on the real per se (*paramārtha*), which is immutable and impartite. The cause as the real is the ground for the effect as appearance.

The Advaita philosophical literature abounds, therefore, in analysis regarding the implication and consequence of this key conception of appearance in its epistemological, logical and metaphysical aspects.

It is commonplace in the philosophical works of the school to analyse a case of empirical illusion – such as the rope appearing as a snake or shell as silver – in order to bring out all the relevant philosophical features of such experiences.

That the Advaita epistemological stand is far removed from that of the subjective idealists becomes at once evident, as one considers the philosophical consequences worked out by its advocates.

The real as the cause (rope, shell) is given, i.e. its existence is not constituted by or dependent on the knowing function. The appearance as the effect (snake or silver) is entirely dependent on the cause, which is a given fact (*vastutantra*). Appearance cannot claim any independent status of its own. Moreover, appearance is always appearance of something given, the real. The philosophical implications of these ideas are worked out in great detail.

But for the purpose of our present study we shall only focus on the Advaita conception of the real as that, to which no change – neither beginning, end nor modification – can be ascribed. This is of immense interest for an understanding of the conception of being as timeless. This specific Advaita Vedānta formulation of the idea of being as timeless is taken up in a separate section. We shall,

4 As e.g. on *Chāndogya-Upaniṣad* 6/1/4 [38].

5 Commenting on *Brahma Sūtra* [39] 2/1/15.

however, discuss briefly the impact of these ideas in terms of their theological consequence.

The quintessence of Advaita Vedānta is often expressed thus – Brahman is real, the world is false, the *jīva* (the individual) is non-different from Brahman.[6] The philosophy contends that the realisation of the world as appearance, which is equivalent to false in Advaita Vedānta appraisal, at once leads to the awareness of the real. This is the salvatory knowledge of Brahman arrived at by negating appearance.

The vital question that arises at this point is, what makes the world a falsity, an appearance?

This is exactly where the analysis of the empirical illusion comes in to clarify what constitutes the criterion of appearance, what is the status of appearance and its implications about the real. The Advaita practice is then to extend this analogically to the idea of world-appearance and to point out its significance.

Advaita Vedānta works out minutely its theory of illusion, termed *anirvacanīyakhyāti*, through a detailed analytical exposition and refutation of all other rival theories propounded by other schools.[7]

In the Advaita-Siddhi [43] an attempt is made at a clear conceptual formulation of what is understood by falsity (*mithyātva*). Some of the illuminating definitions are: The false is subject to negation in all three times (*traikālikanisedhapratiyogitvam*). The real is, by implication, unsublatable (*trikālābādhyam*). Again, the false is that which is removable by knowledge (*jñāna-nivartatvam*). Knowledge, here the non-discursive intuition, reveals the real. The false is also defined as that which is neither real nor totally non-existent (*sad-asad-vilakṣaṇatvam*). Thus, the false/the appearance is termed as indeterminable (*anirvacanīya*), as its sublatability deprives it of being called a real per se, nor can it be classed as non-existent since it appears.

This is precisely the status of the world in the Advaita appraisal. The world as effect signifies that it hs no independent existence apart from its cause. The cause is self-existent, the effect is contingent. Brahman, the real per se, is the very ground for the world appearance.

Thus the Advaita Vedānta position is to be distinguished from the Nyāya-Vaiśeṣika conception of the reality of the world supported by its causal theory, where the effect is taken as an independent existent.

The Advaita Vedānta reduces the problem of creation to a problem of appea-

6 *Brahma satyam jaganmithyā jīvo brahmaiva nāparah.*

7 *Such as sat-khyāti, ātma-khyāti, anyathā-khyāti, akhyāti* and *asat-khyāti*. *Brahma-Sūtra* 1/1/1.

rance. Just as the fact, that the pot has a distinct name and form (*nāma-rūpa*), does not indicate its existence to be independent of the 'earth'; similarly the world as effect has no independent existence without its cause, Brahman.[8]

Here it is interesting to note that the Advaita Vedānta does not accept the theological formulation – as in *Brahmapariṇāma-vāda* – where the world is conceived as a real transformation of Brahman. Advaita Vedānta maintains Brahman as the cause, but cannot accept any transformation (*pariṇāma*) or modification (*vikāra*) of it. The empirical world has no reality of its own, it is entirely dependent on the self-existent Brahman, whereas Brahman is the indispensable ground of the world-appearance. This is the position which is variously characterised as *māyāvāda/anirvācyavāda/vivartavāda*.

It is important to bear in mind, that the idea of appearance does not imply that the world for Advaita Vedānta is merely a subjective dream or illusion. Śaṅkara in and through his refutation of Vijñānavāda, the Buddhist school of subjective idealism, makes the Advaita conception distinctly clear.[9]

In this connection, it is of great theological interest to see the implications of Brahman, the real per se, as cause. The conception of Brahman as the cause[10] of the origin, sustenance and cessation of the world gives expression to the challenge that is faced by all theologians, across cultural boundaries, viz. the formulation of the idea of being as timeless as the very presupposition of the temporal. Here is a search for a formulation of a notion of cause which does not hamper the conception of being as immutable, non-dual.

Brahman as cause, in the Advaita Vedānta philosophical literature, is taken as an accidental or modal definition of it (*taṭastha-lakṣaṇa*). Brahman, conceived as the unmodified ground (*adhisthāna*) of the world-appearance points to the transcendent character of the cause. There are significant theological implications of the *vivartavāda* approach. It intends to bring out that 'the real' is the implicate and not implicatory of appearance; the appearance is implicatory of the real and not its implicate.[11] The world as effect is no ontological real, but Brahman as its ground is self-existent.

Thus the modal definition indicates Brahman as the ground of the world-appearance. The Advaita Vedānta advances, however, a non-relational definition (*svarūpa-lakṣaṇa*) as being-consciousness-bliss (*sat-cit-ānanda*). Much has been

8 See *Brahma-Sūtra* 2/1/14.

9 In his commentary oin the *Brahma Sūtra* 2/2/28 *nābhāva upalabdheḥ* and 2/2/29 *vaidharmyācca na svapnādivat* [39], Saṅkara refutes the Vijñānavāda position, which brings into focus that the world is empirically real. The idea of the falsity or appearance of the world is intended to disclose its entirely dependent status, i.e. it is no real per se.

10 *Janmādyasya yataḥ, Brahma Sūtra* 1/1/2.

11 *The two definitions of Brahman in the Advaita* by T.R.V. Murti [49].

written and discussed on these ideas which are of profound theological consequence. Advaita Vedānta is held as interpreting justly the claim of the *Upaniṣads* that it is the knowledge of Brahman – "by knowing which one knows all".[12] Brahman is the one-reality-without-a-second.

It is, however, important to observe that for Advaita Vedānta the realm of duality and difference is the temporal order – that which is designated as appearance. The real as unchanging and unchangeable is timeless. Where there is no change – i.e. no beginning, end or modification, where there is no room for even a numerical difference, i.e. duality, there is no question of time either. "Within the world of experience time has universal scope". However, the point remains that "the world is not self-sufficient. The temporal is not the real".[13] Thus the problem of time is necessarily a problem of appearance.

(ii) On refutation of the reality of time

In the person of Śrī Harṣa, the system of Advaita Vedānta finds an ardent advocate, who uses his dialectical skill in its defence. A major target of his attack has been the system of Nyāya-Vaiśeṣika realistic pluralism. Śrī Harṣa's analysis [45] aims at showing that the *lakṣaṇas*[1] and the *pramāṇas*,[2] with the help of which the Nyāya-Vaiśeṣika systems have constructed the categories of existence (*padārtha*), are themselves defective. Thus, in the context of the dialectical analysis of the idea of causality, Śrī Harṣa is led to examine the definition of cause as proposed by the Nyāya-Vaiśeṣika philosophers, which, as we shall see shortly, has bearing on the problem of time. Śrī Harṣa's refutation is tantamount to denying the conception of the reality of the objective time as a category of existence (*padārtha*) as held by the Nyāya-Vaiśeṣika schools. It is evident that the goal of Śrī Harṣa, as an Advaitin, is to establish *vivartavāda*, which calls for a dismissal of the realistic approach to the question of causality.

The Nyāya-Vaiśeṣika schools have defined cause as an invariable, necessary antecedent to the effect. The cause as antecedent to the effect necessarily refers to time. The causal operation, involving this idea of temporal precedence (of the cause) and succession (of the effect), in the Nyāya- Vaiśesika system is worked

12 *Chāndogya Upaniṣad* 6/1/3 [3].

13 *Indian Philosophy*, by Radhakrishnan, [8], Vol. II, p. 528.

14 Characteristic marks.

15 Valid means of knowledge.

out – as we have already discussed – in the framework of the notion of unity and reality of time as an objective, ontological category.

Śrī Harṣa's objection is first aimed at the very definition of cause as the temporally antecedent. The chief points of his analysis can be summarised as follows. He raises the question whether these time-distinctions, as past, present, and future, are integral to time as such or not.

If it is held that this distinction of three time-forms is inherent in the very nature of time, in that case the unity (*ekatva*) of the real time, as the Nyāya-Vaiśeṣika philosophers would have it, cannot be maintained. In other words, if our apprehension of the past time, present time, and future time is due to the very nature of time as such, then differences would be integral to time and consequently the notion of the unity of time has to be given up.

On the other hand, if one maintains the unity of time as essential and the differences of time-forms as inherent in it as its three-fold nature, then the designations of past, present and future could be made at random for the want of a strict basis for such usages. This is to say that one cannot accept the differences of time-forms as integral to one time either.

But if, as the Nyāya-Vaiśeṣika philosophers maintain, the time-distinctions are attributed to other external factors such as the solar motion, Śrī Harṣa finds that too equally untenable. His objection is that the solar motion cannot account for the determinations of the different time-forms, since it is used as the common criterion for the distinctions of all three time-forms – past, present, and future. The idea that the same qualifying factor, viz. the solar motion, which distinguishes the past day from the present, also distinguishes the present day from the future, is not a basis for valid argumentation.

If the Nyāya-Vaiśeṣika now urges that although as such the solar moton is the same, distinctions are conceivable with reference to it because of the time-distinctions and thus can account for the conventional usags of past, present, and future, – this too cannot be accepted. Śrī Harṣa brings the charge of the fallacy of circular definition (*itaretarāśraya*) against this argumentation. He points out that the argument is tantamount to saying that the present time is determined by the act, and the presentness of the act is due to time. Moreover, if the time-distinctions are due to the act, then they can be just as well accounted for by the act, making the assumption of one, indivisible, substantial time superfluous.

This discussion, found in the *Khaṇḍaṇakhaṇḍakhadyam* by Śrī Harṣa,[16] is an example of the rejection of the reality of time through a critical analysis of the Nyāya-Vaiśeṣika definition of cause as antecedent to the effect. The temporal determination is the basis which makes it possible to demarcate the effect – as

16 [45] pp. 682-684.

present – from its cause which precedes it. The main aim of the analysis is to expose, that this very definition of cause as entailing time-distinctions requires that the latter are accounted for. Tha Advaita understanding of the indeterminable (*anirvacanīya*) character of the empirical world cannot accept the Nyāya-Vaiśeṣika notion of causal operation implying the reality of time.

The Advaita Vedānta philosophical march aims at the establishment of Brahman as the sole reality, one without a second (*ekamevādvitīyam*). This is evidently, as we have discussed earlier, a conception of being as timeless of which no difference – external (*vijātīya*), internal (*svagata*), or numerical (*svajātīya*) – can be predicated. In this metaphysical structure, therefore, there cannot be any room for a conception of an objective, real time. To accept time as a substantial reality leads to, as exemplified in the Nyāya-Vaiśeṣika structure of thinking, realistic pluralism.

Thus, although there is not much direct involvement with the problem of time in the system, there are documents in the philosophical literature of the Advaita Vedānta on refutation of the Nyāya-Vaiśeṣika position regarding the reality of time.

We have noted an example of that in Śrī Harṣa's work. In the important work called *Tattvapradīpikā* [41] by Citsukha we find still another example of it. The challenge of the reality of time is taken up by the Advaitins as the position cannot be compromised with the idea of Brahman as worked out fully in the philosophy of Advaita Vedānta. To accept time to be real is to make way for pluralism. The world of multiplicity and change cannot be pronounced, in that case, as appearance. In the *ārambhavāda* structure of Nyāya-Vaiśeṣika the theory of causality, *asatkāryavāda*, operates with the conception of the effect as real, as a new emergence. The Advaita Vedānta, which intends to discard pluralism of ontological categories, formulates the problem of causality in a manner so as to clearly distinguish it from both the asatkāryavāda of Nyāya-Vaiśeṣika as well as from the *satkāryavāda* of Sāṅkhya-Yoga. The Sāṅkhya model of causal operation, as we have already studied, is expressed within a framework involving the conception of being as eternal-in-change, viz. Prakṛti. This too as an objective, ontological principle, although closer to the Advaita standpoint than the Vaiśeṣika position, is yet untenable. Advaitins seek to establish *vivartavāda*. The Advaitins have therefore examined and refuted these two theories of causality. Thus, it is in the context of a review of the Nyāya-Vaiśeṣika theory of causality that Citsukha comes to examine the Nyāya-Vaiśeṣika view of time.

Citsukha raises the question as to how the Nyāya-Vaiśeṣika establishes the reality of time. This is in order to scrutinise the *pramāṇas* used for the argumentations in favour of their position. The Nyāya-Vaiśeṣika understanding of the causal operation as involving a sequence presupposes the reality of time. If time were real, the reality of precedence and succession of cause and effect could be established, as a consequence of which the reality of the world too would have to be granted. Thus, by refutation of time as ontologically real, the realistic view of causal operation is also shown as untenable. As a consequence the significance of the world as appearance, as in the *vivartavāda* appraisal, comes into focus.

Citsukha argues to show that neither perception nor inference can establish the reality of time. Historically, the target of Citsukha's attack is the realistic position about the problem of time as advocated in the *Nyāyalīlāvatī* [26] of Vallabhāchārya. The ontological reality of a substance can be established through perception only if – and this is in accordance with the Vaiśeṣika stand – the substance in question can be said to be perceived by vision or touch. Citsukha points out that since it is held that time is without form and is intangible, sense-perception cannot be the source of knowledge, which can demonstrate it as having an ontological status – as the Nyāya-Vaiśeṣikas seek to establish.

His next consideration is whether it could be so maintained that time is known not through external sense-perception but through internal or mental perception (*mānasa-pratyakṣa*). This too cannot be maintained, as internal perception cannot refer back to an objective entity, which cannot otherwise be established by sense-perception. But since the substantial time cannot be, as we have seen, said to be an object of sence-perception, internal perception cannot establish it.

Again, it is possible to point to the existence of such mental states as sadness, happiness, etc. which are known through introspection and need not to be first known by sense-perception. Could time be established in a similar way? Evidently not, as it is only possible for such facts which are subjective (*āntara-vastu*), but time as an objective category of existence cannot be thus established.

At this point it is necessary to recall that the Nyāya-Vaiśeṣika philosophers do not seek to establish the reality of time by perception. It is inference (*anumāna*) which is used as the valid means of knowledge (*pramāṇa*). So Citsukha now turns to examine the validity of the Nyāya-Vaiśeṣika claim that time can be established by inference.

The point of controversy refers back to the Nyāya-Vaiśeṣika contention, that the existence of time is inferred on the basis of such apprehensions as priority and posteriority, which serve as the middle term (*liṅga*) in the said inference. To this Citsukha objects. He points out that inference is possible only where universal relation (*vyāpti*) between the major term (*sādhya*) and the middle term (*liṅga*) can be established. But in this particular case of inference how have the Nyāya-Vaiśeṣika philosophers obtained the knowledge of *vyāpti* (i.e. where there is apprehension of priority/posteriority, there is time) – or universal relation between the middle and the major term? It has never been perceived in any previous experience. Thus, this inference is fallacious. Time cannot be said to be established by inference either.[17]

Citsukha further investigates into the question. He asks whether priority, posterioty, etc. are to be understood as effects (*kārya*) of time or are due to any external adjuncts (*upādhi*). If, he points out, the Nyāya-Vaiśeṣika philosophers would maintain them as effects, then time as an instrumental cause cannot be held as passive (*niṣkriya*) – as the realists would have it. On the other hand, if it is due to such external adjuncts like solar motion, the latter can just as well be said to be sufficient basis in order to account for such conventional temporal usages. In other words, Citsukha points out that in neither case is it essential to postulate time as an ontological category.

The Nyāya-Vaiśeṣika appraisal is however different. To them, priority, posteriority are accidental or relational properties of given entities. The argument thus runs as follows: that (i.e. time) by contact with which entities (*piṇḍa*) get these properties or denominations, (e.g. this body is old, that body is young, etc.) – that must be a universal, ubiquitous substance.

Space (*dik*) cannot substitute for time. The spatial nearness and remoteness cannot account for temporal distinctions of which there is clear apprehension (*pratīti*). Citsukha asks, cannot the self (*ātman*) be a substitute for time? (Note that in Vedānta, *ātman* is universal and has no special property, unlike in the Nyāya-Vaiśeṣika system). This is, however, not acceptable to the realists, for whom the self has special qualities like desire (*iccha*) etc. In other words, it is not sufficiently neutral in character to perform the function of time.

This holds equally true of all other substances (*dravya*) accepted by the realists. It is time alone which can perform the exclusive function which enables the contact between the body (*piṇḍa*) and the solar motion. Earth, water, air, fire, – none of these can replace time as they are not all-pervasive. In other words, the realist search for a substance which is universal, all-pervasive, having no special qualities (*viśeṣaguṇa*) of its own leads to the detection of time as an ontological category.

Citsukha further objects that if time is universal and uniform, how can there be differences in our apprehension of time-distinctions such as day, month, etc.?

17 It is to be noted that the objection raised against this position is due to the fact, that the Vedantins accept only one form of inference (*anvayavyatirekī*), which has for its prerequisite that the association of the middle term with the major term has to be known, e.g. by perception, to make a valid inference.

To the Nyāya-Vaiśeṣika this does not hold true of all forms of inference. The inference of time is a case of *pariśesānumāna* where this requirement need not be fulfilled.

To this, the realist answers that time-divisions are due to such external adjuncts as solar motion. Time as an ontological all-pervading substance has to be accepted as that which makes these conventional usages at all possible.

Note that the solar motion is accepted by both parties as indispensable for accounting for conventional usages of time-distinctions. But whereas the realists are accepting time as a separate substance, as an ontological category, Citsukha finds such an assumption untenable and even entirely unnecessary. It is only needlessy increasing the number of ontological categories (*gaurava*), which is fallacious, going against the law of parsimony.

In conclusion, to an Advaitin the reality of time as a separate ontological category is wholly superfluous. No valid means of knowledge can be said to establish such a contention.

(iii) Being as timeless in Advaita Vedānta

The Advaita Vedānta conception of being as timeless deserves special attention. It is here that one comes across the most clearly pronounced expression of the idea in its philosophical refinement and purity. The conception is formulated with a philosophical rigour and depth, which surpasses all other attempts by the different schools in the Brahmanical tradition.

It is to be noted that the conception of *nitya vastu*, – being as uncaused and indestructible i.e. beginningless and endless – is present throughout the philosophical history of Brahmanism. All the principal philosophical schools have this conception, as their common heritage from the *Upaniṣads*, which plays a predominant role in their respective metaphysical structures. But it is of great philosophical interest to note how the understanding of *nitya vastu* varies from school to school, the philosophical development reaching its culmination in the school of Advaita Vedānta. In this system it gives rise to a strict, rigorous formulation, as an outcome of penetrating analysis bearing on all its implications and consequences.

In the Nyāya-Vaiśeṣika metaphysical realism there is room for a plurality of *nitya vastu*, conceived as ontological categories – beginningless/uncaused and endless/indestructible. It is not only *ātman* which is *nitya*, but so also are space, time, etc. They have distinct existences, where one cannot encompass the other. The *janya vastu*, i.e. that to which beginning and/or end could be ascribed, can be so encompassed. Thus time, a *nitya vastu*, encompasses all that is contingent (*ādhāra-ādheya sambandha*). The multiplicity and the differences of ontological categories of Nyāya-Vaiśeṣika metaphysical pluralism evidently find no room in the Advaita Vedānta scheme of thought.

Again in the Sāṅkhya metaphysical dualism both Puruṣa and Prakṛti are conceived as *nitya*, beginningless and endless, uncaused and indestructible. But Prakṛti, as Sāṅkhya specifies it, is a *pariṇāmī nitya*, i.e. it undergoes modifications. There is change of states (*avasthā*) in Prakṛti. Prakṛti is the underived principle of concrete becoming, movement is intrinsic to it. As we have already discussed earlier, even where the discernible time-phases are not present as in the *visadṛśa pariṇāma* or heterogeneous modification, it still preserves the principle of temporality in its transcendental aspect in the state of *sadṛśa pariṇāma* or homogeneous modification. The Advaita Vedānta has no room for change and becoming in its understanding of *nitya vastu*, which is conceived as unchanging and unchangeable (i.e. *kūṭastha/apariṇāmī*).

The Sāṅkhya conception of Puruṣa comes closest to the Advaita conceptual pattern, in so far as it is conceived as unmodified, unchangeable consciousness, but its obiection to Sāṅkhya would be the latter's idea of the plurality of Puruṣas. In other words, the Sāṅkhya conception of many Puruṣas is against the Advaita Vedānta understanding of the ultimate real. The absence of duality, i.e. numerical difference (*saṅkhyā-rāhitya*) may not be a requisite for the Sāṅkhya conception of *kūṭastha nitya*, but in Advaita Vedānta a plurality of similar (*sajātīya*), eternal (*nitya*) beings, as the Sāṅkhya idea of many Puruṣas implies, has no room. The *nitya* is not only beginningless, endless, unchangeable but also non-dual (*advaya*). Numerical difference is still difference (*bheda*) which belongs to the order of empirical reality (*vyavahāra*). Brahman as Being par excellence is the 'one-without-a-second' (*ekamevādvitīyam*), no change (*pariṇāma*), no duality/plurality (*dvaita*) can be predicated of it.

In this connection it is highly significant to note that the Advaita Vedānta arrives at this conception of being as non-dual, immutable, impartite, through the negative method of denying all differences (*bheda*) to it. This deserves special treatment. The conception of being as timeless – a philosophical idea on which Advaita Vedānta focuses in all intensity – demands a thorough and profound intellectual expression.

We, therefore, turn to *Pañcadaśī*, an important work on Advaita Vedānta by Vidyāraṇya [42], where a summary of the denial of differences is brilliantly worked out. All differences are classified under three heads – *svagata, svajātīya,* and *vijātīya*. As an example of the former kind, *Pañcadaśī* (II, 20) mentions such differences as in a tree, of leaves, flowers, fruits, etc. The difference of one tree from another is an example of the second kind. The third kind of difference is exemplified as that of a tree from a stone. In other words, difference is conceivable as existing within an entity, as difference in species falling under the same class/genus or differences of one class/genus from another.

It is precisely in order to remove all possible doubts about the conception of oneness of Brahman that these three kinds of differences (*bheda-traya*) are to be negated and rejected, thereby arriving at the right understanding of the import of the idea.

Thus, through denying any *svagata-bheda* in Brahman, the impartite character of being is indicated. It rejects the conceptual pattern present in the Sāṅkhya formulation of the notion of Prakṛti. Although beginningless and endless, modification and movement are intrinsic to Prakṛti. Moreover, Prakṛti is composite. As contrast to this, Brahman is conceived as uncomposite, it has no parts. No change of state/transformation can be attributed to it. It is *apariṇāmī*, unchanging and unchangeable.

By rejecting *svajātīya bheda* of Brahman, it is the non-dual (*advaita*) being which is indicated, where there is no room for numerical difference of similar entities. The Sāṅkhya model of many Purusas cannot be permitted.

Moreover, Brahman cannot be conceived as having any *vijātīyabheda* either. The Nyāya-Vaiśeṣika pluralistic model as well as the Sāṅkhya dualism operates with the conception of heterogenous, dissimilar ultimate ontological existents. It is not possible to conceive of an 'other' to Brahman, which is being or *sat*. Non-being or *asat* is non-existent and therefore, as we read in *Pañcadaśī* II, 25, cannot serve as a counter-correlate (*pratiyogī*) to Brahman.

There is, thus, no room for duality or difference in any conceivable form applicable to the idea of being, that Brahman stands for in the philosophy of Advaita.

Let us now observe that the idea of *nitya vastu* has profound philosophical implications. Although all the Brahmanical schools agree in defining *nitya* as beginningless and endless, as unoriginate and indestructible, yet the subtle philosophical differences in their understanding are unmistakable.

The conception of *nitya* as in the Sāṅkhya model of Prakṛti implies eternality, but not timelessness. By insisting that the *nitya* must be *apariṇāmī*, immutable, the Advaita Vedānta is driving towards the conception of being as timeless in contrast to being as eternal.

Moreover, a yet more rigorous formulation is attained through denial of numerical differences, of similar and dissimilar eternal entities. Thus, the Sāṅkhya and the Vaiśeṣika metaphysical structures cannot satisfy the Advaita quest for the being as timeless. There is no room for duality in this framework of thinking, as it operates with the rigorous conception of the ultimate real (*sat*) as 'one-without-a-second'. Brahman is plenitude (*bhūma*), unlimited and impartite (*aparicchinna*), and non-dual (*advaita*).

In this connection it is to be observed that Brahman – the ultimate, non-dual being – is, in some Advaita texts like *Advaitasiddhi* [43], described as *trikālābādhya,* i.e. uncancellable in all three times, past, present, and future. It is that about which one could not say – it is not, it will not be, or it was not. In other words, it is not being-in-time. But if it is urged that the Sāṅkhya conception of Prakṛti is also uncancelled in three times, the difference lies evidently in the Advaita rejection of all modification and change as pertainable to Brahman.

The same question can be discussed with regard to the idea of ever-presentness (*sarvadāvidyamānatva*). The idea of being as ever-present is another way of designating being which no time can cancel. To say that there is no conceivable time where absence or negation of being can be maintained is a mode of indicating its ontological status. Now, again one could apply the idea to the Sāṅkhya or the Nyāya-Vaiśeṣika models of *nitya-vastu.* This is why a thorough rejection of all three kinds of differences is an indispensable and effective conceptual tool for arriving at the idea of being as timeless. Thus, being which is ever-present, in other words, which is uncancellable in all three times, when purged of all the three kinds of differences, leads to the idea of being as timeless.

Moreover, it is not to be lost sight of that, whereas the principle of change qua time is objective and ontological in Sāṅkhya, *avidyā,* the corresponding principle in Advaita Vedānta, has merely epistemic status. Time as a product or as a personification of Prakṛti is real in Sāṅkhya, whereas time as product or as coeval with *avidyā* is only appearance in Advaita Vedānta. The Nyāya-Vaiśeṣika conception of time as an ontological category is, as is evident, totally unacceptable to Advaita Vedānta. This is why all the various modes of defining the timeless Brahman are to be taken as accidental definitions – *taṭastha-lakṣaṇa* – of Brahman. These are attempts to describe or define Being as timeless from the order of time, which coincides with that of the phenomenal and empirical.

IV

(i) Time in Jainism

The metaphysical stand of Jainism, known as *anekāntavāda*, is, as the term designates, an attempt to construct a conceptual structure which makes room for a many-sided view of reality. It aims at formulating a conception of reality, which can accomodate both identity and difference, permanence and change.[1] It therefore seeks to avoid such views which are branded as *ekānta-vāda*, i.e. the extreme one-sided views, which either emphasize the reality of the ultimate identity at the exclusion of change or maintain the reality of perpetual change at the price of identity. The system of Advaita Vedānta, for example, represents the former and Buddhism the latter, which are therefore extreme views, designated by the Jainas as *Brahma-ekāntavāda* and *kṣaṇika-ekāntavāda*, respectively. Jainism seeks to avoid these extreme views and puts forward a comprehensive philosophical position as a metaphysical reconciliation.

This is a broad outline indicating the conceptual goal of the Jaina philosophers, which was eventually worked out in detail, covering such areas of investigation as logic, epistemology, ethics, eschatology, etc. The Jaina contribution to these fields of knowledge saw the development of new concepts in support of its metaphysics. The Jaina philosophical tradition has a distinct flavour, which is un-Buddhistic and un-Brahmanical, in so far as it sets up a metaphysical structure peculiar to its own view of reality.

It is evident, as the philosophical exchanges point to, that the metaphysical compromise of the Jaina philosophy found favour with neither the Brahmanical nor the Buddhist thinkers.

The Jaina attempt to avoid the extreme one-sided views gave rise to a distinct conception of the real, which is formulated by Umāsvāti in his *Tattvārthādhigama Sūtra* [67] as *utpāda-vyāya-dhrauvya-lakṣaṇam sat*, i.e. origin, decay and permanency are the characteristics of the real. In other words, this threefold characteristic of the real is expressing the Jaina conception which allows for

1 cf. *Jaina Sūtra* [70] and *Syād-Vāda-Mañjarī* [71].

difference/change and yet maintains an underlying permanence/identity. This becomes even more clear, as one notes the Jaina conception of substance (*dravya*) which plays an important role in Jaina metaphysics.

It is indispensable to have an overall idea of the metaphysical structure of the system in order to comprehend the conception of time which is eventually the subject of interest for our present study. The Jaina metaphysical system is one of realistic pluralism. The two important terms, that occur throughout the Jaina philosophical literature, are *dravya* and *astikāya*. It is only through our understanding of these concepts that we can grasp the distinct Jaina formulation of the problem of time.

Dravya or substance is defined by Umāsvāti as that which possesses qualities and modes.[2] To talk about a substance without qualities and modes or vice versa is merely an intellectual abstraction which does not do justice to reality. The system lists six substances (*dravyas*) as ultimately real, of which one is time. The various principles that are employed to classify the substances (*dravyas*) according to their characteristics at once focus on the Jaina view of time as such along with its similarities and differences from other substances. The six *dravyas* that are listed as metaphysically real are *jīva, pudgala, dharma, adharma, ākāśa* and *kāla,* i.e. the soul/the conscious substance, matter, the principle of motion, the principle of rest, space and time.

Amongst the six *dravyas* five are called *astikāya,* a concept which is significant for the conception of time, negatively speaking. The term *astikāya,* consisting of two words *asti* and *kāya,* is explained in *Dravya-Saṃgraha* [66], 24, an important Jaina book of which the author is Nemichandra, as follows – *asti* literally means 'exists' and *kāya* means 'body'. The *astikāyas* are therefore those five substances which exist and have magnitude/bodies. Here *kāya* is technically understood as consisting of many indivisible particles (*pradeśa*). Thus, the Jaina text points out, five out of the six substances apart from time can be characterised as *astikāyas*. This becomes clear in the context of the general atomic conception of the universe in Jaina thought, as the notion of *pradeśa* indicates. The five substances are called *astikāya* precisely because the particles of which they are composed are not separate or at least in principle capable of being mixed up. This specification helps one to understand why time (*kāla*) is not classified as an *astikāya* by the Jainas despite that it has existence.

The Jainas propound an atomic conception of time.[3] The characteristic of the time-atoms is, however, such that they are distinct and can never be mixed up.

2 *Guṇaparyāyavat dravyam.*

3 For the internal differences between the Svetāmbara and Digambara Jainas, see Nagin J. Shah, *Nature of Time,* [118] p. 63-87.

This is brought out by saying that *kāla* has one *pradeśa* only, i.e. the time-atoms can never be combined. This explains why time cannot be classified as an *astikāya*. This, again, is a clear way of indicating the difference between the atoms of space, matter, etc. from that of time.

An important understanding pertaining to the time-atoms is discussed in the Jaina text entitled *Pañcāstikāyasāra* [68] (109). Here it is pointed out that the fact, that time has no *corpus* (*kāyatva*) or extension, is generated by such an arrangement that the time-atoms can constitute a mono-dimensional series which is unilateral. This is what in Jaina terminology is called *ūrdha pracaya* as opposed to the *tiryak pracaya* – a multi-dimensional series or horizontal extension. A. Chakravarti writes in his 'philosophical introduction' to *Pañcāstikāyasāra*, "... when the simple elements, say the points, are so arranged in a series, where each term is an item also in another series, we must have the two-dimensional series, which will correspond to surface or extension. Whereever there is such a *tiryak pracaya* we have *astikāya*. But time or *kāla* has only *ūrdha pracaya*. The elements are in a forward direction ...«.

The Jaina understanding of the time-atoms (*kālānu*) as ultimate, absolute and real again points to its distinction from the conventional time (*vyavahāra kāla*). The conventional time-periods, of which we find a long list in *Pañcāstikāyasāra*, 25, range from the minutest moment called *samaya*, through *nimiṣa*, *kāṣtha*, *kalā*, *nāli*, to *muhurta* – equal to two nālis, divārātra – day and night, equal to thirty *muhūrtas*, *māsa* – month, equal to thirty days, *ṛtu* – season – equal to two months, *ayana* – half year – equal to three seasons, *samvatsara* – year, which is equal to two *ayanas*. These divisions and subdivisions are linked to the different units of measurement pertaining to conventional time.

It is said that these distinctions of conventional time-periods are made possible only with the help of some extraneous factors. The units of measurement are generally based on some changes in the physical world, such as the motion of the heavenly bodies. This is why conventional time is never unconditional but dependent on other outside factors, unlike the real, absolute time, which is variously designated as the great unconditioned time (*paramārthakāla*), true time (*niścayakāla*), real time (*dravyakāla*).

The conventional time presupposes the absolute time. In the Jaina text the absolute time is described not only as a real existent but also as being potent, i.e. it brings about changes in the other substances. Birth, growth and decay of things are due to its influence.

It can thus be noted that the very changes, which determine the use of conventional time, are themselves the effects of absolute time. All distinctions that are made of conventional time, short or long and so forth, are dependent on the standard of measurements. They are not intrinsic to absolute time as such, nor can they affect the latter by any means.

The absolute time, consisting of instants, is conceived as having no beginning or end, whereas conventional time have both. This brings into light an important feature of the Jaina understanding of time. The instants arranged unilaterally are conceived as permanent (*nitya*),[4] i.e. beginningless and endless. The Jainas agree with the other atomic views of time (e.g. Yoga, Buddhist views) in maintaining that no two instants can be found simultaneously but unlike them conceive of the instants as unperishable. Time (*kāla*) is *nitya* for Jaina, like the Vaiśeṣika philosophers held it to be, but the difference between them is glaring. The Vaiśesika view of one ubiquitous time is found to be untenable, and the Jainas propound an atomic, plural view of time instead.

The Jaina conception of absolute, real time is to be contrasted to the idea of time as appearance. Time, to the Jaina thinkers, is a substance, having an ultimate status in the pluralistic metaphysics of the system. No modification in the universe can be conceived without time.

It is significant that Jainism with its realistic framework of thinking accepts the reality of change which, in turn, points to the reality of time. To deny the reality of time is tantamount to the dismissal of all change involving birth, growth, decay or motion. It is precisely this position that is avoided by maintaining the reality of time.

Thus, we find that in the Jaina structure the absolute time-atoms are conceived as pervading the space (*lokākāśa*, i.e. the space which is occupied by other substances as opposed to *alokākāśa* signifying void), the instants having no extension or volume (*kāya*). In other words, there can be no question of simultaneous moments, the time series consisting of time-atoms is always to be understood as successive.

The different principles for classifying the *dravyas* in distinct groups are, as already indicated, a source of our knowledge about the Jaina idea of time. In chulika 104 of *Pañcāstikāyasāra*, *dravyas* are classified as *mūrta* and *amūrta*. The substance which is found to have sense-qualities such as contact, smell, colour, sound, etc. is called *mūrta*. Matter (*pudgala*) alone is said to be so, whereas the other five, including time, are classified as *amūrta*, i.e. devoid of sense-qualities. This is indicative of the fact that the absolute time can never be made an object of sense-perception. It is arrived at through knowledge by inference.

Again, according to another principle of classification, on the basis of which substance can be said to have consciousness, we find that *jīva* alone is singled out

4 Chulika 108, *Pañcāstikāyasāra* [68].

as conscious (*cetana*). All the other substances including time are listed as *acetana* or insentient.

The chulika 105 of the same text brings out the conception of time as non-active (*niṣkriya*). This means that causal activity bringing about any change in it is contemplated as inconceivable. On the other hand, no change in matter involving aggregation or disintegration is conceivable without time.

These are the main ideas about time that can be traced from the original Jaina texts.

The Jaina challenge to the Vaiśeṣika conception of time is documented in an illuminating discussion which will now be taken up.

(ii) The Jaina challenge to the Nyāya-Vaiśeṣika conception of singular, ubiquitous time

An interesting account of the plural conception of time as instants – a Jaina conviction sought to be established through a refutation of the Vaiśeṣika conception of one ubiquitous time-is documented in the reputed Jaina work called *Prameyakamalamārtaṇḍa*.[5] The Vaiśeṣikas and the Jainas both accept the reality of change along with the reality of time. Their notions of time, however, have important differences.

To the Jainas, the absolute time consists of the ultimate time-atoms, which are evidently conceived in plural terms, and the conventional time-periods, short or long, are all due to the measurements made on the basis of such extraneous factors as the motion of heavenly bodies.

The Vaiśeṣikas, however, maintain that the absolute time is one and indivisible, the conventional time-usages can be many, made on the basis of such units of change as the solar motion etc. The Jainas find it untenable and raise a philosophical challenge to this notion of one ubiquitous time.

The question raised from the Jaina standpoint is, whether the Vaiśeṣika understanding of time is that of one partless, indivisible substance (*eka-dravya*) or that of a substance composed of parts (*aneka-dravya*). Evidently the reference is to the Vaiśeṣika Sūtra, where the question has been discussed. The Jaina refutation is so formulated as to point out that neither of the two possibilities can be valid thereby demonstrating the vulnerability of the Vaiśeṣika position.

5 By Prabhāchandrāchārva [69].

The Jainas argue that time cannot be taken as an indivisible, partless substance. If it were so, the distinction between time per se and the conventional time – which is accepted by the Vaiśeṣikas themselves – would be impossible. If the essential nature of time is to be ubiquitous, it can never be divided even with the help of any external adjuncts, as that is possible only in the case of a composite substance, made of parts.

On the other hand, if the absolute time is taken as a composite substance (*sāvayava-dravya*), one need not postulate time as a separate substance, space could serve the purpose. Space, in Jainism, is conceived as having parts, which makes the conventional use possible. The same space (*lokākāśa*) is known somewhere as Lankā, and elsewhere as Kurukṣetra. In other words, it is superfluous to accept a notion of time as a composite substance. If time is to be postulated as a separate substance, it is to be accepted as atomic in nature.

The Jaina argument against the notion of time as ubiquitous is that, on the basis of such a conception, it is not possible to account for such conventions as past, present, future, etc. Such usages as past time etc., the Jaina asks, is it due to its relation to past causal efficiency or is it integral to time itself? If one accepts the first alternative, the Jaina objection is, that in that case causal efficiency itself could be the basis for such conventions as past time, and it would be unnecessary to postulate time as a separate substance. Moreover, the further difficulties that will arise here are, how should one determine the pastness of a causal efficiency? If that involves another causal efficiency, the argument would lead to infinite regress (*anavasthā*). On the other hand, if it is urged that the usage of the causal efficiency as past is possible only on the basis of time, and again the usage of time as past is possible on the basis of causal efficiency, it involves the wrong argumentation of mutual dependence (*anyonyāśrayadoṣa*).

The second alternative, that such conventional usages can be accounted for as integral to time itself, is, however, simply unacceptable. A partless substance, as the Vaiśeṣika philosophers hold time to be, cannot have any inherent differences as natural to it.

Again, the Jaina points out that, contrary to the Vaiśeṣika supposition of one ubiquitous time as a necessary basis for accounting for such usages as slowness, fastness, the atomic notion of time as plural has to be admitted for explaining such uses. Slowness and fastness only indicate that which is accomplished by more time or less time – both leading to a conception of time as many. It is quantitative manyness or scarcity of time which is at the back of it, a convention which can never be explained on the basis of a notion of time as one, indivisible and ubiquitous.

The notion of simultaneity is also examined in this connection only to expose the untenability of the Vaiśeṣika conception of time as involving fallacious circular arguments. Simultaneity, when analysed, only shows that though the effects are different, they are produced together. On the basis of this it is needless first to postulate one indivisible time and then to imagine differences in it with the help of adjuncts, i.e. the effects, in this case.

If it is pointed out that the notion of sequence calls for a conception of indivisible time, the Jaina is equally insistent on demonstrating that the very idea of sequence demands an atomic view. Simultaneous or successive (i.e. involving a sequence) occurrences can be accounted for as pertaining to the same or different moments. All these arguments aim at showing, that the conception of indivisible time is to be rejected.

V

(i) The Buddhist idea of instantaneous being

Apart from the conceptual models that the study of being and time have given rise to in the Brahmanical tradition, there is an entirely novel set of ideas introduced by the Buddhist thinkers in their philosophical treatment of these problems.

The Buddhist stand regarding the problems of being and time represented a complete departure from the views hitherto emerged in the pre-Buddhistic period of Indian philosophy. The Buddhists renounced all conceptions of being as permanent, as immutable, as substance and universal. They also rejected all ideas about time as unitary, as an all-embracing receptacle and as a real per se. They maintained, on the contrary, the idea of reality as flux, involving a conception of time as instant and that of being as instantaneous. This has the radical implication, as the technicalities of Buddhist thinking disclose, that difference of time involves difference of being, so much so that at no two instants can a thing be said to remain identical. The position is even more drastic. As we shall see shortly, the Buddhist brings out the idea, that being as instantaneous and time as instant coalesce ontologically, their so-called separation can only be attributed to an arbitrary linguistic convention.

The pressure and the challenge of this radical view gave rise to polemics. With the advent of Buddhism the history of Indian philosophy underwent a long period of growth and multifaceted development. Conflicts amongst the Brahmanical, Buddhist and Jaina schools – leading to a full disclosure of the philosophical implications and consequences of their respective positions – constituted a driving force towards coherency and consistency and thereby contributed to greater maturity of philosophical thinking. Some of these exchanges resulting from philosophical disputes are selected and dealt with in the next section in so far as they are directly relevant and illuminating for a study of the problem of time.

It is a matter of common observation, that destructibility and transitoriness of things have often stimulated philosophical and spiritual thinking. The apprehension of the transitory, the impermanent and the ephemeral has led to the quest for the contrast which is variously described as the permanent, the unchanging and unchangeable, the beginningless and endless, etc. The Brahmanical philosophers, for example, have all admitted such a category in their conceptual frameworks irrespective of their monistic, dualistic or pluralistic bias.

But a remarkable feature of Buddhist thinking is the marked absence of such a category which is exempt from change. Their philosophical investigation focuses on the idea, that all without exception is subject to change. The Buddhist raises a sequel of arguments to demonstrate logically, that what does not change cannot be said to exist. This itself introduces a revolutionary way of looking at the universe, leading to a reformulation of all philosophical problems which have been hitherto conceived in terms of the category of an abiding substance with changing attributes and qualities. A thorough rejection of the substance view and a full exploration of the idea of pure change is no easy intellectual task. One has to watch the steps, by following which the Buddhist insists upon the fact that nothing real can be unchanging. Even more, the Buddhist demonstrates that the real as changing is instantaneous in character. This is to be contrasted with the idea of longer or shorter duration attributed to a changing object by common sense or by systems committed to realism. To the Buddhist, to say that existence is flux implies its essentially momentary character.

Again, this signifies that destruction follows immediately after the moment of origination. This Buddhist view is opposed by those who maintain that destruction is not spontaneous but dependent upon additional, external cause and circumstance, thus involving the idea that the changing object is not necessarily momentary.

Thus, the problem of change and the problem of destruction with their necessary and inevitable implication for the problem of time undergo a revolutionary treatment in the hand of the Buddhist. Change is not modification but substitution of one entity by another; destruction is total and spontaneous. The Buddhist claims that an entity perishes and is replaced by another at every instant. The idea of time as instant and its inseparability from being – as instantaneous – is the key to the Buddhist conceptual structure. An attempt to understand these radical ideas of change and destruction,[1] which are evidently not empirical but transcendental notions involving a specific view of time, would lead us to the heart of Buddhist philosophy and lay bare the Buddhist logic which is urged upon us in support of the position.

The Buddhist doctrine of universal momentariness (*kṣaṇikavāda*) is of vital importance for an appraisal and understanding of this novel philosophical per-

1 See sections V (iv) and VII (iii).

spective, which emerged in the history of Indian philosophical thought with the rise of Buddhism.

Buddhist philosophers of all the three periods, into which the history of Indian Buddhism is generally classified, have all explored the view of the real as momentary The doctrine of universal momentariness, however, has received various interpretations from the Buddhist philosophers of different schools in its different periods of development. We shall take a brief note of these internal differences regarding this doctrine of central importance for all Buddhist thought.

But prior to this let us note how the Buddhist establishes the momentariness[2] of the real. Evidently, it cannot be established by perception. The Buddhist proves it by inference. The Buddhists offered a chain of arguments and analysis with the view of establishing their principal thesis that the real is momentary. Existence and annihilation, change and motion are analysed in order to focus on this very idea. Ideas of duration, extension, permanence and continuity are rejected dialectically in consistency with their principal thesis.

The classical Buddhist arguments formulated by the philosophers of the Sautrāntika school, belonging to the first phase of Buddhism, were to remain famous. The Buddhist scholars in the West as well as in India have noted them in great detail over and over again.[3] It is a landmark in the history of Indian philosophical speculation and opens the source of a new stream of ideas, which challenge the entire structure of Brahmanical metaphysics. The Buddhist argumentation aims at repudiating the permanent, the substance, and the universal.

A summary of the principal steps in their argumentation is attempted here. The criterion that distinguishes the real from the fictitious, the Buddhist argues, is causal efficiency. In other words, that which is real is essentially of the nature of a cause, i.e. it gives rise to effects.[4] The Buddhist attempts to demonstrate that causal efficiency is restricted only to the momentary, the permanent cannot be causally efficient. The Buddhist argumentation is a specimen of apagogic proof,

2 In *Vaibhāṣika Darśana* [60] p. 102 the following definition of momentariness is forwarded, making use of the concept of *abhava, svādhikaraṇa-samaya-prāgabhāvādhikaraṇakṣaṇasambandhittva* – that is, the momentary is non-related to the moment which is the locus of the antecedent non-existence of that moment which is its own locus, e.g. if a momentary thing A occupies a time T_2, then it is non-related to the preceding moment T_1, which is the locus of the antecedent non-existence of T_2.

3 See Stcherbatsky, *Buddhist Logic* Vol. 1 [63] Ch. 1 (p. 79-118) and S. Mookherji, *The Buddhist Philosophy of Universal Flux* [61] Ch. 1-2 (p. 1-38).

4 The Buddhist refutation of other contending theories concerning the criterion of real, although highly interesting, is a separate question and is omitted here.

which is directed towards establishing that the momentary alone can be said to be real through a repudiation of the permanent.

The Buddhist points out that causal efficiency can be exercised in either of the two conceivable ways, viz. in succession or simultaneity, and that the idea of the permanent is incompatible with it. If it exercises causal efficiency in the very first moment, can the permanent be said to exist after that? If so, it would give rise to the same effects in the second and in all succeeding moments, ad infinitum, which is absurd. If it does not produce effects and yet is imagined to be existent, it would then have two contradictory qualities, being efficient in the first moment and non-efficient in other moments. This manifest difference in the nature of the permanent points to the fact, the Buddhist argues, that the entity in question cannot be the same identical entity of the first moment. The Buddhist dictum is: that cannot be one, about which one could predicate contradictory characteristics.[5] In other words, to say that the real or the efficient exercises its causal power in the very first moment of its existence is tantamount to saying that in the succeeding moment it would cease to exist. Efficiency cannot be attributed to a perdurable/permanent entity.

The Buddhist proceeds to show that the permanent can neither be said to exercise efficiency successively. If the permanent has the power to give rise to effects in succession, it may be asked whether during its execution of present efficiency it also has the past and future efficiencies as well. If it has, the Buddhist argues, the inevitable result is that it would exercise them at the same moment – thus reducing the problem to that of simultaneous production, discussed above. If it does not have the past and the future efficiencies, it can never produce the effects. Thus the permanent has present causal efficiency and not the future and the past. To say, that the entity continues to be the same through past, present and future moments, is to commit the fallacy – as pointed out before – of investing it with contradictory qualities, which militates against its identity. At no two moments can the entity remain the same.

The opponents, however, bring forth further objections to the view, playing on the idea of auxiliaries (*sahakāri*) as necessary for the operation of efficiency, although the cause is the same.

Thus, the Buddhists had to defend their position against the following criticisms: (a) the thing may exercise its power, i.e. produce its effect gradually and not all at once, so that it may last for several moments or a period of time. Or (b) it may be that it possesses the power but it does not exercise it. Its power remains latent, owing to some factors which hinder it from being exercised.

5 *Yo viruddhadharmādhyāsavān nāsāv ekaḥ.*

The Buddhists refute both these criticisms by saying that in either case one has to say that the cause waits for some other factors in order to produce its own effect. From this they conclude that if it waits for some other factor, then by itself it has no causal power. For instance, if the cause is A and it has the power to produce the effect E, the Buddhists argue, A will do so, i.e. produce E in the very first moment of its existence. If, however, A waits for B in order to produce E, we should say that A does not have the power to produce E by itself, which contradicts the original hypothesis.

If one says that A cannot produce E, because O obstructs this causal efficiency, the Buddhists would reply that it would be better in that case to say that the causal power does not belong to A by itself, but belongs to A together with the absence of O. To sum up, the Buddhists reject the idea of merely latent power, or of power which is not exercised. If something has power, that power must be at once exercised, and if it is at once exercised, the thing would cease to exist in the next moment. The only other alternative to their thesis, according to the Buddhists, is that anything may last for ever, which is absurd.

Thus the permanent, to the Buddhist, coincides with the non-efficient, i.e. the unreal.

In this connection it is to be noted, that in the framework of Buddhist thought duration and continuity are nothing but conceptual constructions. The notion of duration formed of a chain of successive moments is merely metaphorical, devoid of any reality.

The Buddhist philosophical analysis reveals that the real time is instant. Time as universal receptacle à la Vaiśeṣika is absurd – as it cannot be said to have efficiency apart from the things. Their separation is merely imaginary. The idea of time as a real per se is rejected through a refutation of the ideas of duration and continuity.

Stcherbatsky in the following passage puts in an interesting manner the Buddhist view that duration is a fiction.

»If a thing exists at a moment A, it cannot also exist at some moment B, for to exist really at the moment A means not to have any real existence at the moment B or at any other moment. If we thus admit that the same thing continues to exist at the moment B, this could only mean that it at once really exists and does not really exist at the moment A. If a thing could have real duration through several moments, it would represent a real unity existing at once at different times. Either is the enduring unity a fiction and real are only the moments, or the moments are fictions and real is only duration. For the Buddhists the moments alone are real, duration is a fiction, for if it were a reality, it would be a reality existing at different times at once, i.e. existing and at the same time non-existing at a given moment]« [63], p. 87.

The Buddhist tirelessly points out that there is no real continuity and duration. The homogeneous succession where the posterior moment resembles the antecedent gives rise to the notion of so-called duration. In reality, this similarity is no continuity of an identical entity, but is due to a lack of perception of the subtle distinction of similar moments. In a heterogenous succession the difference is greater, and therefore the discontinuity is noticed, which is technically called the production of a dissimilar moment (*vijātīya-kṣaṇa-utpāda*). This is how the ideas of duration and substance are accounted for from the empirical standpoint. These ideas are forged and constructed out of the ultimate real which is the point-instant (*svalakṣaṇa*) – "the only thing in the universe which is a non-construction, a non-fiction" [63], p. 106.

Evidently this specific formulation of the idea of time as instant is intimately related to the Buddhist conception of cause. A thorough and searching analysis of causation has led to its formulation in terms of functional dependence. The doctrine of *Pratītya-samutpāda* or the law of dependent origination expresses the relation of cause and effect thus: this being that happens (***asmin sati idam bhavati***). This doctrine, again, is of capital importance for all Buddhist thought. Consequently, it has been interpreted and debated by the different Buddhist schools.

For the purpose of our present investigation, however, it is vital to note that to the Buddhist a non-cause is equivalent to the non-existent. That which is real/existent must be causally efficient, and it is only the instantaneous which can be so. Time as instant, again, indicates this ever fluctuating, evanescent character of being with which it is fused ontologically.[6] Being, time, and causality form a conceptual whole in Buddhist thinking.

(ii) Some internal differences regarding the doctrine of momentariness within the Buddhist tradition

The understanding of the doctrine of momentariness by the Vaibhāṣika school, also belonging to the first phase of Buddhism, features important differences from the Sautrāntika interpretation of it, which has been just discussed. The specific mode in which the Vaibhāṣika school formulated the idea of momentariness explains why the term *sarvāstivāda*[7] was especially coined to designate their doctrine. They propounded that all the elements exist in all three times. The

6 For more on the Buddhist understanding of time, see sections V (iv), VI, VII (iii).

7 The philosophy of all existents.

momentariness of the elements consists in their being subject to constant change and mutation. But in their noumenal state, so to speak, they are indestructible. This position has come down in four versions with slight variations. In the *Abhidharmakośa* of Vasubandhu [51] a good exposition of this stand is given. Moreover, both in the *Mādhyamika-Kārikā* of Nāgārjuna [56] and in the *Tattvasaṃgraha* of Śāntarakṣita [54] the view is referred to and refuted.

The first objection to this understanding of momentariness consists in labelling the position as accepting the elements to be permanent (*nitya*), since they are existent in all three times. This, the opponents hold, amounts to giving up the doctrine of momentariness.

The Vaibhāṣikas have answered to this objectio by pointing out that to maintain the reality of the elements (*dharmas*) in three times does not mean to accept them as permanent (*nitya*). Their momentariness is vouchsafed by their being subject to the incessant flow of moments, representing their coming into being (*jāti*), decay (*jara*), and passing away (*maraṇa*) – a sequence which is repeated over and over again. If the real were, so to speak, devoid of this process, the accusation of giving up the idea of momentariness could be made.[8]

It is interesting to note this *Sarvāstivāda* pattern of conceptualisation in the context of Buddhist philosophical treatment of being and time. Naturally, many scholars have found the Sarvāstivāda understanding similar to the idea of three mutations (*pariṇāmas*) described in the Sāṅkhya-Yoga.

A brilliant attack on this interpretation of momentariness is made by Śāntarakṣita in his *Tattvasaṃgraha* [54], who found the Vaibhāṣika understanding totally un-Buddhistic. According to the Vaibhāṣika philosophers the entity is said to exist in past, present, and future. This distinction of three times is made possible due to the difference of causal efficiency.

To this Śāntarakṣita raises the question whether causal efficiency should be regarded as identical with or different from the entity (*vastu*). If it is not identical, he argues, causal efficiency cannot be used as a basis for such usages. But if it were, the problem would still remain, as the present causal efficiency was not there before and will not be there after. In other words, causal efficiency, being only restricted to the present, cannot account for any sequence affecting the real or its continuity in three times.

It is to be noted that the Sautrāntika philosophers maintain, precisely therefore, that *vastu* is existent only at the present moment – when alone it is causally efficient –, neither in the past, nor in the future, thus departing from the Vaibhāṣika pattern of understanding, which is found akin to the Brahmanical Sāṅkhya and equally un-Buddhistic.

8 *Vaibhāṣika Darśana*, [60] p. 5.

Again, if it is urged that causal efficiency is restricted not only to the present, but is also there before and after as well, the consequence would be that the causal efficiency pertaining to the three times is to be taken as one and the same. This would lead to the acceptance of the *vastu* as permanent (*nitya*). The Vaibhāṣikas cannot, therefore, demonstrate the momentariness of the real on this premise, as they intend to do. A more serious objection would be that if *vastu* is taken as permanent, the entire chain of arguments, discussed in the previous section, would support the Sautrāntika thesis, that causal efficiency cannot be predicated of it; only the fluxional, the momentary entity can be causally efficient.[9]

The central insight, that is operating in this analysis, is that an investigation into the nature of *vastu* clearly reveals, that the idea of its enduring in three times is impossible to maintain. It is equally important to note the conceptual interdependence of causality, being and time in the Buddhist formulation. The critique of causality is at once disclosing being and time as ontologically inseparable. It is a total rejection of a static view of reality. Thus, the doctrine of momentariness contains the fruit of the Buddhist exploration of the problems of being and time.

Again, in the second phase of Buddhism, which saw the rise of Mādhyamika-Śunyavāda, the doctrine of momentariness received an altogether different interpretation. which is described by some as a 'dangerous crisis' for the doctrine [63] p. 110.

The protest against the substance-view was there at the very root of Buddhist thinking. The Mādhyamika school of Nāgārjuna offered a major challenge to the Ābhidhārmika position current in the first phase of Buddhism. If the Brahmanical model of being was rejected already in early Buddhistic thinking, the Śunyavādin Mādhyamika philosophers now attempted to expose dialectically the illusive character of the point-instant.

The dialectical method employed by them is used for the purpose of revealing that 'the world has only phenomenal existence and things are neither transient nor eternal, neither produced nor destroyed, neither transient nor eternal, neither produced nor destroyed, neither the same nor different, neither coming forth nor passing away except in appearance.[10]

The Mādhyamika standpoint, which sought to transcend the two extreme positions represented by the *ātma*- and *anātmavādas*, reveals a critical awareness about the limitations not only of the Brahmanical position, but also equally of the difficulties of the philosophical positions that emerged in the first phase of Buddhism.

9 *Tattvasaṃgraha* 1786-1856 *Kārikā: Traikālyasiddhi* [54].
10 *Indian Philosophy*, Vol. 1, p. 655 by S. Radhakrishnan [8].

The *Ratna-Kūta-Sūtra* (Kāśyapa Parivarta), belonging to the earliest Mahāyāna texts, anticipates and expresses the middle position represented by the school thus:

»'That everything is permanent' is one extreme; 'that everything is transitory' is another ... 'that *ātman* is' (*ātmeti*) is one end (*antah*); 'that the *ātman* is not' another; but the middle between the *ātma* and *nairātmya* views is the Inexpressible ... It is the reflective review of things (*dharmāṇāṁ bhūta-pratyavekṣā*)".[11]

In Nāgārjuna's *Mādhyamika-Kārikā* [56] (Chapter 19: *Kālaparīkṣā*) and its commentary by Candrakīrti one finds a dialectical analysis directly involving the problem of time. This investigation has for its aim to expose the untenability not only of any idea of time as unitary and absolute, but also of the notion of the reality of time as instant.

The motivation for the Mādhyamika dialectic, however, remains the same in all cases:

"It is the consciousness of the inherent contradiction present in the attempts of Reason to characterise the unconditioned in terms of the empirical. The dialectic exposes the pretensions of speculative metaphysics which seeks illegitimately to extend thought-categories beyond their proper field" [62] p. 75.

The analysis touches upon the pertinent questions which invariably arise for a study of time, viz. the conception of time-divisions, the idea of an empty time as a real per se or even the idea that treats time as coalesced with being, only to focus on the eventual untenability of these positions.

The existence of time is inferred by some as a basis for the apprehension of the three time-divisions such as past, present, and future. The validity of these time-discinctions is itself questioned by the Mādhyamika philosophers. They challenge the basis on which these time-distinctions are made to rest. The three time-distinctions are found to be made in relation to one another, such as the time-divisions of present and future are dependent on the past. But in what sense are they dependent? The time-divisions are never there all at once; when one is present the two others are absent. On the other hand, if they were co-present, they would be indistinguishable from one another. Again, if it is argued that the time-divisions are not made relative to one another, the question still remains as to what serves as basis of these distinctions. A non-relative past, present or future is not conceivable. In other words, the attempt to infer the existence of time on the basis of the usage of time-divisions is not justified, as the latter is not established on a sound philosophical premise. Again, it is significant that time is never apprehended independently of the time-divisions. Thus to argue that there is time as a real per se apart from the time-divisions makes no sense, as it cannot

11 Quoted by T.R.V. Murti in The *Central Philosophy of Buddhism* [62] p. 27-28.

be established without the latter as vital to its conception. On the other hand, time cannot be established on the basis of the apprehension of time-divisions, as the analysis has already disclosed its untenability. The Mādhyamika philosopher, therefore, concludes that a refutation of the validity of time-divisions (*kāla-traya-khandaṇa*) amounts to a rejection of time as a real per se.[12]

But the opponents protest. They insist on the existence of time as a real per se. They point out that since time has magnitude (*parimāṇa*), e.g. moment, day, month, etc., it must be existent, as a non-existent thing cannot be said to have magnitude, like the sky-lotus. The Mādhyamika remarks in reply that only when the existence of an entity is established, the question of its magnitude can arise. But a want of such a philosophical demonstration – as has already been shown – only indicates that the idea of magnitude itself is merely a superimposition and, therefore, cannot be used as a ground for accepting the entity in question. In other words, the existence of time cannot be established, neither on the basis of the apprehensions of time-divisions or time-magnitudes nor independent of them.

The Mādhyamika philosophers equally demonstrate the unsoundness of the argument involved in the idea of the existence of absolute time as cause for the origin, duration and destruction of all that can be characterised as contingent. This, evidently the realists' postition, is neither acceptable. The idea of time as absolute, invariable and uniform is incompatible with the idea of cause. The causally efficient can never be permanent (unchanging) – the arguments for that are well-established in the first phase of Buddhism. Moreover, the self-contradictory character of such notions as origin, duration and destruction has already been shown by the Mādhyamika dialectical analysis.[13] The Mādhyamika directs its criticism against those who maintain, that although the idea of time as unitary, absolute, etc. is not tenable, the idea of time as instant is valid. The exponents of this view point out, that the Mādhyamika rejection of the empty, unitary time is based on the fact, that time is never apprehended apart from the changing entity. The reality of time as instant in relation to the changing entity is therefore to be admitted.

As an answer to this the Mādhyamika points out, that if the existence of the changing entity can be established, the reality of time as instant could be accepted. But as the former (*bhāvapadārtha*) has already been shown to be untenable by prior dialectical analysis,[14] the reality of time as instant is also to be rejected.

12 *Yataśca evam vicārane kālatrayam nāsti, tasmāt kālo na vidyate, kālābhavācca bhāvasadbhāvo'pi nāsti iti siddham;* from the commentary *Prasannapadā* by Candrakīrti on *Mādhyamaka Sāstra* of Nāgārjuna [57] 19/4.

13 *Mādhyamika Kārikā* [56] 7/33.

14 *Mādhyamika Kārikā* 1/5-9.

The analysis amounts to a refutation of all views about time, which the Mādhyamika would label as dogmatic, the aim being to point to its phenomenal character.

It is interesting to note that although the doctrine of momentariness can be said to have received a severe blow in the second phase of Buddhism, the theory regains its central importance again in the third phase of Indian Buddhism. It saw the rise of Yogācāra-Vijñānavāda, the school of Buddhist idealism, which makes a bold use of the idea once again. But here too, there can be traced an interesting difference of opinion concerning the status, so to speak, of momentariness – as to whether it holds good only of the empirical or is to be accepted as an ultimate metaphysical truth. This question will be discussed in section VII (i), 'time and consciousness'.

(iii) Controversies centering on the Buddhist doctrine of momentariness (*kṣaṇikavāda*)

The history of the philosophical development of Brahmanical, Buddhist, and Jaina thought bears the stamp of mutual influence through interaction and confrontation of ideas. The philosophical disputes have played a significant role in shaping the views in their actual, full-fledged forms and even in influencing the specific orientations of the different schools.

An appraisal of the different philosophical stands regarding the problem of time, therefore, calls for an analysis of the polemics launched by the schools against their opponents and their defences put forward in reply to criticisms of their respective positions.

In this context of philosophical controversies one becomes aware of the impact of a specific view of time on the remaining major concepts in a given system. Time is a fundamental problem of philosophy, and any position taken regarding time is bound to influence the entire conceptual structure where it happens to figure.

The decisive role that a specific conception of time plays in a given system thus becomes immediately evident as one examines Buddhist thinking. Here one encounters the radical consequence, which a serious involvement with the problem has given rise to. In the Buddhist universe of thought the understanding of time as instant has carved out a conception of being entirely restricted to the instant which alone has causal efficiency. The idea of time as instant is so vital to

Buddhist thought that it can be said to be "the fulcrum on which the whole edifice of reality was made to rest" [63] p. 85.

A searching analysis has convinced the Buddhist that, ontologically speaking, neither is there any empty time nor any being which is non-temporal – positions which can be found in un-Buddhistic conceptual structures. The Buddhist understanding of the fusion of being and time, i.e. the ontological inseparability of the instant and the instantaneous, has revolutionary impact on all pertinent branches of conceptual enquiry, viz. logic, psychology, metaphysics, eschatalogy, etc., – all bearing witness to the presence of this view as being of central importance.

A study of the contending philosophical stands regarding the problem of time is not complete, if it is based only on the expositions of views found within the framework of specific philosophical schools. The immense value of the philosophical controversies is undeniable, as they bring into focus the consequences that a specific view of time has on other major philosophical issues which also have to be reckoned with. They are consequently indispensable for a proper assessment of the strength of the philosophical argumentations in support of the respective views of time.

Note, for example, the consequence of the Buddhist idea of the point-instant, which asserts that reality is through and through kinetic, leaving no room for any stable, stationary entity. This amounts to a total rejection of any so-called eternal metaphysical entity or principle, which is cherished in the non-Buddhistic conceptual structures. Buddhism has been thorough in its repudiation of even the so-called enduring empirical object, which is explained as nothing but a conceptual construction, a function of our imagination. Thus the discrete, discontinuous, atomic view of time is seen as detrimental and destructive of the Brahmanical and Jaina metaphysics, demolishing the conception of being that is hailed in these traditions. The idea of instantaneous being is therefore vehemently opposed by the Brahmanical and Jaina philosophers.

The history of Indian philosophy, thus, covers long records of controversies centering on the Buddhist doctrine of momentariness. To its opponents the doctrine has appeared to be both against reason and experience. The details of these exchanges can make volumes, which handle the problem from various angles and on different levels. In a set-up where free philosophical exchanges were in full swing, where no religion could survive without a philosophical backing, the challenge of Buddhism was taken up with utmost seriousness.

On the other hand, the Buddhist philosophers too were fully aware of the challenges that the doctrine of momentariness offered to the Brahmanical as well as the Jaina thinkers. Referring to the idea of instantaneous being, the reputed philosopher Kamalaśīla remarks,

"... By proving this our fundamental thesis alone, we could have repudiated at one single stroke the God (of the Theists), the eternal Matter (of the Sāṅkhyas), and all the wealth of (metaphysical) entities imagined by our opponents. To examine them one by one, and to compose elaborate refutations at great length was a perfectly useless trouble, since the same could have been done quite easily. Indeed, no one of our opponents will admit that these entities are instantaneous, that they disappear as soon as they appear, that their essence is to disappear without leaving any trace behind. We, indeed, are perfectly aware that by proving the instantaneous character of Being in general, these (metaphysical) entities would have been eo ipso repudiated".[15]

The Brahmanical and the Jaina schools, on their part, took up the challenge squarely. It is fascinating to go through the wealth of philosophical literature recording the battle of controversies, attacks and counterattacks in the realm of ideas.

A survey of these exchanges indicates that the main charges, that the opponents brought against the Buddhist stand, can be classified under three principal headings. They point out that the theory of instantaneous being is incompatible with the idea of causation, that it cannot account for such phenomena as perception, memory, recognition, etc., that it renders ideas concerning moral retribution, bondage and salvation meaningless.

It is interesting to see that if the Buddhists have repudiated the permanent on the basis of its incompatibility with the idea of causal efficiency, the opponents now raise the objection that no invariable concomitance can be established between the momentary and causal efficiency. The target of the argumentation is evidently to demonstrate that the so-called momentary entity can by no means give rise to an effect.

In Jayanta Bhaṭṭa's *Nyāya-Mañjarī* [27] one finds a relevant and pertinent discussion about these issues. He objects to the Buddhist definition that causal efficiency is the criterion of real. The fictitious entity can exercise efficiency as well. Moreover, even if it is granted that real is the causally efficient, it would be impossible to establish that the causally efficient be momentary.

The challenge, that he puts forward against the Buddhist position is centered on the question regarding the establishment of invariable concomitance (*vyāpti*) between momentariness and causal efficiency in the inference by means of which the principal Buddhist thesis 'all that is real is momentary' (*yat sat tat kṣaṇikam*) is sought to be proved.

The details of the discussion focus also on various aspects of the problem of causality. One of the points in the chain of arguments is to focus on the idea that

15 A condensed translation from *Tattvasaṃgraha-Pañjikā* [63] p. 80.

in order to give rise to an effect an entity must be existent at least in the moment following its production. An entity which exists but for a moment can by no means be admitted as causally efficient.

In this connection, it is of interest to recall the Nyāya-Vaiśeṣika formulation of causation and their classification of cause as material (*samavāyi*), non-material (*asamvāyi*), and as instrumental (*nimitta*) – ideas which indicate a conceptual structure operating with a conception of time entirely different from that of the Buddhists.

In Śrīdhara's *Nyāya-Kandalī* [19] an elaborate discussion can be found regarding the problem of causation focusing on the idea of subsidiaries and auxiliaries essential for the production of an effect. An admission of auxiliary cause amounts to a refutation of the Buddhist position.

It is to be noted that the Buddhists, fully aware of this, have rejected the idea of auxiliary cause. The critique of causality occupies a central position in Indian philosophy. The difference in the views indicates the different manner of conceiving time.

Controversies between the Nyāya and the Buddhist philosophers constitute a prolonged chapter of Indian philosophy. The adherents of the respective schools carried on the dispute through the centuries, covering a whole range of problems of fundamental importance.

Udayanācārya's *Nyāyakusumāñjali* 1/16 [24] contains significant analyses of the idea of momentariness of the real only to demonstrate the untenability of the Buddhist doctrine. One of the various objections that he raises is that no perception is possible on the Buddhist premise. Perception presupposes a contact between the visual organ and the entity, a possibility which is outrooted by the proposition, viz. that which exists is momentary. This amounts to saying that perception cannot be used as a valid means (*pramāṇa*) for establishing the momentariness of the real. Again, the Buddhist thesis can neither be established by inference for the want of invariable concomitance between the middle and the minor terms. Again, in the *Ātmatattvaviveka*[16] one comes across elaborate logical analyses aimed at disproving the Buddhist position. Kumārila Bhaṭṭa, a principal exponent of the Mīmāṃsā school, has been a strong adversary to Buddhist thought. He points out that no cognition could be explained if the real were momentary, as the Buddhists claim. In his *Ślokavārttika*[17] he elaborates his criticism against the Buddhist doctrine of momentariness. An analysis of the knowledge-situation shows that there cannot be any cognition without an object. The object is the cause of knowledge, the latter being effect of it. This

16 By Srī Udayanācārya [23].
17 [32] *Kārikā* 152-159.

causal relation between the two, which is the very presupposition for all our knowing, cannot be accounted for on the Buddhist premise. The causal relation can be effected only if the cause is present when the effect is produced. But if the object ceases to be at the moment when knowing is to take place, no cognition can at all happen. The argument is aimed at emphasising that the idea of sequence is basic to the idea of causation. The antecedence of the cause is to be accepted for the production of an effect. Moreover, the cause must not cease already before the effect arises. If these conditions are fulfilled, a satisfactory explanation for cognition can be found, but it disproves by the same stroke the Buddhist doctrine of momentariness.

It may be said in support of the Buddhist view, that the object and cognition of it are simultaneous, i.e. they appear at the same moment. To this Kumārila Bhaṭṭa remarks that the idea of simultaneity of cause and effect cannot be accepted. However minute, and therefore imperceptible, the difference of time may be that intervenes between the cause and the effect, e.g. between the lamp and its light, the notion of a necessary, invaribale sequence is indispensable for the constitution of causal relation. The simultaneous existence of two facts does not constitute a causal relation between them. The production of an effect implies that its cause is prior to it. Thus, an investigation into the relation between the object and its cognition shows the untenability of the Buddhist view that all existents are instantaneous.

The principal objection of the Jaina philosophers against the Buddhist view is also akin to the preceding, exposed above. The Jainas also insist that no knowledge can be explained on the premise, that all that is real is momentary. No knowledge is objectless. The object is prior, knowledge is posterior. If the Buddhist idea is to be taken seriously, it would imply that when knowing should occur the object is not existent, and when the latter is present, knowing is not yet effected. To maintain that these two are simultaneous is as ridiculous as to say that the two horns of a cow are the cause of one another.[18]

The impact of the doctrine of momentariness has been most devastating for the Brahmanical philosophers regarding the problem of self (*ātman*). The idea of a permanent self constitutes the very foundation of the Brahmanical tradition. The Buddhists, however, in consistency with their principal thesis, has denied an unchanging and unchangeable self in their account of the subjective aspect of mental phenomena. The cherished Brahmanical doctrine of the permanent self is replaced by the idea of everchanging fleeting states of consciousness, succeeding

18 *Ārhata-Darśana* from *Sarvadarśanasaṃgraha* [5] p. 53.

one another, – momentariness and causal interdependence remaining its important features.[19].

The Brahmanical philosophers have attacked the idea of momentariness on the ground that such mental phenomena as memory or recognition cannot be accounted for by the Buddhist theory. The Mīmāṃsaka philosopher points to the fact of recognition as clearly indicating the identity of an entity experienced at different points of time. If the entity were different at different times – as would be the consequence of the Buddhist idea of momentariness – the phenomenon of recognition would be impossible.[20] Again, without the notion of an identical subject, the phenomenon of memory cannot be explained. The one who experiences and the one who remembers have to be taken as identical subjects, a fact which clearly disproves the idea that all is momentary.[21]

The Buddhists, on their part, have not shirked from these persistent attacks launched against their position. They firmly guarded their own stand and insisted that the entire series of problems ranging from that of causality, phenomena like memory, recognition, ideas of action, and even that of rebirth can be explained and accounted for in consistency with their own stand.

The Buddhists have refuted all the different doctrines of soul which in any way can be a vestige of the permanent, in the guise of a spiritual or a mental substance. They have attempted to demonstrate that memory, recognition etc. do not require the postulation of a permanent self. It is indeed with admirable logical skill and philosophical depth that the Buddhist philosophers have explained the problem of unity of consciousness and the question of ethical responsibility all in accordance with their no-substance stand. A brilliant summary of the main objections is given by the outstanding Buddhist philosopher Śantarakṣita in his *Tattvasaṃgraha* [54] in which he subsequently analyses and refutes these objections in defence of the Buddhist stand.

It is not possible here to go into details of these marvellous philosophical exchanges. What remains, however, worthy of notice for the present investigation of the problem of time, are the drastic consequences which emerge from a particular view about time. In other words, all these controversies touching upon various problems of philosophy can be said to bear witness to the impact of how time is eventually conceived by the contending philosophical schools. The problems of being and non-being, creation and annihilation all, implicitly, are formulated according to a conception of time that a particular scheme of philosophy cherishes. As an instance we take up in the next section the problem of

19 See section VII (i).
20 *Śabdanityatā' dhikaraṇam, Kārikā* 414-415 *Ślokavārttika* by Kumārila Bhaṭṭa [32],
21 *Kārikā* 440-444, Ibid.

annihilation vis-a-vis time, a sample of the many controversies which took place between the Nyāya and the Buddhist schools.

(iv) Annihilation and time – a Nyāya-Buddhist controversy

The problem of annihilation, akin to the problem of change, has been an interesting topic of debate between the Nyāya and the Buddhist philosophers. Their specific philosophical stands regarding the problem at once indicate the differences in their respective views about time, which implicitly underly the mutual exchanges and argumentations.

The Nyāya-Vaiśeṣika metaphysical framework makes room for the perishable and the imperishable as two distinct and mutually exclusive categories of the real. The former covers the range of all that is produced i.e. caused and therefore has necessarily being in time. The latter includes all that is classified as uncaused, consequently indestructible, and therefore can be said to be outside of any influence of time (*kālaprabhāvamukta*).

Time itself is conceived in this system of pluralistic realism as a real per se, without which no talk of annihilation or production is possible. No beginning or end can be attributed to time, as it is only on the presupposition of time as the universal receptacle that any beginning or end is conceivable or possible.

To the Buddhist, however, the annihilatory character of existence is universal. In other words, the Buddhist argumentation is directed against the idea of any imperishable category of existence – which the Brahmanical tradition cherished. The Buddhist insists that all, without any exception, is subject to annihilation.

It is evident that the thesis, that annihilation characterises all existence, is implicit in the principal Buddhist tenet that all existence is momentary. The philosophical argumentation for establishing the momentariness of all existence has already been exposed in a previous section.[22] Here we are to note how the Buddhist analysis of the problem of annihilation is worked out consistently with their principal thesis viz. that causal efficiency being the criterion of real, all that is real is momentary. The momentariness of the existent primarily indicates its evanescent character. This implies – as the Buddhist radically formulates it – that annihilation of an entity in question is not dependent on any external agent, but is inherent in its very existence, meaning that annihilation is to follow immediately after the moment of production.

22 See section V (i).

The Nyāya challenges the Buddhist view. It is to be noted that both the parties in dispute agree that all existents that are produced are liable also to destruction. (However, to the Nyāya-Vaiśeṣika metaphysical thinking, there are the absolute, eternal entities which are uncaused and imperishable). But the Nyāya understanding of annihilation is distinctly different from that of the Buddhist. The polemic between the two schools regarding the problem is recorded both in the Nyāya and the Buddhist literature. The Nyāya insists on the fact that annihilation does not necessarily follow in the very next moment of the production of an entity, nor can annihilation be said to be without an external cause. This is to say that according to the Nyāya the contingent entity continues to exist until the causal agent necessary for its destruction appears on the scene.

In the *Ātmatattvaviveka* [23] we find a firm statement of the Nyāya position and its objections against the Buddhist view. On the other hand, in *Tattvasaṃgraha* there is a brilliant record of the dispute summarising the Nyāya objections and the Buddhist answers to them. The exchanges are especially significant for understanding the differences in their views, which by implication reveal that the respective mode of conceiving annihilation is eventually based on their conception of what is the nature of ultimate real and its immediate bearing on the understanding of time. The pluralistic realism of Nyāya-Vaiśeṣika not only lists space and time and a host of other entities to be ontologically real, it also admits non-existence to be an objective category of reality. It is, in Nyāya terminology, a *padārtha*, that is, not merely a thought construction. The Nyāya insists that non-existence[23] of the jar (*ghatābhāva*) is produced by the stroke of the hammer.

The Buddhist, on the contrary, does not grant reality to anything but the point-instant. He maintains that non-existence has no objectivity. Annihilation of an entity implies its substitution by another. In other words, whereas for Nyāya non-existence is something over and above the entity annihilated, to the Buddhist it is nothing other than the replacement of one entity by another.

The controversy leads to pointed exchanges. The Buddhist attempts to lay bare the absurdity of the realists' position that annihilation depends on any special cause. The Buddhist points out that since existence and non-existence are not on a par, non-existence cannot be said to have a cause similar to existence.[24] To say that annihilation is caused is to admit that the so-called cause produces nothing, which implies that the cause is unreal (since it gives rise to nothing). Consequently, the implication would be that non-existence cannot be said to be real.

23 *Pradhaṃsābhāva*. For the Nyāya-Vaiśeṣika classification of non-existence see p. 231.

24 It is part of the Buddhist understanding of cause, that it should give rise to a positive entity.

The Nyāya refutes the argument with the view of disclosing the absurdity of the Buddhist claim by pointing out, that if annihilation were to be taken as uncaused, it could never take place. To be uncaused implies that the event in question is either fictitious or an eternal fact. Annihilation is an event in time, it is real, so it must have a cause.

This leads to a clarification of what the Buddhist exactly means by annihilation. Annihilation implies the instantaneity of being. The production of a point-instant implies the annihilation of the previous point-instant. Annihilation is not passing into non-being (*abhāva*), to which Nyāya grants objective reality. That is a hypostatised notion, a conceptual construction. The Buddhist, on the contrary, maintains that no external agent can make an entity cease to exist if it were not inherently perishable. Again, to grant that it is perishable by nature is also to admit of its momentary character. In other words, the Buddhist maintains that for annihilation no other additional factor or circumstance is necessary. Being is automatically i.e. by its very nature evanescent. But the Nyāya realists insist that if annihilation were not contingent upon any other factor, space and time are to be accepted as auxiliary causes. To this the Buddhist answer is that the very idea of auxiliary cause is unacceptable (as has been shown in Sec. V (i)). The Buddhist is fully aware of the incompatibility of the idea of auxiliary cause with the idea of instantaneous being, which he is advocating as real, as free from any conceptual construction or interpretation. This is why the Buddhist urges that if an entity could continue after the moment of its production, it could – so to speak – keep on existing forever. This is also why the Buddhist insists that annihilation is uncaused (*ahetuka*) and denies non-existence any ontological status. The treatment of the problem of annihilation is similar to that of change. The core of the Buddhist argument remains the same viz. two or more opposed qualities cannot be predicated of the same entity. Thus, in every next moment there is not to be found the slightest trace[25] of what was existent in the previous moment.

The Nyāya evaluation of the problem of annihilation is based on a conception of time which is widely different from that of the Buddhists. To maintain that annihilation must have a cause indicates that the contingent may endure until the appearance of the cause for its destruction. This, in other words, is to deny momentariness to be the universal character of being in general – as the Buddhists would have it.

The conception of total annihilation, pertaining to the Buddhist understanding of being as instantaneous is – as Stcherbatsky[26] puts it – transcendental as distinguished from empirical destruction, which is caused as in the example

25 *Niranvaya-vināśa*.
26 [63] p. 94.

cited, viz. the destruction of the jar by the stroke of the hammer. The idea of total annihilation which is not produced by any external cause is another way of pointing to the same fact that instant and the instantaneous coalesce. Śāntarakṣita boldly formulates the idea – 'the instantaneous thing represents its own annihilation'.[27] The evanescent character of being is brought out in this startling manner. This analysis of annihilation brings out the radical Buddhist position that the dynamicity of the ultimate real[28] is based on the understanding of the fusion of being and time. The evanescence of the instant also implies the annihilation of the instantaneous. The difference between the terms 'instant' and the 'instantaneous' has no ontological basis.

The precision with which Kamalaśīla [54] brings out the exact Buddhistic understanding of the terms instant and the instantaneous is remarkable. It makes it clear that the instant – in Buddhist terminology – is nothing other than the nature of being itself, which consists in its annihilation immediately after its production. The instantaneous refers to the entity which has this nature. The verbal distinction between the two terms has no corresponding ontological difference, it is linguistic and conceptual in character.

Stcherbatsky [63] p. 92 gives a pointed summary of the Buddhist stand, following the Buddhist text of *Tattvasaṃgraha-Pañjikā*, thus:

'... just as existence ... is nothing but a name for the things existing, efficiency is the efficient thing itself. Time and space are nothing besides the things residing in them, these again are nothing over and above the point-instants of which they represent an integration ... finally non-existence or the annihilation of a thing is also a mere name, nothing over and above the thing annihilated'.

To focus on the views of time on the basis of their respective analysis of annihilation, it is vitally important to note that for the Nyāya philosophers absolute time is the substratum, with reference to which events like production as well as annihilation of an entity are at all conceivable. As the further elaboration of the Nyāya philosopohical argumentation points to, time, being instrumental to all events, is all-pervasive, a real per se.

Annihilation is thus an event in time, dependent on the external agent responsible for the destruction of the entity in question. The fact that annihilation is experienced at a given moment and not at any other indicates its causal dependence on some factor outside of the entity in question. This, they maintain, cannot be explained on the Buddhist premise that all that is real is necessarily momentary. The contingent is subject to annihilation, but its annihilation is not uncaused, and therefore the entity cannot be said to be automatically

27 [63] p. 95.
28 *Calabhāvasvarūpa*.

evanescent immediately after its production. This analysis is evidently carried on in a conceptual framework which operates with a view of time which is un-Buddhistic to its core.

To the Buddhist, on the other hand, to accept that destruction is contingent upon any external agent would be tantamount to giving up his principal thesis, that momentariness is the universal character of all that is real. Moreover, as their sharp analysis of being and time indicates, the moment and the momentary are inseparable ontologically, the distinction being merely conceptual. Thus time as an independent real per se – like the Nyāya philosophers would have it as a support for understanding annihilation as an objective fact – is foreign to the Buddhist mode of thinking. Annihilation does not imply that it is something apart from the annihilated entity, no more than it is dependent on any external destructive agent. The momentary entity represents its own annihilation. Efficiency and evanescence are intrinsic to that into which the instant and the instantaneous are coalesced ontologically.

The different analysis of annihilation bears witness to the radically opposed views about time that are implied in the Nyāya-Buddhist controversy. To Nyāya, the fact of annihilation itself is an event which presupposes time as an imperishable real per se. It is with reference to and in the substratum of this ontological real that the non-existence of the contingent is conceivable or is possible. To the Buddhist this conception of unitary, absolute time is nothing but a thought-construction, having no basis in reality. The real time is the discrete instant, which is by its very nature perishable. Moreover, the perishability of the instant implies the annihilation of being. Being and time are inseparable ontologically, expressed as the point-instant whose evanescence is not dependent on any additional external cause. This constant annihilation is at the very root of the Buddhist understanding that real is dynamic.

VI

A note on the problem of time in the perspective of philosophy of language and the idea of the timeless as inexpressible

The philosophy of time knows of inner divergence of many sorts. Some hold time to be ubiquitous, others as atomic; some maintain it to be a purely subjective construction, others insist that it is an objective fact – a real per se.

However, the linguistic usage of the word 'time' is current not only in common parlance but also in the philosophical literature of the different schools. In this connection the question can be raised that if the word 'time' is universally used, is it not necessarily a pointer which indicates that there is a corresponding reality? To put it differently, can there be a category of language without a category of being?

The different schools of Indian philosophy are fully aware of the various problems concerning the question of the import of words. The implications of language as the universal tool of expression itself underwent in due course a careful philosophical scrutiny. The history of Indian philosophy of language can be traced all the way back to the *Vedas*. The ancient school of grammar and the school of Mīmāṃsā are well-known for their intense preoccupation with many subtleties pertaining to the area of philosophy of language, and which contain to a large extent a systematic working out of the suggestions found in the *Vedas*. It is an enormous field of enquiry giving rise to theories about the origin of language, about the relation between the sounds, the letters and the word, regarding whether language reveals or distorts reality etc. etc.

For the present investigation on time, however, only certain aspects of some theories and their implications will be considered with the view of noting how in a given system the philosophy of time and the philosophy of language can be shown to be in harmony with one another.

The understanding of the interconnection between language, thought and reality are open to diverse interpretations. The rival views have, at least implicitly, specific metaphysical presuppositions. The Nyāya-Buddhist controversies are repeated once again in this area.

The realistic schools of Nyāya-Vaiśeṣika assert boldly that the nameable (*abhidheya*), the knowable (*jñeya*) and the real (*prameya*) are in one to one relationship. Language, according to the Indian realists, reveals reality. Thus, the linguistic usage (*vyavahāra*) of time (*kāla*) at once indicates it as knowable and as objectively real. They maintain that words and facts are congruent with one another. It is the objective reality which underlies all linguistic usages. Thus, the ontological reality of time in the Nyāya-Vaiśeṣika philosophy corresponds to the category of language.[1]

Turning to Buddhism, however, one faces an entirely opposed understanding of the significance of words. The realists' position, that words necessarily refer to reality, is interpreted by the Buddhist as nothing but an unwarranted assumption. They point out that words deal with concepts which are again nothing but subjective constructions. But the ultimate real, for them being the point-instant, the uniquely particular (*svalakṣaṇa*), is necessarily inexpressible. It is thought which constructs the empirical reality (*samvṛti-sat*) which is utterable (*abhilāpya*), imposing imaginary (*kalpita*) general essence (*sāmānya-lakṣaṇa*) on the unutterable, unconstructed ultimate real.

The Buddhist understanding is nominalistic – "Indeed the name can express its own meaning only by repudiating the opposite meaning".[2] This Buddhist doctrine of *apoha* is particularly significant in connection with their understanding of duration as metaphorical and the point-instant as the ultimate real.

With reference to the analysis of the Buddhist doctrine of momentariness previously discussed it is clear, that in the Buddhist conceptual framework there is no room for an idea of being which endures more than an instant. The being as instantaneous is efficient. It is the object of pure sensation which is said to be free from any trace of construction. It is evidently not fused with any verbal expression. The image of the object, invariably associated with a verbal expression, is formed in the subsequent moments. The idea of duration is thus a conception and therefore a construction, following the first moment of sensation, which alone grasps the unutterable particular that the point-instant is.

In this context it is interesting to read the following lines, which explicitly bring out the Buddhist understanding as opposed to that of the realists':

"When a word is said to denote an object, it does not do anything more than this: the word only generates in the subject's mind a conceptual image, which is distinct and different from other concepts and this conceptual image is believed

1 See p. 41 for Vallabhāchārya's comment indicating the reality of present time from linguistic usages.

2 As quoted and translated from *Pramāṇa-Samuccaya* of Dignāga [63] p. 459.

to be an external reality existing ahead and independently of the thinking mind" [61] p. 119.

The problem of time drew the attention of the great grammarian philosopher Bhartṛhari. He has devoted a long section of his outstanding work *Vākyapadīya* to the various philosophical considerations about time. This treatise, entitled *Kālasamuddeśa* [74] is an interesting document not only for understanding Bhartṛhari's reflections on the subject, but also because it provides a sort of catalogue of views and opinions that were current regarding the problem of time.

As a grammarian philosopher Bhartṛhari is deeply concerned about the problems that arise with the question regarding the tense-distinctions in the sanskrit language. This forms a natural step leading towards the problem of time. His involvement with the problem is not, however, merely in order to speculate about the metaphysical nature of time. The distinct goal and method, that a philosophy of grammar involves, is not lost sight of. After a summary of a host of varied philosophical positions dealing with time, it is pointed out in *Kālasamuddeśa* (*Kārikā* 58) that "whether it (time) is only something having an existence in the mind or whether it has an existence outside the mind, expression in words is not possible without recourse to the notion of time" [75].

Although records of reflections on time from the quarter of the grammarian school are scanty, it can be seen that the interest in the notion of time is natural to a grammarian as it forms the very basis of tense-distinctions. Speech is incomplete without verbs. Verbs invariably refer to one of the three time distinctions, past, present or future. As no sentence is meaningful without a verb, all expressions in words can be said to have a necessary temporal dimension. To a grammarian the terminations, which are added to the verbal roots, indicate time as the basis of tense-distinctions.

In this context reference may be made to the great grammarian Pānini [*Sūtra* 3/1/183]. He refers to the present-tense terminations as indicating the present time – 'from the commencement of the desired action to its end'.[3]

In the *Mahābhāṣya* of Patañjali [72], one comes across the same idea, that time is the basis for the tense-distinctions of verbs.[4] Here the question – shifting from grammar to metaphysics – is, if time were not granted a distinct existence, how could the tense-distinctions of verbs be accounted for? Despite the same verbal root e.g. √*pac* (to cook) the meaning of the three verbs "cooks", "will cook" and "cooked" are at variance with one another. Grammarians reflecting on the question tend to admit the reality of time, which is understood as the instrumental cause for the tense-distinctions. In other words, an analysis of the

3 *prārabdhāparisamāptam* – *Vaiyākaraṇabhuṣaṇasāra* by Kunda Bhaṭṭa [73] p. 140.
4 *kriyābhedāyakālastu.*

nature of verbs – found to be indispensable for any meaningful expression in words – gives rise to a philosophy of time, which seems close to that of the Vaiśeṣika realists. As for example, in Patañjali's *Mahābhāṣya* 2/2/5 one comes across the idea of time as that, in association with which bodies grow and decay. Again, the usages of day and night etc. are described as possible due to the movement of the sun in connection with time.

Now, to return to Bhartṛhari again, it is important to note that the problem of time equally touches upon his ingenious analysis of 'the word'. This implies the necessity of understanding the special significance it obtains as he delves into the philosophical considerations about the nature of the word. A brief sketch of the principal ideas is attempted here.

Bhartṛhari emphatically declares in his *Vākyapadīya* that there is no cognition in this world, which is not intertwined with the word.[5] Bhartṛhari's understanding of the word, however, is to be sharply distinguished from all other linguistic analysis found in the various schools of Indian philosophy such as Nyāya, Mīmāṃsā and the schools of Buddhism. Bhartṛhari's thought, as we shall see shortly, acts as a conceptual bridge between philosophy of grammar, metaphysics and theology, converging in the common quest for the Ultimate Reality.

Pushing the analysis of the word to its furthest limit, Bhartṛhari comes to hold that the ultimate nature of the word – which is also for him the Ultimate Reality (*śabdatattva Brahman*) – is such that it is of the nature of consciousness, that it rests in itself, indivisible, without any trace of sequence.

For a further clarification of the idea and its relevance for the problem of time it is to be noted, that for Bhartṛhari the overt speech is not the essence of the word. His analysis reveals that three levels of it can be distinguished as involved in the process of externalisation of the word which is at first internal. The uttered word represents the stage of *vaikharī* where it is fully externalised and has a 'fully developed temporal sequence' [76]. In between these two, the internal and the external, lies the stage of *madhyamā vāk*, where the word is not yet uttered but is already conceived. The temporal sequence is in a subtle form. The innermost stage is termed *paśyantī vāk* where no temporal sequence can be traced.

All verbal communication presupposes these stages. The concern with the problem of time is tied to the analysis of the situation of verbal communication, which necessarily involves the sequence of sounds. What is to be emphasised here is that neither the speaker can utter the sounds nor can the hearer hear them simultaneously, yet the sounds having sequence manifest the meaning-content in its totality. The fundamental idea is that the indivisible, sequenceless word (*akramā vāk*) is present in both the speaker and the hearer. This is why the sequence

5 *Vākyapadīya-Brahmakānda* 123 *Kārikā* [75a].

of multiple sounds can manifest, as in the case of the speaker, and awaken, as in the case of the hearer, the sequenceless word-unity.

This doctrine of *sphota*, as it is called, has brought Bhartṛhari to delve into metaphysical speculations. Time is described as a power (*śakti*) of the Word-Principle which is the Ultimate Reality. It is by virtue of this power, that what is essentially one can appear as many and yet maintain its unity just as discussed with reference to the multiple-sounds and the word-unity.

However, there is difference of opinion amongst scholars in discerning the question as to whether Bhartṛhari propounds a doctrine of *vivarta* as is found in Śankara or not[6]. The word *vivarta*[7] figures in his work as well as the word *pariṇāma*[8]. Metaphysically, the status that would be ascribed to time by him is dependent on the solution of the above problem. If he is taken to hold a position similar to that of Śankara's *Brahmādvaitavāda*, according to which all change and multiplicity is reduced to a problem of appearance, the power called time (*kālaśakti*) would then be similar to that of Māyā – the inscrutable quasi-positive principle which makes the one appear as many, the unchanging and unchangeable as undergoing mutation. But if *vivartavāda* is not the proper conceptual model for interpreting Bhartṛhari's ideas about the status of change, time would yet have to be understood as non-different (*abheda*) from the Ultimate Reality as a non-dual principle. The closest parallel for the metaphysical pattern would be that of Kashmir Śaivism.

It is also of significance to note that on the basis of this conception, Bhartṛhari worked out the idea of salvation as a raising of the consciousness in order to attain union with the Word (*śabdapurvayoga*), where all sequence is finally transcended. Thus, so to speak, the boundary between theology and philosophy of grammar is crossed in the common quest of the Ultimate Reality as the presupposition of and yet transcending all manifstations involving temporal sequence.

It is interesting in this connection to note the Advaita Vedānta evaluation of language.[9] The objective, empirical language relates words to their referrents in terms of species, action, quality or connection. If that is so, the import of the word 'Brahman' becomes an important matter for philosophical scrutiny. The chief exponents of the philosophy of Advaita Vedānta like Śaṅkara, Vidyāraṇya etc. have discussed the question at depth, giving rise to the understanding that the timeless non-dual real cannot be expressed in language in its fullness. No

6 Cf. *Bhartṛhari* by K.A. Subramania Iyer [76] and *Philosophy of Word and Meaning* by G.N.Sastri [77].

7 *Vākyapadīya, Brahmakānda-Kārikā* 1.

8 *Vākyapadīya, Kālasamuddesa-Kārikā* 13.

9 cf. K.S. Murty [48].

word can be said to express it, as the texts point out that Brahman has no species, no qualities, no activity, no connection, as it is the non-dual real which has no internal difference in it and no other to confront it. The idea of the Ultimate Reality as inexpressible is worked out in Advaita Vedānta in tune with the Upaniṣadic (*Taittirīya*) saying – *yato vaco nivartante* (wherefrom words turn back).

Yet the *Upaniṣads* teach about the inexpressible Ultimate Reality through words. The Advaitins are fully aware of this predicament. The function of the revealed text here is to indicate and not to describe the Ultimate Reality. This is why the value of the negative method (*neti neti*) is stressed, precisely in order to point out that the important function of language is first to superimpose (*adhyāropa*) false descriptions only to negate (*apovāda*) it hereafter.

The definitions of Brahman are understood in this manner by the Advaitins who are fully aware of the implications of their philosophy of language which mirrors the Advaita ontology. Thus such statements as that Brahman is real (*sat*), consciousness (*cit*), bliss (*ānanda*) or even infinite (*ananta*), one (*eka*), are not to be understood in the Advaita context as qualities pertaining to the Ultimate Reality. There is explicit warning that there is no internal difference in Brahman, no substance – quality relation can be attributed to it. The purport of the words is to negate unreality or illusoriness, materiality, suffering, finitude and multiplicity of it. The words are intended, in all cases, to indicate the non-dual real – which is timeless.

VII

(i) Time and consciousness

A series of problems of philosophical and theological importance can be fruitfully studied under this heading. The area of investigation is broad, and it is basic to philosophical and theological conceptual structures across cultural boundaries.

In Indian philosophy itself a study of consciousness, as it is recorded in the philosophical texts of the different schools, involves a complex set of ideas. Analytical and critical investigations covering a wide range of issues have been carried out, focusing on various aspects of this important problem. The history of Indian philosophy contains a rich variety of views about consciousness, which arose as a consequence of intricate and elaborate enquiries of logical, epistemological and metaphysical character.

In the following discussion, however, only a few selected issues will be raised where there is direct bearing of the problem of consciousness on that of time. It is interesting in the given historical context to examine some conceptual patterns in order to note, how a specific formulation about consciousness is interrelated with a certain interpretation of the time-experience.

Let us first return to the Sāṅkhya account. It has been noted, that in Sāṅkhya the problem of time coincides with the problem of change. The pattern of conceiving change in this system, with reference to an underlying permanent substratum (Prakṛti), is distinctly different from that of the Buddhist conception of change as a total substitution of one entity by another.[1]

In this section, the Sāṅkhya understanding of change is to be appraised on the background of the dichotomy of matter and consciousness. It is evident that the postulation of the two principles – Puruṣa and Prakṛti – as ultimate and ontologically independent of one another is highly significant for a study of time and consciousness. The metaphysical dualism of Sāṅkhya involves a deep phi-

1 See section VII (iii).

losophical interpretation of the problem of change qua time as well as the problem of consciousness.

The elaborate arguments for the postulation of Puruṣa as underived and uncaused, distinctly different from Prakṛti, which are worked out fully in the *Sāṅkhya-Kārikā* (17,18,19) and ably commented upon by Vācaspati Miśra in his *Tattva-Kaumudī,* are directly relevant here as they bring out in this process the philosophical implications of the principle of change for that of consciousness.

The principal argument for the postulation of the principle of consciousness, i.e. Puruṣa, seems to be implied and required by the very composite nature of Prakṛti. The Sāṅkhya argument is, that all which is composite is meant for another's use (*saṃghāta-parārthatvāt, Sāṅkhya-Kārikā* 17). Prakṛti, constituted of three *guṇas* and thereby complex, is indicative of a teleology or a purpose and hence implies the existence of another principle, Puruṣa. Puruṣa, in turn, cannot again be said to be composite as this would otherwise lead to the assumption of composite objects ad infinitum. Thus, in Sāṅkhya, if Prakṛti is conceived as composite, everchanging and object of experience, the principle of consciousness, i.e. Puruṣa, is understood as uncomposite, un-changing and subject of experience. Thus, the Sāṅkhya text further elaborates the uncomposite nature of consciousness by saying that there is absence of the three *guṇas* in Puruṣa. In other words, that which goes into the very composition of Prakṛti as dynamic material principle, is denied of the Puruṣa, the principle of consciousness. Consciousness as the subject is characterised in Sāṅkhya in diverse ways: as the controlling agency,[2] as the one who experiences.[3] It is not what Prakṛti is, viz. the common, objective, productive, composite principle of matter.

The *Sāṅkhya-Kārikā* 19 brings forth the further important notions of Puruṣa as witness (*sākṣī*) and seer (*draṣṭā*), developed from the understanding of Puruṣa as conscious and non-object. Prakṛti, as the unconscious object principle, cannot be made to fulfil the function of witnessing, seeing. Puruṣa, the unchanging, uncomposite conscious subject, witnesses what Prakṛti exhibits as it evolves. The perceptible, experiencable nature implies that there is an observer and experiencer, which is Puruṣa. It is un-productive (*aprasavadharmī*), inactive (*akartṛtvam*). It is the ever-constant (*kūṭastha*) consciousness witnessing the manifold evolutes of the ever-active Prakṛti.

Thus, it is at this point that we have to note that to Sāṅkhya, the principle of materiality with its built-in movement is an irreducible ultimate, as is the principle of consciousness which is ever-constant. This dichotomy, worked out in fullfledged philosophical formulations, contains the very significant insight,

2 *Adhiṣṭhānāt – Sāṅkhya-Kārikā* 17.

3 *Bhoktṛbhāvāt – Sāṅkhya-Kārikā* 17.

which has important bearing on the problem of time and consciousness, viz., that which changes cannot take note of itself as change, being an unconscious principle; that which, on the other hand, takes note of change, is the principle of consciousness and is itself devoid of all change.

The Sāṅkhya system conceives of a teleological bond between the *guṇas* and the Puruṣas, thus accounting for the co-operation between the two ultimate principles – Puruṣa and Prakṛti – for all worldly experiences as well as salvation. The interdependence of the two principles – consciousness and that of change qua time – is conceived in clear terms by the school. The principle of change, which is held as independent and objective, can be said to be known only when consciousness illuminates it, when the unconscious principle of changing matter is presented to the unchanging (*apariṇāmī*) principle of consciousness.

Thus, the time-experience, in the Sāṅkhya conceptual framework, can be said to be dependent on the duality of Puruṣa and Prakṛti. The principle of objective succession is an aspect of the heterogeneous becoming of Prakṛti which, as we have noted earlier, is not conceived as an event in an empty time. The temporal aspect of concrete becoming involves that it is noted by consciousness as a sequence.

In this connection it is also interesting to note that consciousness, in Sāṅkhya, is not understood as an attribute or quality of the self. Consciousness is the self. Moreover, the constantly changing mental states are just as much a part of Prakṛti.

The Sāṅkhya non-distinction of self and consciousness equally holds true of the Advaita Vedānta. But the Advaita Vedānta metaphysical non-dualism does not make room for any plurality of selves in the final analysis, all plurality belongs to the empirical, the phenomenal (*vyavahārika*).

But Sāṅkhya, unlike Advaita Vedānta, admits of a plurality of subjects as ultimate and final. It is maintained, as *Sāṅkhya-Kārikā* 18 points out, that it is only on this hypothesis that birth, death, differences in activities, etc. pertaining to different individual subjects can be accounted for. The Nyāya-Vaiśeṣika schools also make room for a conception of plurality of selves in its metaphysical pluralism.

The conceptual pattern of the self (Ātman) as unoriginate and indestructible is uniformly present in all the Brahmanical schools, despite their internal differences. In their confrontation with the Buddhists, it is to be emphasised, that the principal target of attack was the doctrine of momentariness, precisely because its inevitable consequence is a denial of Ātman – the permanent essence, untouched by the march of time.

Evidently, the philosophical considerations that lead Sāṅkhya to postulate the unchanging principle of consciousness is teleological in character, whereas for the Nyāya-Vaiśeṣika the permanent self is posited as a substance in which inhere qualities such as knowledge, volition, etc.

But here too, the distinction between the Nyāya-Vaiśeṣika conception of consciousness and that of the other Brahmanical schools is to be noted. Consciousness is conceived by the Nyāya-Vaiśeṣika schools not as identical with the self but as a quality of the self. Time, space and even the mind (*manas*) are all accepted as separate substances. In Sāṅkhya, however, these are regarded as evolutes of Prakṛti, arising from the combination of the *guṇas*. These differences are reflected equally on their theories of causality. The Sāṅkhya formulation of the effect as an actualisation of the potential and that of Nyāya-Vaiśeṣika as a production of a new existent, as we have noted previously, are worked out within conceptual frameworks where the understanding of time is distinctly different.

With the advent of Buddhist thought, as has been noted already, the emphasis on the idea that 'all is impermanent' (*sarvam anityam*) has its inevitable sequel in the thesis that 'all that is, is without substance/self' (*sarvam anātman*). The doctrine of momentariness is incompatible with the idea of a permanent, persisting self. A consistent carrying out of the claim, that the real is the causally efficient and hence momentary, leads to the rejection of the idea of an unchanging self, which stands behind the changing states of consciousness. The Buddhist stand of 'no-self' (*anātmavāda*) is of great consequence for a study of time and consciousness.

The Buddhist idea of universal instantaneousness leaves no room for any abiding 'mental substance' in the flux of consciousness – the stream of sensation, perception, volition, etc. The conscious moments, however, follow one another not haphazardly but according to the law of dependent origination, i.e. are causally inter-chained: one happening, the other happens.

The Buddhist philosophers have discussed the problem on both logical and psychological levels. The fascinating conversation between the monk Nāgasena and King Milinda recorded in the early Buddhist text *Milinda-Pañha* [55] bears witness to the novelty of the Buddhist doctrine of no-self, the questions that arise in reaction to it and the Buddhist responses.

As mentioned earlier, the Buddhists had to meet the challenge of the objections that the Brahmanical philosophers brought against the idea of no-self. The Buddhists attempted to account for such mental phenomena as memory, recognition, and even the idea of moral responsibility in conformity with their stand – the no-self theory.

To give up totally the idea of self and to replace it by a chain of conscious moments is no easy task. Even amongst the Buddhists exceptions to the idea can be noticed. The Vatsīputrīyas, who also claimed themselves to be Buddhists, for example, are said to have maintained a notion of a quasi-eternal spiritual substance[4]. They conceived the principle of individuality (*pudgala*) neither as distinct from the mental aggregates (*skandhas*) nor as identical with them.

It is interesting to see that the Vatsīputrīyas attempted to avoid the charge of eternalism by denying the *pudgala* or the principle of individuality to be distinct from the mental aggregates. On the other hand, to account for the unity of consciousness, to give meaning to the idea of action with its moral bearing (Karma) they found it necessary to deny the identity of the principle of individuality with the mental aggregates.

The Sautrāntika philosophers have strongly opposed the idea as un-Buddhistic and have rejected it along with the different theories of soul that were current. With great philosophical skill they have pointed out, that the idea of a permanent self is not only an unnecessary postulate for accounting for mental phenomena such as memory, recognition, etc., it is indeed an obstacle for moral responsibjility, bondage and salvation.[5]

The Buddhist philosophers held that the mental phenomena of memory, recognition, as well as the unity of mental life, can be explained with the help of the idea of the law of dependent origination and does not call for the postulation of a substratum underlying the succession of conscious units.

In this connection it is also important to note, that although the doctrine of soul is rejected by the Cārvāka materialists as well, the Buddhist understanding is distinctly different from the former. The materialists held consciousness to be a by-product of matter. Death of the physical body meant a complete cessation of the stream of consciousness. They insisted that a denial of a permanent self underlying the variable conscious units ought to make the Buddhists accept their position. The Buddhist philosophers, however, were operating with the idea of a beginningless consciousness-continuum, which does not cease with death.

The denial of any idea of substratum of the chain of conscious states does not, however, amount to a negation of soteriology. Śāntarakṣita faces the materialists squarely on various issues in his *Tattvasaṃgraha* [54]. It is, indeed, fascinating to observe how the ideas of bondage and salvation are worked out fully in harmony with the no-self stand within the Buddhist framework. The idea of salvation (Nirvāṇa) is, of course, of central importance to all schools of Buddhism. There exist voluminous discussions on the subject unfolding different interpretations, emerging in the various phases of the history of Indian Buddhism.[6]

4 See *The Soul Theory of the Buddhists*, by Th. Stcherbatsky [65].

5 A good review of the controversy can be found in *The Buddhist philosophy of universal flux* by S. Mookherjee [61].

6 See *The Conception of Buddhist Nirvāṇa*, by Stcherbatsky [64].

It is impossible here to go into the details of the different accounts of how the various Buddhist schools dealt with these problems. But what is of utmost significance for the present study is to note, how a specific mode of conceiving time is bound to have its impact on a chain of inter-connected issues, which are theologically and philosophically of capital importance.

The problem of salvation and time, for instance, falls within the general discussion on time and consciousness. It may be asked whether the temporality of consciousness is only empirical and is annulled in the state of Nirvāṇa.

Reputed Buddhist scholars have debated the question. We shall only refer to the Yogacāra Vijñānavāda – the school of Buddhist idealism – as an example of the type of controversy concerning Nirvāṇa, that has relevance for the problem of time and consciousness. This school, emerging in the third phase of Indian Buddhism, maintained the ontological reality of consciousness.

A difference of opinion arose amongst the earlier and the later exponents of this school regarding whether the absolute consciousness in the state of Nirvāṇa is to be considered as momentary or not. According to some, the doctrine of momentariness is applicable only to the empirical. One can trace an objective succession of moments, following the causal chain, in empirical consciousness. But consciousness in the state of Nirvāṇa is beyond the chain of causality; here no trace of objective succession can be found. From this it is concluded, as did the great master Vasubandhu,[7] that the pure consciousness is beyond time. But others like Dignāga, Dharmakīrti and Śāntarakṣita denied this understanding and vehemently stuck to the position that momentariness is a basic feature of consciousness, empirically as well as transcendentally.

This leaves the question open as to whether these later Buddhist philosophers were searching for a conception of consciousness as a flux, which is to be understood neither as a chain of objective succession of momentary states nor as an unchanging eternal substance.

Thus, a whole series of questions can be raised which are intertwined with the problem of time and consciousness. It may be asked, what does the awareness of time/change imply about consciousness itself? That which takes note of change, is it itself to be conceived as changing or must it be an unchanging principle? The Buddhist would cling to the first position, the Brahmanical philosophers e.g. of Sāṅkhya-Yoga to the second. Again, the analysis of change would yield different philosophical results. Sāṅkhya admits the reality of change, but no category of time apart from it. The principle of change implies, for Sāṅkhya, the principle of consciousness as unchanging. The analysis of change, for the Nyāya-Vaiśeṣika philosophers, points to the reality of time as an ontological category. The idea of

7 *Vijñaptimātratāsiddhi – Triṃśikā* 30 [52].

the permanent self features as a vital constituent of their metaphysical pluralism. To the Advaita Vedānta, the unchanging consciousness is the ontological reality, the problem of change qua time is a problem of appearance.

Issues, such as whether consciousness of object and consciousness of consciousness involve a temporal sequence, or are simultaneous happenings, could also be fruitfully studied with reference to all the different schools of Indian philosophy. These questions are taken up, and answers have been worked out both from the Brahmanical and the Buddhist premises. The Nyāya-Vaiśeṣika philosophers advocated the first stand, that consciousness of consciousness is subsequent to the consciousness of object (*anuvyavasāya*), whereas the Vedāntins maintained consciousness to be self-revealing (*svaprakāśa*). The Buddhists also insisted on the self-luminosity of consciousness (*svasamvedanā*) and developed the idea fully.

Despite all their internal differences, the schools of the Brahmanical tradition remained loyal to the original Upaniṣadic understanding of the self as unchanging and unchangeable. The idea finds its full-fledged expression in the philosophy of Advaita Vedānta. Consciousness as the ultimate non-dual ontological real is characterised as *trikālābādhya* – i.e. unsublatable in all three times. Profound philosophical considerations lead them to emphasise that in no experience is this self/consciousness (Ātman) ever cancelled.

The famous expression of the Advaita text, *Bhāmatī*, of Vācaspati Miśra [39] puts it thus – 'that which is constant in whatever is variable is different from the latter, as a string from the flowers'.[8] The philosophy of Advaita Vedānta stands as the culminating point of the Brahmanical understanding of consciousness as timeless.

(ii) A comparative note on the concept of instant (*kṣaṇa*)

Instant (*kṣaṇa*) is a term used not only in common parlance, but also in the philosophical literature of the different schools. No study of the problem of time can neglect to take note of the divergent technical employment of this term. A philosophical analysis, however, discloses the different views of time, which determine the import and significance of the idea of instant in the conceptual framework of each school.

8 *Yesu vyāvartamāneṣu yad anuvartate tat tebhya bhinnam, yathā kusumebhyah sūtram.* Translation taken from *The Philosophy of Advaita* by T.M.P. Mahadevan [47].

It is indeed interesting to focus on the question as to how the concept of instant is formed and evaluated by the different schools of philosophy, whose approach and commitment to the problem of time are widely divergent, even conflicting with one another. From our survey of the distinct positions developed regarding the problem of time we note, that in all the three philosophical traditions of India – the Brahmanical, the Buddhist and the Jaina – the term instant is abundantly used in the philosophical literature. An analytical exposition of the different views of time in such systems as Yoga and Vaiśeṣika, the Buddhism and the Jaina enables one to make a comparative note of the concept of instant which acquires a special technical significance in each school of philosophy.

The Vaiśeṣika school, as we have seen, is committed to a view of time as unitary, objective and absolute. Instant as time is explained, like any other plural uses of time e.g. hours, days etc., as being due to the utilisation of external adjuncts such as solar motion for pragmatic purpose which, however, leave the essential unitary, indivisible time as a category of existence untouched. In *Bhāṣa-Paricchedа*[9] we find a pertinent discussion on how in four different ways one could designate the use of instant with the help of qualifying adjuncts such as action. To the Vaiśeṣika philosophers the use of instant or for that matter any other pluralistic employment of 'time' presupposes the universal substratum of the time-substance (*kāla-dravya*), which is a metaphysical reality. The universal, unitary time is an independent, absolute existent, whereas the instant is a relative, pragmatic conception dependent upon its relation to an event. It is an abstraction.

In the Yoga metaphysical structure the concept of time as unitary and as an independent category of existene is challenged. The Yoga school declares that the idea of time as instant is objectively real, but the idea of time as duration, involving a collection of instants e.g. day, month etc., or that of a sequence, implying an objective series of preceding and succeeding instants, is a thought-construct, it is an ideal representation. In the *Yoga-Bhāṣya*[10] 3/52, we find an explicit, clear-cut commitment to the idea of reality of the instant and the merely subjective, conceptual construction of the sequence, being devoid of objectivity. Two moments cannot co-exist. Thus the idea of time as a continuum or as a substance in the Vaiśeṣika sense is unreal (*vastu-sūṇya*) for Yoga. But time as instant is real (*vastu-patita*).

The philosophical opposition between the Vaiśeṣika conception of time as unitary and the Yoga view of discrete time is evident. Thus emerges the conflict

9 By Viśvanātha [22].
10 Vyāsa's commentary on *Yoga-Sūtra* [10].

regarding the concept of instant in a philosophical appraisal of the views of time within the fold of the Brahmanical tradition.

For all schools emerging in the Buddhist tradition the idea of instant is philosophically of primal importance. The Buddhist philosophers reject the idea of the unitary, all-pervading time-substance of the Vaiśeṣika philosophers. The notion of time as an all-embracing receptacle of all that is contingent is attacked dialectically in order to show the inner contradictions of the idea. The Buddhists advocate a discrete view of time. However, the discrete view of time based on the reality of the instant alone acquires altogether a different philosophical dimension at the Buddhist's hand.

The Yoga view obviously is a close parallel to that of the Buddhist, in so far as it grants reality only to the present instant and denies objectivity to the past or the future instant. Moreover the Yoga interpretation of sequence (*krama*) as a mental construction bears similarity to the Buddhist understanding.

However, the interesting analogy between the two views has its serious limits which must not be lost sight of. The common denial of the ubiquitous time as a unitary, objective reality in the pattern of the Nyāya-Vaiśeṣika does not lead to a common understanding in their conception of becoming and being. The distinctness of the two views is clear and pronounced.

The understanding of time as instant in Buddhism has a profound impact on the entire philosophical thinking of that tradition, which leads to a radical transformation of the conception of being – as has been discussed earlier, –, which entirely demarcates the Buddhist conceptual model of being and time from all the diverse models, emerging from the Brahmanical tradition.

In the Buddhist formulation, being and time coalesce with one another. The conception of time as instant at once implies the notion of being as instantaneous. Even more, the instant and the instantaneous form an inseparable unity. The instant and the instantaneous, in this conceptual structure, are not conceivable one without the other. This understanding of the problems of being and time is a radical departure from the traditional Brahmanical thinking and marks Buddhism as a distinct philosophical tradition. It is to be also noted in this connection, that the radical understanding of time as instant leads to a specific understanding of consciousness, which is peculiar to Buddhism. Unlike the Brahmanical mode of conceiving a permanent self, the Buddhist works out a discrete view of consciousness, accounting for all subjective phenomena on that premise.[11] In other words, the point to be brought into focus is that the idea of time as instant has so radical an impact, that it leads to a reformulation of all the basic philosophical issues in harmony with this insight. Thus, the doctrine of

11 See section VII (i).

momentariness (*kṣaṇikavāda*) is of fundamental philosophical importance for all Buddhist thinking, despite all other internal differences between the various schools of Buddhism.

The idea of time as instant in the Yoga school has its own distinct philosophical implication. The evanescent character of the instant does not hold true of being. In Yoga thinking time as instant does not imply being as instantaneous. The conception of *dharmī* as explicitly brought out in *Yoga-Sūtra* III, 14 focuses on a conceptual model of being which is quite evidently distinct from the Buddhist model, where two moments imply two things. According to the Buddhist emergence and evanescence of the instant and the instantaneous cannot be conceived as distinct events. More precisely, the two conceptions of time as instant and of being as instantaneous are fused together. Obviously, the pattern of conveiving birth/production, death/destruction is markedly different here from the Yoga system, as a logical consequence of pursuing this mode of philosophising.

In the Yoga system, the substance is conceived as enduring, as persisting through changes. The analysis of *pariṇāma* or becoming in Yoga presupposes the substratum of Prakṛti which continues and supports the process of evolution. Again, consciousness is unchanging and unchangeable, for Yoga, in its essential nature. The system remains true to the *ātmavāda* tradition, conceiving the self as timeless.

For the Buddhist, on the other hand, the understanding of the instant is so thoroughgoing, that it leaves no room for any category of existence which is not instantanous. We have noted the logical persuasion of the Buddhist which goes to show that what is existent is causally efficient and consequently instantaneous in character. There is no exception to this rule.

Another distinct expression of a discrete view of time can be found in the philosophical literature of the Jainas. The Jainas challenge, in a like manner to the Buddhist and the Yoga, the Nyāya-Vaiśeṣika conception of ubiquitous time.[12] However, an analytical exposition of the Jaina conception of time as instant clearly indicates the difference of the view from that of the Yoga school or the Buddhist.

The Jainas, taking their stand on the reality of time, advocate an atomic conception. The real, objective time is of the character of instant. This is the ultimate and absolute nature of time, which is conceived as a mono-dimensional, asymmetrical series constituted of the time-atoms (*kālānu*). The conventional time-periods as collections of instants are usages dependent on extraneous factors such as any standard motion. It is thus a relative, conditional concept dependent on extraneous factors, whereas the real, objective time-atoms are

12 In *Prameyakamalamārtanda*, see section IV (ii).

discrete and in reality can never be combined. The Jaina conception of time-atoms has to be distinguished from the Yoga or the Buddhist notion of time as instant. To the Jainas the time-atoms are not only real and objective but also eternal, i.e. no beginning or end can be ascribed to them. The main difference between the space-atoms and the time-atoms is, that whereas the former are capable of combining, the latter are not. The instants are many, conceived as forming a linear order.

Thus, the Yoga, the Buddhist and the Jaina views of discrete time, although they all entail a refutation of the Vaiśeṣika view of time as unitary, differ fundamentally in their understanding of time as instant.

(iii) The views about time and the problem of change

The interdependence of specific formulations of the problem of change and the different views of time is evident, as one attempts to analyse the positions held by the various schools of Indian philosophy. There is an abundance of philosophical speculations regarding the problem of change. On the one hand is the metaphysical dispute as to whether it is essentially a problem of appearance or not, on the other hand lies the various contending views proposed by those who accept the reality of change. It is indeed interesting to study the different positions about time, viewing them as diverse conceptual models for understanding the problem of change.

The experience of change is universal, as appearance and disappearance of an entity, or as a modification of its states and qualities. Reflections about the problem of change are necessarily connected with time. For instance, does change imply a lapse of time? Is time, then, something apart from the changing object? Does change mean modifications of states/qualities of the identical entity or does it involve, on the contrary, a replacement of one entity by another?

The drive for consistency and precision in formulating answers to such questions has given rise to a variety of philosophical stands. Each system deals with the problems in a distinct manner, keeping in harmony with the general characteristics of the tradition it stems from.

In the Brahmanical tradition, the reality of time is expressed in clear terms by the Nyāya-Vaiśeṣika system of metaphysical pluralism. It maintains time to be a separate, independent reality, outside and apart from all-that-is-in-time i.e. the contingent. No change of any kind is conceivable – whether as occurrence, disappearance, modifications of states and qualities – without reference to time.

Events are in time. The beginning, continuation or end of an entity is explicable only on the basis of an idea of time as an ontological reality. One can meaningfully talk about the production of an entity only as its first conjunction with time, its destruction refers to its disjunction with time. Time is, therefore classed as a *nitya-dravya* –, a substantial reality, which is beginningless (*anādi*) and endless (*ananta*). As it is the very presupposition of all contingency and of every possible mode in which change is conceivable, no contingency can be predicated of it. Time is absolute, ubiquitious and unitary.

That the contingent bears a necessary temporal reference, is amply brought out by the Nyāya-Vaiśeṣika theory of causality – *asatkāryavāda*. The theory, as has been already exposed, focuses on the idea of the effect as a beginning (*ārambha*) of a phenomenon in time. Similarly, the destruction of the contingent is the termination of its contact with time. This model for understanding change underlies the Nyāya-Vaiśeṣika conception of time as the receptacle (*ādhāra*) of all that is contingent (*janya*). The production, continuation and destruction of the contingent are all events-in-time. To put it differently, that which is conceivable as not in time, is either a fictitious entity or an absolute entity like god, space, etc., entities listed as *nitya* in the Nyāya-Vaiśeṣika pluralistic metaphysics. In other words, only the uncaused is conceivable as bearing no reference to time. The contingent is caused, and all causal operation presupposes time, conceived as all-pervasive (*sarvavyāpī*).

It is to be noticed that if according to the Vaiśeṣika philosophers change points to the existence of time, time itself is not conceived as changing or moving. Time is the static (*niṣkriya*) background which makes change possible and explicable. Again, the Vaiśeṣika philosophers are aware that time can be measured by movement e.g. the solar motion, but movement is by no means identical with time. This leads to the further question regarding the passage of time. The Vaiśeṣika philosophers account for such conventions of past, present and future time as involving no real movement or division of time but as due to external determinations, which leave the unitary nature of time unaffected. In other words, what changes is in time, but time itself cannot change. Therefore, such conventional usages do not imply any change of time but are, on the contrary, made possible by the ontological existence of absolute, indivisible time. Thus, for the Nyāya-Vaiśeṣika philosophers, the reality of change can be explained only on the basis of reality of time. In fact, the changing entity is indeed a valid premise for inferring time as an ontological category, which is also indicative of why space cannot be made to function for time.

In the Vaiśeṣika literature, the difference in the apprehension with reference to the body of an old man and a youth is analysed only to focus on the idea, that changes in the body of the old man point to the reality of time as their instrumental cause. The Vaiśeṣika conviction, that the solar revolutions cannot alone be made to account for changes in the bodies, is emphasised. The existence of an ubiquitous, all-pervading substance called time is pointed out as necessary for explaining, how the solar revolution can mediate its influence on the body, with which it has no direct connection.

Now that the relevance of the problem of change to the particular view of time in the Nyāya-Vaiśeṣika structure is clear, including the system's pattern for understanding production, continuation and destruction of an entity, we turn to the Sāṅkhya-Yoga conception of the problem.

In the dualistic metaphysics of Sāṅkhya-Yoga, the conception of Prakṛti stands for the reality of change. The conceptual model for explaining change, including events as production, continuation and destruction, is however markedly different from that of the Nyāya-Vaiśeṣika. A careful review of the Sāṅkhya theory of causality – *satkāryavāda* – immediately discloses the pattern. The formulation of the problem of change here does not call for a notion of unitary time as a separate category of existence. The conception of time as a receptacle, an idea cherished by the Nyāya-Vaiśeṣika philosophers, is rejected in this conceptual structure as superfluous, even as merely a thought construction.

In Sāṅkhya, the process of becoming as a movement from the potential to the actual is identical with the causal process. *Yuktidīpikā*,[13] commenting on *Sāṅkhya-Kārikā* 15, hints time to be identical with this process. In other words, the reality of change does not necessitate a conception of time as apart from the changing stuff, unlike in the Nyāya-Vaiśeṣika system.

Satkāryavāda, the Sāṅkhya theory of causality, as has been pointed out previously, does not require to operate with any notion of vacant time. Change, in Sāṅkhya, implies a succession of states of the substance, which persists identically through them. Change and identity are not mutually exclusive in Sāṅkhya as in Buddhist thinking.

The analysis of the conception of *lakṣaṇa-pariṇāma* clearly reveals the problem of change in relation to time as conceived in the Yoga philosophy. It is indicated that the substance (*dharmin*) is that, which remains common to all the three stages of its changing qualities, which when sub-latent is called the past, when rising, present and when indeterminable, future. Thus the empirical time is intimately related to the changing qualities of the substance in its successive phases. Shortly, there is no event-in-time conception in this system. The ultimate substance as Prakṛti is beyond the three phases of empirical time. Prakṛti is eternal-in-change.

13 Author unknown, edited by R. C. Pandeya [13].

Production and destruction in Sāṅkhya do not involve any notion of a passage from non-being to being – the effect is pre-existent in the cause; or from being to non-being – destruction is a going back to a sub-latent state and not annihilation. The substratum is a stable reference for understanding any change as its different phases.

Thus we have noted briefly, how the reality of change is understood and accounted for on the basis of distinct formulations of the problem of time in the Nyāya-Vaiśeṣika and the Sāṅkhya-Yoga schools, all stemming from the Brahmanical tradition.

The conception of reality of change and along with it that of time is challenged in the philosophy of Advaita Vedānta, a system which marks the culmination of the Brahmanical tradition. A radical formulation of the conception of being discards any understanding of it as changing – as could be found in the idea of Prakṛti in Sāṅkhya. Change is ascribed an empirical reality, having no ontological status. Moreover, the ontological being is pronounced as non-dual – a conception which rejects all pluralistic/dualistic views of being. The idea of being as timeless is focused on in the Advaita Vedānta. Time and change are conceived as appearance. The ontological being and the empirical time are realities of two orders.

The problem of change, however, undergoes a radical transformation in Buddhist philosophy. Change here is not an accidental feature, but it is the very core of reality. The idea of a stable stuff with changing qualities is totally unacceptable to the Buddhist. An entity cannot change and yet remain the same. Change and identity are mutually exclusive. The radical understanding of change as expressed in this philosophy is, that it implies a total substitution of one entity by another.

Time is conceived as instant, one instant being superseded by another. At no two instants can the entity remain identical. The idea of time as instant and being as instantaneous and both as fused one with the other is a philosophical event, which at once places Buddhism as an original tradition, breaking away completely from the *ātmvāda* comceptuel framework.

The Buddhist conceptual model for understanding production, destruction is thus quite distinct. Nothing endures, at every instant the entity is replaced by another. The succeeding point-instant represents the annihilation of the former. Thus the conventional idea, that a thing is experienced to exist through a flow of instants, is a conceptual construction and does not correspond to reality, but – as the Sautrāntika Buddhist would say – the annihililation of the entity is followed by a similar entity in the next instant.

Let us note that the idea of time as universal receptacle for all that is contingent is unacceptable to the Buddhist philosophers. In the Buddhist framework there is no room for a conception of time as apart from the contingent entity. The conceptual model of point-instant is a mode of conceiving contingency, which is in total opposition to that of the Nyāya-Vaiśeṣika conception.

On the other hand, the Nyāya-Vaiśeṣika philosophers accept the reality of change, but do not accept the Buddhist view that change is replacement of one entity by another. In other words, the contingent is not necessarily momentary – as the Buddhist would have it. The Nyāya-Vaiśeṣika realists maintain time to be absolute and an independent category of reality, the instant being intelligible only on the background of the universal, unitary time.

The Buddhist rejects the idea of universal time, the instant alone is real. It is clear, that the Buddhist understanding of change is thorough and total, there is no room for any notion of unchanging substance, no category of reality as beginningless and endless (i.e. *nitya*). Thus in the Buddhist framework a conception of time as that of the Nyāya-Vaiśeṣika philosophers can have no place. Time as instant, being as instantaneous, are the inevitable concepts, when the problem of change is understood in the Buddhist manner. Even more, the instant and the instantaneous are conceived as coalesced, as fused with one another, giving rise to the Buddhist model of the point-instant. The interpretation of change in Buddhism is radical, giving rise to a novel conceptual model of being and time.

Now, let us turn to review the Sāṅkhya-Yoga understanding of the reality of change and compare it with that of the Buddhist. We find that the conception of Prakṛti as eternal-in-change is an idea, which the Buddhists have attacked vehemently, as here again there is a model of being, where identity and change go hand in hand – unlike in the Buddhist model. The problem of change is a central problem for both Sāṅkhya-Yoga and Buddhism. Considerable effort and involvement towards understanding change/becoming is evident from the profound analyses of the problem in all its aspects found in their philosophical literature. Noticeable is, however, the sharp and subtle difference in their respective conceptual models.

Stcherbatsky, in his *Buddhist Logic* Vol. I, pointedly summarises the difference between the Sāṅkhya and the Buddhist patterns of conceiving movement. To the Buddhist, he writes, "movement consists of moments, it is a staccato movement, momentary flashes of a stream of energy", whereas for the Sāṅkhyas "movement is compact, is a legato movement, the momentary changes of a fluctuating substantial stuff with which they are identical." "Everything is evanescent", says the Sāṅkhya, "because although never at rest, it represents fundamentally one and the same stuff" [63] p. 19.

The radical difference in their formulation of the problem of change is reflected in their respective distinct formulations of being and time (see section VII (iv)).

In the Jaina tradition, where emerges a conceptual scheme which seeks to compromise the reality of change with the idea of being as unchanging, time is conceived in order to fit this metaphysical pattern. Here we find a conception of time as real and absolute but not as unitary. Time as instant is real, but these instants are present in a linear order. In other words, the position agrees with the Buddhist's in maintaining the reality of time as instant and in rejecting the idea of universal time. On the other hand, it agrees with the Nyāya-Vaiśeṣika realistic conception of time as absolute, unchanging, but disagrees with the idea that time is unitary. In brief, the reality of change as conceived by the Jainas necessitates time as instants, which are many, but an absolutely existing category of reality.

The problems of change and time, involving at once the problem of causality, evidently form a set of interconnected problems, which are basic to the constitution of distinct conceptual structures. As the historical record of ideas shows, a specific stand regarding any one of these problems necessarily influences the formulation of the views concerning the others.

The problem of change is a challenge faced by the Bṛahmanical, the Buddhist and the Jaina philosophers; each, however, sets forth a model, which is in consistency with his own metaphysical stand. As the study shows, in each system the thought-pattern is different. Despite the internal differences, it seems that the understanding of time and change is greatly influenced by the conception of being in each tradition.

The Brahmanical tradition, loyal to the Upaniṣadic conception of Ātman as the unchanging and unchangeable reality, developed the alternative metaphysical structures, giving considerable thought to the problem of time and change. The Nyāya-Vaiśeṣika and the Sāṅkhya-Yoga schools formulated differently their positions regarding the problems of change, causality and time, but both systems despite their serious involvement with the aforesaid problems modelled their formulations following the conception of being in the *ātmavāda* tradition. In their metaphysical systems – dualistic and pluralistic – the important core remained – viz. the Ātman, an ontological category, untouched by time.

In the system of Advaita Vedānta, where the Brahmanical tradition expresses its conception of being in its radical form, the metaphysical structure rejects pluralistic, dualistic models. The system, as the very name indicates, advocates a philosophy of non-dualism, focuses on the reality of the unchanging and unchangeable Ātman as the one and only reality, thus expressing conceptually the Upaniṣadic vision of Ātman as *ekamevādvitīyam*. Consequently the problem of change is reduced to a problem of appearance. Time is no more an ontological reality but phenomenal (*vyavahārika*). The Nyāya-Vaiśeṣika conception of time as a metaphysical reality is, therefore, untenable in the Advaita structure. As we have noted, in his *Khaṇḍanakhaṇḍakhadya* Śrī Harṣa – an

Advaitin – directly challenges the Nyāya-Vaiśeṣika conception of time and attempts to refute it by pointing out the inner contradictions involved in such a conception.

The Buddhist tradition on the other hand upholds a metaphysical perspective, which is in total opposition to that of the Brahmanical. It challenges the entire conceptual structure of *ātmavāda* – in all its diverse forms. It rejects and refutes all philosophical conceptions which are modelled on the *ātma*-pattern. The unchanging and unchangeable reality – a conception which dominates the Brahmanical tradition of *ātmavāda*, finds no root in the Buddhist intellectual soil, a tradition consequently known as *anātmavāda*. There is no room here for any unchanging ontological entity. On the contrary the Buddhist maintains firmly, that whatever does not change does not exist. This philosophical stand is based on the idea of causal efficiency as the criterion of reality. Their theory of causality – the doctrine of *pratītyasamutpāda* – expresses the radical conception of change fashioned after the Buddhist vision of reality. It is clear, that the problem of change takes an altogether new dimension with the emergence of the Buddhist tradition. The involvement of this tradition with the problem at various levels – logical, epistemological, metaphysical – uniformly and consistently focuses on the idea of reality as flux.

It is clear from the above review of different conceptions of change, that each position grasps the problem in accordance with its view of time. The attempts to formulate the conceptions with precision bring their mutual differences into focus.

(iv) Being and time

Being and time constitute the fundamental problems that lie at the heart of any systematic philosophical enquiry. A perusal of the history of Indian philosophy discloses their central role in all the contending conceptual structures. It is evident that the problems of being and time have direct bearing on one another. A study of time necessarily involves the understanding of the various conceptual patterns of 'being' as it is clear from a critical investigation into the different schools of philosophy. Thus, the whole spectrum of philosophical stands regarding time, which has been the subject of the present study, can be said to display along with it the distinct formulations of the problem of being. All views about time are intertwined with specific philosophical interpretations of being. In this section we shall note explicitly the various formulations of being, which are implied by the different views of time.

In the conceptual structures developed in the Brahmanical philosophical traditions there can be found a variety of formulations.

In the Nyāya-Vaiśeṣika philosophical scheme, being (*sattva*) is an universal (*jāti*). The technical significance of the term becomes clear as one examines their conceptual scheme. Being is an objective fact, and it is the universal which makes it possible to include all entities falling into the categories of substance (time is one of the substances), quality, and action, under one class-concept. Non-being, which is also taken as an objective category in this system, naturally is excluded from it. Moreover, positive categories such as universal, particular and inherence are technically ascribed a self-existence (*svātmasattva*), but cannot be classified under the universal being. This understanding of being has received severe criticism from the Buddhist philosophers, which will be pointed out shortly.

The Sāṅkhya-Yoga understanding as to what constitutes the essence of *sat* or being is not, however, without similarity to that of the Buddhist, in as much as the schools recognise it to be efficiency (*arthakriyākāritva*)[14]. Prakṛti is *sat*, as it is for enjoyment (*bhoga*) and salvation (*apavarga*) of Puruṣa. Puruṣa, on the other hand, is *sat* as it is the presupposition (*adhisṭhātā*) for the evolution (*pariṇāma*) of the inert Prakṛti. But it is needless to say, that the Buddhist understanding of the universal instantaneous nature of being is totally unacceptable to these schools. The Brahmanical adherence to the supremacy of being is steadfastly maintained by both Sāṅkhya and Yoga. The *Yoga-Sūtra* itself contains a refutation of the Buddhist doctrine of momentariness (*kṣanikavāda*). The concept of Puruṣa is modelled after the Upaniṣadic view of Ātman, the unchanging and unchangeable essence in man. Even the concept of Prakṛti – being that transforms itself (*pariṇāmī nitya*) – defies the Buddhist understanding, where change does not presuppose an underlying permanence.

The philosophy of Advaita Vedānta contains the most radical expression of the Brahmanical conception of being. That alone is declared to be *sat* which is unsublatable in all three times (*trikālabādhya*).[15] Being (*sat*) is further identified with the self-revealing consciousness (*cit*). In the *Bhāmatī* (I,1,i) of Vācaspati Miśra we find a refutation of three distinct views regarding being, only to focus on the Advaita conception of being as timeless.

The first view is that of the Buddhists, which maintains causal efficiency to be the criterion. This is shown to be unacceptable. The argument seeks to bring out

14 *Puruṣārthakriyaksamam sat*, see the explanation of Vācaspati Miśra on *Yoga Sūtra* 2/19, in his *Tattva-Vaiśāradī* [10].

15 See section III (iii), 'Being as Timeless in Advaita Vedānta'.

that if causal efficiency is being, then the former has to be again shown as the object of a prior causal efficiency leading to the fallacy of *regressus ad infinitum*. Moreover, the illusory object can also be demonstrated as causally efficient.

The second view is that, according to which being is an universal – historically held by the Nyāya-Vaiśeṣika philosophers. It is pointed out that it will be impossible to establish this view philosophically, which insists on being as an universal, as being itself cannot be brought under the scope of another universal, thus leading to a contradiction.

The third of these views under scrutiny regards as being anything which makes impression on us, i.e. is apprehensible, attributed to the Prabhākara Mīmāṃsaka. This view, it is pointed out, fails to give a criterion, by means of which the erroneous could be discriminated from the right knowledge of reality.

All the above criticisms are intended finally to focus on the Vedāntic thesis, viz. Being *par excellence* is that which no time can cancel.

To the Buddhist, on the other hand, none of these formulations are acceptable. He insists causal efficiency to be the criterion of being (*sat*). Moreover, as further analysis discloses, whatever is causally efficient is bound to be instantaneous in character (*yat sat tat kṣaṇikam*). The chain of arguments that the Buddhists used to demonstrate, that an entity cannot be said to exist previous or consequent to the moment when it exercises efficiency – and thus denying causal efficiency to the permanent – has already been discussed.

However, it is interesting to note that the Nyāya-Vaiśeṣika philosophers did not approve causal efficiency to be the criterion of being. They insisted that it is not only being, which can exercise causal efficiency, but non-being (*abhāva*) can also just as well. They pointed out that it is not merely conceivable, that non-being can exercise causal efficiency, it is even a presupposition for practical life, e.g. the absence of physical obstruction can not only be conceived, but is also an indispensable condition for movement. It is to be recalled that in the Nyāya-Vaiśeṣika scheme non-being is accepted as an objective category of reality. The Buddhists, on the other hand, have vehemently criticised the Nyāya-Vaiśeṣika understanding of being. All the categories of relations such as universal, inherence etc. are demonstrated in the Buddhist analysis to be false, which the Nyāya-Vaiśeṣika philosophers take as objectively real.

At the close of this study it is evident, that at the very core of the philosophical tension between the Advaita Vedānta – as the culmination of the Brahmanical tradition – and Buddhism, lies their radically opposed understanding of being and time. The Brahmanical tradition in and through its metaphysical pluralism, dualism and monism has attempted to carve out a conception of being, which is outside the influence of time. In the philosophy of Advaita Vedānta 'being as timeless' is alone granted the ontological status (*paramārtha-sat*), which reduces being-in-time to the phenomenal, empirical order (*vyavahārika-sat*). The Advaita dialectical attack on the realistic conception of absolute time is motivated precisely to bring out, that it cannot be accepted as a real per se. In order to save the complete philosophical integrity of this conception of being, that is uncancellable in all three times (*trikālābādhya*), the Advaita Vedānta has modelled its metaphysical structure with a sharp and subtle philosophical caution – it has abandoned the pluralistic, dualistic and monistic structures and, as its very name signifies, commits itself to an ontology of non-dualism, which steadfastly focuses on a conception of being – the one-without-a-second (*ekamevādvitīyam*).

Turning to the Buddhist tradition, one is faced with the radical idea of time as instant which is integral to being. The course of the history of Buddhism bears witness to the more and more stringent formulation of the idea of being as instantaneous, disclosing the strong impact of this key idea about time on a specific manner of understanding being as instantaneous. We have noted that the Vaibhāṣika school modelled its conception of being close to that of the Sāṅkhya view of Prakṛti. Their idea of the ever-changing character of being, which yet in its noumenal character (*dharma-svābhāva*) remains in three times, did not satisfy the Sautrāntika, who ridiculed the conception as a vestige of the permanence and therefore as un-Buddhistic. A more philosophically drastic interpretation of time as instant discloses its, so to speak, complete infiltration, into being. A new conceptual model for understanding being emerges. Not only the conception of being as immutable and impartite is abandoned; the pattern, in which the Vaibhāṣika school of the first phase of Buddhism conceived of being, is also found to be a half-way position, a compromise. No idea of being, as in the Sarvāstivāda framework, despite its mutations yet existing in three times, is amenable.

An uncompromising philosophical follow-up of the idea of instant reveals, that being is entirely restricted to and partakes of the nature of the instant. The fleeting character of time, understood in its radical implications, brings out the idea of being as instantaneous. There is no room for the idea of being enduring in three times in the manner Sāṅkhya conceived of Prakrti or the Vaibhāṣika Buddhists understood it to be.

It is very significant that, although this radical interpretation of time and being undergoes severe attack from the great Buddhist dialecticians of the Mādhyamika school of Buddhism itself, it yet survives and makes a bold re-appearance in the history of Indian Buddhism in its third phase. This understanding of time is of capital importance for the Buddhist tradition giving it the flair of originality and distinction. A compromise in this philosophical interpretation of time would have meant a loss of identity for the Buddhist tradition as the analysis of the late Vijñānavāda philosophers clearly brings out.

It is interesting to note in this connection that, although the conceptual models for understanding being and time remain the same in the Sautrāntika and Vijñānavāda schools of Buddhism, the conflict between them is centered around a realistic or an idealistic interpretation of reality. The Sautrāntika philosophers were realists. They abandoned the idea of substance in conformity with the general pattern of Buddhist thinking. They accepted a chain of conscious moments on the subjective side and a flow of discrete elements on the side of the object. The epistemological situation is conceived along the line of realism. But the Buddhist school of idealism, Yogācara Vijñānavāda, developed in the third phase of its history, launched an attack on the realistic claim of the independent existence of object apart from consciousness.[16] They accepted wholly the Buddhist thesis that being is instantaneous, but being (*sat*) here is identified with consciousness alone.

But even at this point there arises a conflict amongst the Vijñānavādins themselves. This is a crucial point in our understanding of the vital role, that the idea of time as instant plays in Buddhist thought. The point of dispute, referred to previously in the study of time and consciousness, centers around the question as to whether this instantaneous character of consciousness is to be understood as ultimate or not. It is a focal point of interest, as it puts into relief how far-reaching and consequential is the notion of time coalesced with being in the Buddhist tradition.

This oscillation between declaring absolute consciousness to be permanent (*dhruva, nitya*) – as in Vasubandhu – and instantaneous (*kṣaṇika*) – as in Śāntarakṣita and others – seems natural in a tradition, whose basic postulate was to deny the substance-view (*ātmavāda*) with all its implications.

On the Brahmanical side, in the philosophy of Advaita Vedānta, being (*sat*) is also identified as consciousness (*cit*). The philosophical steps leading to the disclosure of being as consciousness is, however, not along the line of subjective idealism. Śaṅkara, championing the philosophy of Advaita Vedānta, rejects, as is well-known, the Vijñānavāda analysis of the epistemological situation. The absolutism of Advaita Vadānta goes along with epistemological realism.

The philosophy of Advaita Vedānta fulfills the task that the Brahmanical tradition sets before itself, by bringing forth to a triumphant glory the idea of Being – Consciousness – Bliss (*sat-cit-ānanda*). It discards the view of time as a real per se, as considered by Nyāya-Vaiśeṣika, and it denies change and multiplicity ontological status, as advocated by Sāṅkhya-Yoga, reducing them to the

[16] *Bahirārtha-parikṣā* [59].

realm of phenomena. The doctrine of Māyā advocated by Advaita Vedānta is indispensable for establishing the idea of Being *par excellence* (Brahman).

Thus, if the Brahmanical tradition is seen as achieving a pure conception of being freed from any trace of time, so to speak, in the philosophy of Advaita Vedānṭa, the Buddhist tradition can be viewed as reasserting its original intuition of the inseparability of being and time in the late Vijñānavādins' insistence on the instantaneity of consciousness as ultimate. The persistent adherence to the idea of time as instant and as ultimate, fused with the absolute consciousness, is philosophically highly significant.

Basing itself on the teachings of Buddha, the Buddhists attempted to carve out a distinct and original philosophical tradition, breaking away completely from the Brahmanical metaphysical pattern. In order to achieve this, the Buddhist philosophers embarked on a new conceptual model of being for which their main philosophical tool was a thorough new interpretation of time. The ontological fusion of the instant with being gave rise to the entirely novel idea of being as instantaneous.

The Brahmanical philosophers, on their side, clearly perceived the philosophical consequence of the Buddhist interpretation of time for all the varying conceptual models of being that emerged in the course of its history. The total attack on the Buddhist doctrine of momentariness launched by all the Brahmanical schools without exception emerges as a philosophical necessity in the light of this understanding.

Thus, the problem of time emerges as central and basic to the conflict between the Brahmanical and the Buddhist traditions in and through the various stages of their philosophical history. At the nucleus of these philosophical traditions lies inevitably an interpretation of the problem of time.

VIII

(i) The problem of time – an inter-cultural perspective

Before this study comes to its close, it is valuable to take an over-all view of the problems, related to time, hitherto discussed within the framework of the Indian philosophical tradition. Here we attempt to extend the field of enquiry to a still wider framework such as to include some broad features of the Greek and Judeo-Christian contributions, which are exceedingly important sources of ideas which go into the making of the very fabric of contemporary western thinking.

Evidently, this could lead to voluminous studies, as the problem of time has offered challenge to the theologian and philosopher across the cultural boundaries. Consequently, the literature covering analysis and expositions of different views of time is enormous.

Our intention here is only to bring into focus a few of the questions directly or indirectly relevant for a study of the problem of time, which at once help to understand the distinct philosophical tradition of India, side by side noting the general conceptual pattern of the Greek and the Judeo-Christian thinking.

We shall first and foremost take note of the different ideas of creation in order to discern the main guiding principle which shapes a tradition. It is needless to say that all cosmological speculations inevitably have implications about the problem of time.

A detailed investigation into this material is outside the scope of this work, but reference to it is indispensable, as these ideas have bearing on the problem of time, opening up an intercultural perspective. Another significant outcome of such a study is that when fully explored, it could provide a basis for a fruitful dialogue for a possible theology of encounter of religions, to which we shall later on make a brief allusion.

Let us examine the Brahmanical tradition, which offers several distinct philosophical formulations resulting from the cosmological speculations of the principal schools.

We have already noted the idea of mechanical combinations of atoms in the Nyāya-Vaiśeṣika attempt to understand creation. God is conceived as an efficient cause (*nimitta kāraṇa*), the principle of material causation is independent of God. The atoms are beginningless and endless, creation and destruction involve their combination and separation.

In the Sāṅkhya-Yoga structure, as we have noted, Prakrti is conceived as an independent, beginningless, endless principle – functioning as the material, the instrumental and the formal cause – to use the Aristotelian categories. The concepts of potentiality and actuality come into play in this structure. Creation is an actualisation of that which was potential, whereas destruction involves a return to the sub-latent state.

We have discussed previously in detail the *ārambhavāda* of the Nyāya-Vaiśeṣika schools along with the specific theory of causality, viz. *asatkāryavāda*, and observed its difference from the *abhivyaktivāda* of the Sāṅkhya-Yoga schools and their understanding of causality, viz. *satkāryavāda*. We shall not further elaborate these positions, but only keep in focus their common and steadfast adherence to the principle that being cannot come out of nothing or be reduced to nothing.

The *Bhagavadgītā*, hailed by all denominations, fractions and schools of this tradition, clearly expresses the maxim thus:

nā'sato vidyate bhāvo
nā'bhāvo vidyate satah

'Of the non-existent there is no coming to be;
of the existent there is no ceasing to be.'[1]

The interpretations, that it receives in the hands of the commentators, vary according to the conceptual structure of each system. But the tradition does not make any exception to this fundamental idea.

In the philosophy of Vedānta emerge other ideas in keeping with the same principle. In the Viśiṣṭādvaita school of Rāmānuja the world is conceived as the body of God whereas in the school of Advaita Vedānta the problem of creation is reduced to a problem of appearance. The doctrine of Māyā advocated by Advaitins focuses on the world as neither having the ontological reality of Brahman nor being totally non-existent like the sky-lotus.

All the different metaphysical structures along with their respective theories of causality weave different conceptual patterns, but never violate the principle *ex nihilo nihil fit*.

It is also important, in this connection, to recall the different philosophical positions regarding the problem of time, which our study has brought into

1 *Bhagavadgītā* 2/16 [2].

focus. The thought models are widely divergent, ranging from time as unitary to a discrete view of time, from time as a distinctly separate existent to the view of time as inseparable from the process of concrete becoming, from time as a real per se to the view of time as appearance.

The contrast of the views of time in different models of cosmological speculations has to be observed clearly for the purpose of the discussion concerning the question of the notion of so-called cyclic time, which will be taken up shortly.

We shall not dwell any further on the analysis of the various problems regarding the views of time and the cosmological models used by their advocates. We shall return to it after noting the conceptual pattern, as it is manifested outside the boundaries of the philosophical traditions of India.

Let us turn to the history of Greek philosophy and note the pattern of cosmological speculations. There is no conception of absolute creation and destruction to be found here. The pattern of cosmological speculations, however much at variance from one another, are in keeping with the principle of *ex nihilo nihil fit*. A steadfast adherence to this formula runs through the pre-socratic philosophies, just as much as in the writings of Plato and Aristotle.

A powerful formulation of the idea can be found in the philosophy of Parmenides in his rigorous conception of being, which was to have strong impact on subsequent Greek philosophisations. He writes – "only Being is, Not-Being is not and cannot be thought", (Fr. 4,6 f.) Again, "... Being cannot have a beginning or cease to be, for it cannot be created from Not-Being or reduced to Not-Being, it was never and never will be but is now, continuous and undivided" (Fr. 8,5 f.) "... It is motionless and unchangeable, everywhere similar to itself ...".[2]

It is interesting to note that this conception of being finds its radical metaphysical opposite in the philosophy of Heraclitus. Heraclitus, the immediate predecessor of Parmenides, found in the incessant principle of change – which he identified with the substance of fire – the fundamental law of the universe. The flux, that he conceived reality to be, is expressed in his writings, claiming "that everything flows, nothing is permanent. One can never step twice into the same river", (Fr. 91).

The metaphysical opposition is total. The problem of change has opposite significance in each case. To the Parmenidean view of reality change is illusory, to the Heraclitean it is permanence which is unreal. Both regarded them, however, as due to the deception of sense. This clash of ideas has obvious parallels in the Indian tradition – between the *atmavāda* and *anātmavāda* in their radical expressions.

2 Zeller, *Outlines of Greek Philosophy*, [85] p. 49.
See also [85] for references to *Fragments*.

The natural outcome of the presence of the two extreme views was the rise of the three compromise systems of Empedocles, Anaxagoras and Democritus. All of them, as their cosmological speculations bear witness to, agreed with Parmenides that an absolute creation and destruction is impossible, since being cannot come out of nothing, on the other hand the influence of Heracleitos' thought was also strong.

Zeller quotes Empedocles as holding the view that "what is called creation and destruction is in reality the mixture and separation of eternal and unchangeable basic substances" (Fr. 8,9) [85] p. 55.

For Anaxagoras, "all coming into being consists only in a combination, and all ceasing to be in the separation of already existing substances, and each change of quality rests on a change of material composition" [85] p. 61.

The third compromise system saw the rise of the atomists. The school, founded by Leucippus, found its chief exponent in the person of Democritus. Here, once again, an attempt is made to reconcile the extreme positions of Parmenides and Heraclitus. Democritus maintained all coming into being as a combination of atoms and all ceasing to be as due to their separation. But the atoms themselves "have neither come into being, nor can they cease to be ... capable of no qualitative change, but only a change of position ..." [85] p. 66.

In Plato's cosmology we find, however, a different formulation. The Platonic conception of creation, as found in his *Timaeus*, is as follows: "The god took over all that is visible – not at rest, but in discordant and unordered motion and brought it from disorder into order" [78] 30A.

Aristotle, as is evident from his *Metaphysics* [80] Bk. IV Ch. V 1009 a, developed the concept of potentiality as differentiated from that of actuality precisely in order to conceive change in keeping with the principle of *ex nihilo nihil fit*.

The following comments by Stace, a historian of Greek philosophy, is of interest in this connection.

"Aristotle claims, by means of the antithesis of potentiality and actuality, to have solved the ancient problem of becoming, a riddle, propounded by the Eleatics, which had never ceased to trouble Greek thinkers. How is becoming possible? For being to pass into being is not becoming, for it involves no change, and for not-being to pass into being is impossible, since something cannot come out of nothing. For Aristotle, the sharp line drawn between not-being and being does not exist. For these absolute terms he substitutes the relative terms potentiality and actuality, which shade off into each other. Potentiality in his philosophy takes the place of not-being in previous systems. It solves the riddle because it is not an absolute not-being. It is not-being inasmuch as it is actually nothing, but it is being because it is potential being. Becoming, therefore, does not involve the impossible leap from nothing to something. It involves the transition from potential to actual being. All change, all motion is thus passage of potentiality into actuality, of matter into form" [84] p. 279-280.

We have now taken some representative examples of the thoughts of pre-Socratic Greek philosophers as well as that of Plato and Aristotle – which undoubtedly show the flowering of ideas of great diversity – but nowhere have we found a transgression of the principle of *ex nihilo nihil fit*.

It is to be noted that an analysis of the history of philosophical ideas points to the fact, that even in systems where the problem of time is not studied as a distinct philosophical problem, the metaphysical kernel of thinking centering around such basic questions as being and becoming implicitly contains different shades of ideas about it. The relevance of such metaphysical formulations for the problem of time can be seen gradually taking shape in the thoughts of the later exponents pursuing the same line of thinking. As an example of this, from the history of Greek philosophy itself, one could mention the impact of Parmenides on subsequent Greek thinking regarding the problem of time. It was precisely in support of Parmenides' philosophy of being as motionless and unhangeable that Zeno formulated his famous paradoxes. Zeno's dialectics directed against the reality of motion at once revealed the challenge that is inherent in the problem of time, the conception of motion being necessarily connected with the conception of space and time. The aim of the dialectics was to silence the opponents of Parmenides by pointing out the absurdities involved in no matter which way motion may be conceived – as continuous or as discontinuous.

Zeno's paradoxes, lending support to the thesis of motionless being of Parmenides, demonstrated the unreality of time as well – a theme which has occurred again and again in the history of philosophical traditions across the cultures. Again, in the history of Greek philosophy itself, this trend of thought can be traced much later in the philosophy of Plato, where time is characterised as appearance. It is to be noted here that the dialectical defence of Zeno against the notion of multiplicity and motion and the philosophical pattern of Platonic thought are both deeply influenced by the Eleatic conception of being. The influence can still be traced later in neo-platonic philosophy as well. Time as appearance – a metaphyical insight which has its advocates in all traditions – is a logical sequel of a conception of being, which in its radical formulation denies becoming an ultimate metaphysical status.

The Platonic conception of time unites in it both the Pythagorean and Eleatic trends of thinking. Let us first take note of the myth of the creation of time in *Timaeus* [78] 37C-38C,

"... so as that pattern is the Living Being that is for ever existent, he sought to make this universe also like it, so far as might be, in the respect. Now the nature of that Living Being was eternal, and this character it was impossible to confer in full completeness on the generated thing. But he took thought to make, as it were, a moving likeness of eternity; and, at the same time that he ordered the Heaven, he made, of eternity that abides in unity, an everlasting likeness moving according to number – that to which we have given the name time.

For there were no days and nights, months and years, before the Heaven came into being; but he planned that they should now come to be at the same time that the Heaven was framed."

Again, a significant idea about time can be read in the following lines,

"Be that as it may, time came into being together with the Heaven, in order that, as they were brought into being together, so they may be dissolved together, if ever their dissolution should come to pass; and it is made after the pattern of the ever-enduring nature, in order that it may be as like that pattern as possible; for the pattern is a thing that has being for all eternity, whereas the Heaven has been and is and shall be perpetually through all time".

Time thus, for Plato, belongs to the world of appearances. However, he conceives it as a numerical moving image of eternity, which is related to the movement of the planets:

"... in order that time might be brought into being, Sun and Moon and five other stars – 'wanderers', as they are called – were made to define and preserve the numbers of time".

Plato's contribution to the problem of time is worthy of notice. Time is not understood as an existing frame of the universe but as generated by celestial revolutions and yet it is not real. The Platonic understanding of time will again be taken up, while we shall attempt to understand the Greek cosmological formulations and their relation to time.

Let us first take note of the Aristotelian contribution to the problem of time. It is in his writings, it can be noticed, that the problem of time takes on a philosophical depth which is hitherto not found in the Greek philosophical literature. Although time is as such not a key problem in the Aristotelian conceptual framework, yet considerable reflection on the problem of time is witnessed in his writings, viz. *Physics*, Book IV, Chapter X to Chapter XIV [79].

These pages of *Physics* cover a wide range of questions and problems, which necessarily come up as one delves into a serious philosophical investigation about time. Fully conscious of the enigma that time is, his analysis seeks to detect what considerations "might make one suspect either that there is really no such thing as time, or at least that it has only an equivocal and obscure existence.

1) Some of it is past and no longer exists, and the rest is future and does not yet exist; and time, whether limitless or any given length of time we take, is entirely made up of the no-longer and not-yet; and how can we conceive of that which is composed of non-existents sharing in existence in any way?

2) Moreover, if anything divisible exists, then, so long as it is in existence, either all its parts or some of them must exist. Now time is divisible into parts, and some of these were in the past and some will be in the future, but none of them exists. The present 'now' is not part of time at all, for a part measures the whole, and the whole must be made up of the parts, but we cannot say that time is made up of 'nows'.

3) Nor is it easy to see whether the 'now' that appears to divide the past and the future (a) is always one and the same or (b) is perpetually different" [79] Bk. IV Ch. X, 217 b-218 a, (p. 373, 375).

The many facets of the problem of time, which puzzle the philosophical intellect across cultures, find a clear expression as Aristotle proceeds with his investigation. The subtle analysis, that follows the above formulation, leads to important questions as to how time is related to movement and change, to number, to non-existence, even to consciousness. His comments are illuminating in each case. We can only cite a few examples of his brilliant analysis. Considering the problem of time and movement, he writes,

"Now the most obvious thing about time is that it strikes us as some kind of 'passing along' and changing; but if we follow this clue, we find that, when any particular thing changes or moves, the movement or change is in the moving or changing thing itself or occurs only where that thing is; whereas 'the passage of time' is current everywhere alike and is in relation with everything. And further, all changes may be faster or slower, but not so time; for fast and slow are defined by time, 'faster' being more change in less time, and 'slower' less in more. But time cannot measure time thus, as though it were a distance (like the space passed through in motion) or a qualitative modification, as in other kinds of change. It is evident, therefore, that time is not identical with movement; nor, in this connection, need we distinguish between movement and other kinds of change" [79] Bk. IV Ch. X, 218 b (p. 377,379).

"On the other hand, time cannot be disconnected from change, ... Plainly, then time is neither identical with movement nor capable of being separated from it ..."

Many important issues are raised in this connection, and it can be seen with what ingenuity he tries to disentangle one concept from another. It is, indeed, a pioneering work, of which he is himself aware. After his first formulation of the puzzle that time is, he writes – "But what time really is and under what category it falls, is no more revealed by anything that has come down to us from earlier thinkers than it is by considerations that have just been urged", [79] Bk. IV Ch. X, 218 a (p. 377).

We shall for the moment, terminate the discussion of Aristotle after giving another example of his awareness of the necessary problem that a study of time has to face, viz. that of consciousness. Since the present study has covered the problem of time and consciousness in some respects, it is interesting to observe how this eminent Greek philosopher conceived of the problem.

Aristotle is aware that "the relation of time to consciousness deserves examination ...". This is followed up in the next paragraph, which runs thus,

"The question remains, then, whether or not time would exist if there were no consciousness; for if it were impossible for there to be the factor that does the counting, it would be impossible that anything should be counted; so that evidently there could be no number, for a number is either that which has actually been counted or that which can be counted. And if nothing can count except consciousness and consciousness only as intellect (not as sensation merely), it is impossible that time should exist if consciousness did not; unless as the 'objective thing' which is subjectively time to us, if we may suppose that movement could thus objectively exist without there being any consciousness. For 'before' and 'after' are objectively involved in motion, and these, qua capable of numeration, constitute time" [79] Bk. IV Ch. XIV 223 a (p. 419, 421).

Aristotle's contribution is of great importance. Ariotti[3] remarks, that "Aristotle ... not only carefully examined their views, but went on to formulate a nearly complete theory of time ...".

Now that we have noted, however briefly, the philosophical pattern of cosmological speculations and some analysis of the problem of time in the history of Greek philosophy, we turn to the Judeo-Christian tradition.

The doctrine of creation *ex nihilo*, which Christianity holds in common with Judaism, stands in contrast to the cosmological speculations found in the Greek philosophical conceptualisation. The doctrine denies that the universe is unoriginate or everlasting. "It also excludes the Platonic notion of a Demiurge fashioning the world out of a formless matter and the Neo-Platonic notion of the physical universe's coming to be by emanation from the Absolute. In distinction to these ideas the doctrine of creation *ex nihilo* asserts, that the universe has been summoned into existence out of nothing (that is, not out of anything) by the creative will and purpose of God."[4]

Philo of Alexandria is aware of the difference between the Judaic conception of creation and the Platonic. He writes, "God when he gave birth to all things, not only brought them into sight, but also made things which before were not, not just handling material as a demiurge, an artificer, but being Himself its creator", *De Somniis*, [91], 14, 76.

Obviously, the formulation of the conception of creation out of nothing in the

3 *The Study of Time* II [102]. Here "their" refers to "his predecessors'".

4 *The Encyclopaedia of Philosophy* Vol. 2, p. 105 [105].

semitic account of the absolute beginning of the universe is a departure from the Greek mode of conceiving the problem of creation. The confrontation of these ideas is naturally a challenge to the respective traditions. Let us note in this connection the two following statements, each representing boldly its own philosophical stand –

"... Non-existence being changed by the Divine Power into Being" – says St. Gregory of Nyssa.[5]

"Nothing is ever produced by divine power out of nothing" – says Lucretius.[6]

Our task here is, however, only to search for such exchanges in this controversy, which would throw light on the problem of time eventually.

Let us first enquire into the term 'creation *ex nihilo*'. Erich Frank points out that the term "is a rational expression evidently coined as a counterpart of the philosophical formula *nihil ex nihilo fit*. It is foreign to scripture, where the idea of creation did not yet constitute a philosophical problem. It first occurs in the second century B.C in the Greek version of the Maccabeans (7.28). Subsequently, the formula is used by Christian thinkers, whenever they wish to express their idea of creation in terms of Greek philosophy" [91] p. 74-75.

Evidently, the idea did not find favour with the Greeks. The opposition is however not centered merely in this rational expression, on the contrary, it can be said to bear witness to all other differences in ideas which are to emerge.

Amongst all the new concepts, which the idea of 'creation out of nothing' has brought along, is what is claimed as a linear conception of time as opposed to the cyclic understanding of the Greeks. But before we ponder on this important question, which has given rise to polemics of different sorts, of inter-cultural dimension, it is important to understand the Judeo-Christian conceptual model, which is in obvious opposition to that of the Greek cosmological speculations – as reflected by these 'rational expressions'.

However, as one penetrates into the thought behind the formulation of 'creation *ex nihilo*' and their objection to the Greek cosmological understanding, the theological motive comes to the forefront.

In this connection, let us read from the writings of important representatives of both Judaism and Christianity the theological considerations that are operating, as they attempt to interpret the texts in Genesis – as 'In the beginning God made the heaven and earth'.

The significance of 'beginning' is to be understood as related to time as well as with regard to, in what sense precisely it is a challenge to the Greek mode of conceiving the origin of the world, etc.

5 Quoted by Florovsky in *Creation and Redemption* [90]

6 Quoted by Frank in *Philosophical Understanding and Religious Truth* [91].

Philo of Alexandria, whose lifetime is supposed to cover that of Jesus Christ and John the Baptist, but apparently knew nothing of their life and work, already pondered on the question. Equipped in both Judaic and Hellenic thought and ideas, he reflects on the account of the world's creation given by Moses, distinguishing the idea from the Greek cosmological speculation. He writes, "There are some people who, having the world in admiration rather than the Maker of the world, pronounce it to be without beginning and everlasting, while with impious falsehood they postulate in God a vast inactivity; whereas we ought on the contrary to be astonished at His powers as Maker and Father, and not to assign to the world a disproportionate majesty" [86] p. 10.

Philo's main objection is that "those who assert that this world is unoriginate unconsciously eliminate that which of all incentives to piety is the most beneficial and the most indispensable, namely providence. For it stands to reason that what has been brought into existence, should be cared for by its Father and Maker" [86] p. 11. He argues further, "... but between that which has never been brought into being and one who is not its Maker no such tie is formed". Philo therefore condemns it as "a worthless and baleful doctrine, setting up anarchy in the well-ordered realm of the world, leaving it without protector, arbitrator, or judge, without anyone whose office it is to administer and direct all its affairs. Not so Moses. That great master, holding the unoriginate to be of a different order from that which is visible, since everything that is an object of sensible perception is subject to becoming and to constant change, never abiding in the same state, assigned to that which is invisible and an object of intellectual apprehension the infinite and undefinable as united with it by closest tie; but on that which is an object of the senses he bestowed "genesis", "becoming", as its appropriate name. Seeing then that this world is both visible and perceived by the senses, it follows that it must also have had an origin. Whence it was entirely to the point that he put on record that origin, setting forth in its true grandeur the work of God".

Thus, the theological considerations underlying the idea that the world has a beginning are quite clear, and in the process Philo has also pointed out what considerations make him decline the other contending cosmological model which claims the world to be unoriginate.

The utter theological character of these arguments becomes further clear as one ponders on the Judeo-Christian understanding of this idea of 'beginning' vis-a-vis time. Philo is also aware of this question and has reflected on the implication of 'beginning' in relation to time.

When Moses says that "in the beginning God made the heaven and earth" what he does is, Philo writes, "... taking 'beginning' not, as some think, in a chronological sense, for time there was not before there was a world. Time began either simultaneously with the world or after it. For since time is a measured space determined by the world's movement, and since movement could not be prior to the object moving, but must of necessity arise either after it or simultaneously with it, it follows of necessity that time also is coeval with or later born than the world. To venture to affirm that it is elder born would be to do violence to philosophic sense. And since the word 'beginning' is not here taken as the chronological beginning, it would seem likely that the numerical order is indicated, so that 'in the beginning He made' is equivalent to 'He made the heaven first'".

This gives us a concrete basis for understanding what creation 'out of nothing' signifies to the Judaic intellect, reflecting on the question, and in what consists their polemic with the Greek mode of thinking.

Let us now turn to Saint Augustine in order to note the Christian understanding of the text of Genesis vis-à-vis the question of time, which he analyses remarkably in his theological masterpiece – *The Confessions.*

His reflection very clearly puts it into focus that "In the Beginning Thou madest the heaven and earth ..." ([87] Bk. XI Ch. IX) does not signify a beginning in time. He writes,

"At no time then hadst Thou not made any thing, because time itself Thou madest. And no times are coeternal with Thee, because Thou abidest, but if they abode, they should not be times" [87] Bk. XI Ch. XIV (p. 262).

The problem of time acquires a new dimension when considered in the perspective of the idea of being as timeless. There is no doubt room for various interpretations, as the different conceptual structures indicate.

However, what is of great interest at this point is to note that the conceptions of time and the timeless offer challenge to the theological and philosophical minds across the traditional boundaries of all cultures. History of ideas bears witness to the formulation of such concepts over and over again.

It is obvious that a formulation of any conception of the timeless in a given conceptual structure has necessary implications for the problem of time. Examples of the conceptual model of being as timeless are found in all major traditions. The Brahmanical tradition especially in itse school of Advaita Vedānta expresses a total commitment to a most rigorous formulation of this conception. Parallel ideas are not lacking, despite structural differences, in the Greek and Christian world of thinking. The formulation of the conception of timeless as not only beginningless, endless, but also as that which knows of no change whatsoever can be found in all these traditions despite their other important differences.

The equivalent to the conception of *kūṭastha nitya*[7] can be found in *De mor. Manich.*[8] as well as in *The Confessions*[9] of St. Augustine, which also points out the theological hierarchy that is there: the timeless as *sui generis*, the temporal having a dependent status.

Another characteristic way of pointing out the conception of being as timeless – which has parallels across the traditions – is to characterise the timeless as ever-present (*sarvadā-vidyamānatvam*). In other words, being as timeless cannot be sublated at any time (*trikālābādhyatvam*). About it one cannot say that it is not, it was not or it will not be.

Plato in his *Timaeus* points out that 'was' and 'shall be' are forms of time and that "we are wrong to transfer them unthinkably" to the being which is not subject to time. He continues:

"We say that it was and is and shall be; but 'is' alone really belongs to it and describes it truly; 'was' and 'shall be' are properly used of becoming which proceeds in time, for they are motions. But that which is for ever in the same state immovably cannot be becoming older or younger by lapse of time; nor can it ever become so; neither can it now have been, nor will it be in the future; and in general nothing belongs to it of all that Becoming attaches to the moving things of sense ..." [78] p. 98 (38A).

A proper appraisal of the conceptual models of time and timeless, because of their very universality, opens up a bridge for further exploration of theological and philosophical structures, varying from tradition to tradition.

(ii) A note on the cyclic and the linear notions of time

The study of time in its inter-cultural perspective poses a variety of problems which call for clarification. The existing literature on the subject is naturally enormous, as no philosophical/theological tradition can avoid reflecting on a problem of such fundamental importance.

The attempts at a global appraisal is risky and, as can be seen, often based on insufficient informations about other traditions. Not only the philosophical ideas but images, symbols and myths stemming from a particular cultural set-up

7 See section III (iii).

8 Quoted in section VIII (iv) p. 162

9 [87] Bk. VII Ch. XI, quoted in section VIII (iv) p. 162

are liable to misrepresentation and misinterpretation without an intimate acqaintance with them.

To cite an example, – in a confrontation of the Greek, the Judeo-Christian and the Indian traditions regarding the problem of time, the most familiar observation that is made is centered on the idea of cyclic vs. linear time. It is held that the Greek and the Indian traditions have cherished a cyclic conception of time, whereas the Judeo-Christian traditions have maintained a linear conception. This common point of difference which is often focused upon has, evidently, important bearings on different problems connected with time.

What does the cyclic conception and the linear conception entail about time? These are obviously notions drawn on the analogy of geometrical figures, intended symbolically to represent ideas about time.

It is, however, not quite so easy to lay one's hand on a proper formulation of these notions, granted that these comments as such are so widespread. Loose observations are, however, obtainable which are valuable but not sufficient for a proper evaluation.

The linear notion of time in the biblical context implies that time has a beginning and an end, the cyclic does not grant that. Some consider a cyclic time as advocating reversability, others point out that the order of events as such is irreversible, but any future event is also a past event – the beginning and the end coincide in a cycle. The linear time advocates the unrepeatability, the uniqueness of the particulars, it makes room for progress, it makes history meaningful, freeing it from mechanical recurrences. It is evident that any attempt at a precise formulation would indicate the complexities and difficulties that are involved in such geometrical representations of the understanding of time in the different traditions.

Now that we have already discussed the different views of time within the philosophical traditions of India, we shall withhold any further comment until we take note of the nature of the conflict, as it took shape, philosophically and theologically, in the confrontation of the Greek with the Christian thinking. The theme of cyclic vs. linear time has already been an issue for a battle of ideas. Let us, therefore, note carefully the objections that are raised against the so-called cyclic idea of time by its opponents, as this would provide valuable clues to understand the implications that are read into it.

At a rather early date of the Christian era, we find Saint Augustine in his *City of God* [88] attacking the idea of circular time, as in Bk.XII, Ch.XIV, XVIII, XXI. Thus, in Ch.XIV (p. 63) we read:

"as those others think, the same measures of time and the same events in time are repeated in circular fashion; on the basis of this cyclic theory, it is argued, for example, that, just as in a certain age the philosopher Plato taught his students in the City of Athens and in the school called the Academy, so during countless past ages, at very prolonged yet definite intervals, the same Plato, the same city, and the same school with the same students had existed again and again, and during countless ages to come will exist again and again. Heaven forbid, I repeat, that we should believe that. For Christ died once for our sins, but "rising from the dead he dies no more, and death shall no longer have domain over him"" [88] Bk. XII, Ch. XIV (p. 63).

From this significant passage it is possible to gather some of the important ideas that are associated with the notion of circular time. 'The same measure of time' repeats itself 'in a circular fashion' and along with it recur the same events to such minute details that it brings about the same individuals etc. in all exactitude.

In a closer analysis, one can discern a complex of ideas which underlies the concept designated as 'circular time' by Augustine. It involves, for example, a view about the cosmological processes as strictly periodical. This entails exact repetition of all events in the cosmos including the destinies of the individuals. In this scheme of thought, thus, there cannot be any room for salvation, which is, of course, a matter of great theological consequence.

These ideas, that Augustine reads into the notion of 'circular time' and challenges, are expressed thus in the following passages:

"... there will likewise be hereafter an uninterrupted series of revolving ages that come and go by. Either these cycles took place in a permanent world or else the world, rising and setting at fixed intervals, always displayed as though new the same events as had happened in the past and were to come again in the future. From this whirligig they are quite unable to free their immortal soul even though it has attained wisdom, for in its own uniterrupted circular course it moves back and forth between false happiness and genuine unhappiness.

For how can that happiness which has no assurance of eternity be genuine when the soul either is totally uninstructed in the truth so that it knows nothing of its future unhappiness or in its happiness has a most unhappy apprehension of it?" [88] Bk. XII, Ch. XIV (p. 61).

We have now before us certain concrete features of the idea of circular time and some of its important implications as viewed by Augustine.

Let us now turn to the history of Greek philosophy in order to obtain more information and insight on the topic in question. We find that the cosmological models of the Greek thinkers are in conformity with the dogma, which Aristotle declares to be "common to all the physicists, that 'nothing can come out of what does not exist'" [79] Bk. I, Ch. IV, 187 a (p. 43).

The differences in cosmological speculations amongst the Greek thinkers can be seen from the critical exposition of such views by Aristotle in his *Physics*, where he critically reviews the positions of his predecessors. To cite an example, the difference between the views of Empedocles and Anaxagoras, as he says, lies in "that Empedocles supposes the course of Nature to return upon itself, coming round again periodically to its starting-point, while Anaxagoras makes it move on continuously."

However, the idea of world-periods/world-cycles involving a chain of creation and dissolution of the cosmos has run through the history of Greek thought. Anaximanes, Heraclitus, Empedocles, as well as the stoics all indicate the belief that the cosmos is eternal but periodically changes and renews itself, so to speak. There are, however, different modes in which genesis is conceived, but no idea of absolute beginning can be found.

An important basis for the idea of world-cycle is the astronomical observation of the periodical recurrences of the positions of heavenly bodies. It is in this connection that the Greek idea of the 'Great Year' (*Eniautos*) is formed, being the time-period in which the cosmos completes one cycle. This is followed by a new cycle and so on infinitely.

The idea of an exact repetition of the cosmical revolutions along with recurrence of all events in exact details has been referred to the Pythagoreans. Eudemus, a student of Aristotle has referred to this view as follows: "... if one may believe the Pythagoreans ... then someday I myself, with this staff in my hand, shall talk to you who will sit in front of me, just as you are sitting now, and the same will be true of everything else".[10] This bears witness to the fact that the idea of exact recurrence of cosmic processes and that of every event of individual lives has been a trend of thinking present in Greece, accounting for 'a sense of fate'[11] that was common in the pre-Christian era.

It is, however, difficult to arrive at a fair evaluation regarding the question as to how widespread and accepted the idea was to all concerned or whether it was rather one amongst various views that were current. It is clear, nevertheless, that the idea of time as associated with circular movement has more than one version. It is in Aristotle's *Physics* we find, that some such views have been taken up for a critical review. The views of his predecessors about time have been noted and commented by Aristotle in the following lines.

"(a) Some have identified time with the revolution of the all-embracing heaven, and (b) some with that heavenly sphere itself. But (a) a partial revolution is time just as much as a whole one is, but it is not just as much a revolution, for any finite portion of time is a portion of a revolution, but is not a revolution. Moreover, if there were more universes than one, the re-entrant circumlation of

10 Quoted by E. Frank [91] p. 83.

11 *Creation and Redemption*, by Florovsky [90] p. 127.

each of them would be time, so that several different times would exist at once. And (b) as to those who declared the heavenly sphere itself to be time, their only reason was that all things are contained 'in the celestial sphere' and also occur 'in time', which is too childish to be worth reducing to absurdities more obvious than itself" [79] Bk. IV, Ch. X, 218 b (p. 377).

This is instructive as it acts as a check on too hasty a generalisation about what could have been the understanding of time in a philosophical tradition like that of Greece, which knows of a variety of views regarding specific problems.

Moreover, the particular Greek view of time that Augustine has in front of him – according to which 'the same measure of time' repeats itself 'in a circular fashion' – does not seem to have been cherished by at least Aristotle, as we read the following passage.

"Moreover, though time is identical everywhere simultaneously, it is not identical if taken twice successively; for the change it measures, likewise, is one when considered as present, but not if considered as partly past and partly future. And time considered numerically is concrete, not abstract; whereby follows that it changes from the former to the latter 'now', inasmuch as these 'nows' themselves are different; just as the number of a hundred horses is identical with that of a hundred men, but the horses enumerated are different from the men enumerated. Now note further that as there may be movement (of rotation to wit) that covers the same course over and over again, in like manner we mark off time by the year or by spring or autumn" [79] Bk. IV, Ch. XII, 220 b (p. 397, 399).

It is illuminating, in this connection, also to read the philosophical explanation that Aristotle gives as to why rotation is accepted as a standard for measuring time and in what precise sense one habitually speaks of the 'circle of time'. We quote again from his *Physics*:

"And now, keeping locomotion and especially rotation in mind, note that everything is counted by some unit of like nature to itself – monads monad by monad, for instance, and horses horse by horse – and so likewise time by some finite unit of time. But as we have said, motion and time mutually determine each other quantitively; and that because the standard of time established by the motion we select is the quantitive measure both of that motion and of time. If, then, the standard once fixed measures all dimensionality of its own order, a uniform rotation will be the best standard, since it is easiest to count.

Neither qualitative modification nor growth nor genesis has the kind of uniformity that rotation has; and so time is regarded as the rotation of the sphere, inasmuch as all other orders of motion are measured by it, and time itself is standardised by reference to it. And this is the reason of our habitual way of speaking; for we say that human affairs and those of all other things that have natural movement and become and perish seem to be in a way circular, because all these things come to pass in time and have their beginning and end as it were 'periodically'; for time itself is conceived as 'coming round'; and this again because time and such a standard rotation mutually determine each other. Hence, to call the happenings of a thing a circle is saying that there is a sort of circle of time; and that is because it is measured by a complete revolution, and the whole measurement of a thing is nought else but a defined number of the units of its measurements" [79] Bk. IV, Ch. XIV, 223 b (p. 423, 425).

Again, in *Problems,* Aristotle has directly posed the question, and his answer at once indicates that the closest he could get conceptually to the notion of cyclic time would still be not identical to the view that Eudemus or Augustine have referred to. The passage is as follows:

"As therefore in the movement of the heavens and of each star there is a circle, what is there to prevent the birth and death of perishable things from being of this nature, so they are born or destroyed again? So they say that human affairs are a cycle. The suggestion that those who are continually being born are numerically identical is absurd, but we could accept that they are the same in 'form'" [82] Bk. XVII, 916 a (p. 367).

We shall not, however, pursue the discussion in the Greek context any longer but turn to the Indian philosophical scene in order to investigate the import of the label of cyclic time in the Indian conceptual framework. The ideas associated with the notion of cyclic time – as have emerged in Greek thought and especially in its confrontation with Christian thinking – provide a significant background for the discussion, as it enables one to discern the distinct characteristics of the traditional Indian position regarding the problem.

It is commonly held that the Indian conception of time is cyclic. Here too the designation is often granted and accepted without much further attempt at a clear-cut, well-defined understanding regarding the conceptual content of this notion. It is, however, important to analyse this designation of cyclic time in the Indian context in order to remove any possible misinterpretation regarding its implications.

The idea of world-cycle (*kalpa*) is a general feature of Indian mythology and philosophy. In the literature of the *Purāṇas,* one encounters a grandiose conception of the cosmological process in terms of repeated creation and dissolution. As an example of the gigantic scale of measurement for time one could refer to the *Vāyu Purāṇa* where a world-cycle is conceived as a day of Brahmā, the creator god, followed by his night, i.e. cosmic dissolution (*pralaya*). The time-span of a world-cycle is divided and sub-divided according to different scales as equivalent to so many *manvantaras, mahāyugas, yugas* etc. The whole process is calculated in terms of billions of human years. It is very likely that the idea is associated with Vedic astronomy. The world-cycles can be compared to one another in terms of generic similarity just as one day resembles another, but the idea of exact repetition involving the return of the particulars does not occur. The idea of world cycles occurs in the epics as well as in the *Upaniṣads.*

The idea of transmigration is equally a general feature of the conceptual framework in India. It is, however, to be understood as a necessarry sequel of the doctrine of Karma. These ideas, in different versions, are current in the Brahmanical, Buddhist and Jaina traditional thinking. To think of transmigration as equivalent to mechanical recurrence, which debars the possibility of moral progress, is a distortion of the idea. The doctrine of Karma implies the inexorability of the moral law, formulating the age-old insight of 'as you sow, so you reap' in its utmost consequence. The idea focuses, on the one hand, on that man creates his destiny through action. The present actions determine the future. On the other hand, the idea entails that one cannot escape the consequences of the actions, once performed.

"It is wrong to identify the doctrine of Karma with fatalism. Karma is not an external destiny driving man to his doom, nor a blind mechanical framework from which there is no escape".[12] The idea of Karma refers back eventually to the idea of transmigration – metempsychosis, viewing the human existence as going beyond birth and death. This idea, shared by the Jaina and the Buddhist along with the Brahmanical tradition can be seen, in the long run, as an attempt to answer the problem of evil. To pronounce *saṃsāra,* the chain of existences, as beginningless is strongly motivated by the urge for an understanding of the problem of evil – a problem which no theological structure can evade. This has been found to be incompatible with the idea of absolute beginning, a conceptual possibility which has been also considered. If the problem of an ultimate basis for individual differences, in all its different aspects, is left to the play of sheer chance, the idea that action determines and conditions the human situation/destiny cannot be established in all strictness. Moreover, in the theistic frameworks,[13] to make God solely responsible for these undeniable differences would be tantamount to attributing to Him injustice, which is inappropriate to the divine nature. Thus, the complex set of ideas, that goes along with the doctrine of Karma, has as one of its necessary implications the idea of pre-existence.

12 Mahadevan, in "*The religio-philosophic culture of India*", [4] vol I p. 163-181 (p. 179).

13 It is so pointed out by different Brahmanical schools. See *Nyāya Sūtra* 4/1/19 and Śaṅkara's commentary on *Brahma Sūtra* 2/1/34-35.

Transmigration is, however, not understood by any of these traditions as equivalent to a mechanical recurrence of the same individual destiny, as the Greek model of the idea which we have considered. The idea of Karma itself would be a rebuttal to such an idea of exact repetition, as the idea of actions bringing forth consequences cannot be relevant in that scheme. All the stories of *Jātaka*, for example, mythologically express the importance of action, seen in the perspective of many lives, in the making of a Buddha.

Moreover, these ideas, involving transmigration, Karma, etc., often symbolised as the 'wheel of becoming' is viewed theologically as having salvation for its goal (*mokṣāyate saṃsāraḥ*). All the traditions have sought to conceive 'salvation', each in its own conceptual scheme, as a final freedom from the 'ocean of death-bound existence'.[14] This idea of salvation must not be overlooked in an appraisal of Karma, transmigration. Even the idea of world-cycle can be understood in a theistic context in the following manner, as Radhakrishnan exposes it:

"The universe once created persists through an entire *kalpa*, or world-period, after which it returns into the supreme God, only to issue again from Him. The cause of this re-issue is that the works of the soul still survive and demand a fresh creation or a renewed existence for their expiation". ([8] Vol. I p. 514).

It is to be noted that the wheel of becoming, in the Indian context, does not involve a mechanical repetition of the particular/the individual, neither does it preclude salvation, nor by any means imply that a released soul can be pulled back to this death-bound existence again.

It is interesting to note the following remark of Śaṅkara, as he criticises the Vaiśeṣika categories. Although taken from quite a different context of conceptual analysis, still his retort has relevance for our present discussion.

"If we once allow assumptions, there is no reason why there should not be assumed a further hundred or thousand things, in addition to the six categories assumed by the Vaiśeṣikas. Anybody then might assume anything, and we could neither stop a compasionate man from assuming that this transmigratory world which is the cause of so much misery to living beings is not to be, nor a malicious man from assuming that even the released souls are to enter on a new cycle of existences".[15]

It is needless to say that in order to do justice to all these complex sets of ideas it requires detailed analysis of the subject in question in the framework of the

14 *Bhagavadgītā* XII, 7.

15 *Vedānta-Sūtra*, I,2,17 by Śaṅkara [40] p. 398.

various schools of thought belonging to the different philosophical traditions. In matters of such profound speculations there is room for several versions, as the ideas are worked out in each system. Thus, for example, the idea of repeated creation and dissolution is accepted by all Brahmanical schools except Pūrva-Mīmaṃsā. Again, the conception of a final dissolution (*mahā-pralaya*) is to be found in the school of Advaita Vedānta, and it can be understood only in the light of the conception of universal salvation (*sarvamukti*).[16]

These ideas, as for example in the Brahmanical traditions those of transmigration, Karma, world-cycle, salvation, are all built into an inter-connected system of ideas which have bearing on each other. They are interrelated and meet at a theological frontier.

Let us note the different ideas in the texts of the *Bhagavadgītā* [2]. There is a direct allusion to the idea of periodic emergence and dissolution of the world, using the metaphor of day and night:

"At the coming of day, all manifested things come forth from the unmanifested and at the coming of night they merge in the same, called the unmanifested." Here the unmanifested is Prakṛti'. (VIII, 18)

Note the idea of the Transcendent,

"But beyond this unmanifested,[17] there is yet another Unmanifested Eternal Being who does not perish even when all existences perish." (VIII, 20)

Again,

"Veiled by My creative power (*yogamāyā*) I am not revealed to all. This bewildered world knows Me not, the unborn, the unchanging." (VII, 25)

Note the idea of transmigration,

"As the soul passes in this body through childhood, youth and age, even so is its taking on of another body. The sage is not perplexed by this." (II, 13)

And the idea of salvation,

"From the realm of Brahmā downwards, all worlds are subject to return to rebirth, but on reaching Me, O Son of Kunti (Arjuṇa), there is no return to birth again." (VIII, 16)

It is not possible, however, to sort out relevant passages from each tradition and to develop them in a coherent, fullfledged form here. Even when the traditions operate with similar ideas, a wide variety of views develop as attempts are made

16 cf. Warrier [50].

17 Meaning Prakṛti.

at systematic philosophical formulations with all the concequences and implications that follow within the conceptual framework of the different systems.

The basic reason for bringing up this discussion is to point out the importance of understanding rightly the appellation of the so-called 'cyclic or circular time', if the term is not to be a misnomer. A sculptural image of 'the wheel of becoming' has to be interpreted in the light of the tradition where it is used significantly.

There is reason to be cautious when we use the same label of 'circular time' for characterising the Greek as well as the Indian philosophical models of speculations. The presence or absence of certain ideas ought not to be the basis for any rash appraisal of traditions. We have noted already that the Greek and the Indian conceptual models for cosmological speculations (whatever their ultimate ontological status) are developed in strict adherence to the principle of *ex nihilo nihil fit*. Again, the presence of such ideas as world-cycles, transmigration can be found, in different versions, in these Greco-Indian fields of speculations. But the important differences of the Indian ideas from the Greek model – that Augustine has in front of him – must by no means be lost sight of. The Greek conceptual model of 'circular time' is completely deterministic, fatalistic. Despite all the internal differences within the boundary of philosophical speculations in India, that Greek model of 'circular time' is nowhere to be found. The ideas of the transcendent and salvation pulsate throughout these traditions. The materialistic school of Cārvāka, of course, does not operate within this framework at all.

The relevance of this discussion, which as such would be outside the scope of this work, is to draw attention to this common appellation of 'circular time' – apparently a designation which stands for a complex set of ideas – to the Greek as well as to the Indian world-view. It is precisely the similarities of certain ideas which has been a basis for misunderstanding. Not to speak of much baseless polemics, even western authors, who have made important contributions to intercultural understanding, have this Greek conceptual model in mind while evaluating and confronting the complex world of Indian philosophy.[18]

18 Toynbee, in his *A Study of History* characterizes the cyclic image of Hellenic and Indic civilisation as 'a counsel of despair for humanity' [103] p. 487, cf. the following passage from [103] p. 157-158: 'This philosophy of sheer recurrence, which intrigued, without ever quite captivating, the Hellenic genius, came to dominate contemporary Indic minds. ...

Are these 'vain repetitions' of the Gentiles really the law of the Universe and, therefore, incidentally the law of the histories of civilizations? If we find that the answer is in the affirmative, we can hardly escape the conclusion that we are the perpetual victims of an everlasting cosmic practical joke, which condemns us to endure our sufferings and to overcome our difficulties and to purify ourselves of our sins – only to know in advance that the automatic and inevitable lapse of a certain meaningless measure of time cannot fail to stultify all our human exertions by

This points to the importance of understanding the significance of myths and symbols of a culture. A proper understanding and evaluation of symbols, verbal or pictorial (such as *bhava-cakra*, the wheel of becoming), presupposes an intimate knowledge of the philosophical background from where it stems. The want of a conceptual apparatus to decipher and appraise symbols and myths coming from unfamiliar cultural set-ups leads to misinterpretations. These, in turn, cause barriers for intercultural understanding, block the possibility of a fruitful encounter.

The theological motives operating behind the 'linear model' can be seen in the writings of Augustine. The cycle represented mechanical recurrence, complete determinism, no possibility of a final salvation. The ideas of an absolute beginning – as creation *ex nihilo* – and an absolute end – eschatology – provide the theological framework, along with the specific understanding of the saviour, in which the significance of linear time is to be understood.

Taken merely as an empirical concept, outside of this theological frame, the idea of time, geometrically represented by a finite line, i.e. itself having a beginning and an end, would lose its conceptual worth. We have to be aware of the pitfalls of such geometrical representations of time as a circle or a line. These have to be understood as theological symbolisms, whose intended spiritual significance can be grasped within their theological, conceptual structures.

It is indeed fascinating to go through the records of how the human mind has waved to and fro in its considerations of the alternate positions regarding whether the world can be said to have a beginning and an end, or is it beginningless but has /has no end or has a beginning but no end. We find illuminating discussions on the subject by Aristotle in his *On the Heavens* [81] Bk. I Ch. X-XII (pp. 94-129). Again, as Augustine breaks away from the traditional Greek thinking, he reflects on the matter at length in his *City of God* [88] Bk. XII Ch. X, XVI. In addition to these contributions from the Greek and the Christian world of ideas we have the immense mythological and philosophical insights and concepts, all contributing to the spectrum of speculations, from the rich variety of the Indian traditions.

reproducing the same situation again and again *ad infinitum*, just as if we had never exerted ourselves at all.'

Cf. also Zimmer [9] p. 18-20. His interpretation of the myth of the *Purāṇa* is illuminating. He captures the moral significance appropriately, yet his understanding is dominated by the Greek model of circular time to which he alludes.

(iii) Some parallel ideas in the investigation on time in Western philosophy

Investigations into the problem of time display across cultural boundaries some similar trends in terms of the questions, that arise in the course of analysis, as well as in the formulations of the actual positions. History of ideas provides many interesting parallels despite the differences in conceptual structures of given systems of thought.

A spectrum of divergent views pertaining to the problem of time is recorded in the history of Western thought. However, in this section reference will be made only to some analyses and views contributed by Western thinkers, which are also of special interest for the present study regarding the problem of time in Indian philosophy.

We have noted the principal views regarding time in Indian philosophy and their bearing on the divergent analysis and interpretation of other major philosophical concepts, which are indispensable for the various specific structures.

Here, we shall first refer to the classification of the existents and a specific aspect of the problem of non-existence found in the Nyāya-Vaiśeṣika schools in order to focus on their analysis in the perspective of Aristotelian discussion on the problem of time.

The Nyāya-Vaiśeṣika philosophical interpretation of time is evidently closely tied to their general conceptual scheme. In their metaphysical pluralistic structure, the universe of existents (*bhāva-padārtha*) is classified as *nitya* and *anitya*. Time is itself listed in the first category, as one amongst the entities conceived as unproduced and indestructible. Here, it is of significance to emphasise that the other entities, which belong to the same category as time, do not exist in time. It is the existents of the second category – liable to production and destruction – which are precisely those which have being-in-time. In other words, the contingent is necessarily in contact with time, a real per se. Absolute time is considered the receptacle (*ādhāra*) of all that is contingent (*janya*).

It is to be noted that the above classification is made on the basis of how the existents are related to time. To exist is not necessarily to be in time. No beginning or end can be attributed to the entities classified as *nitya*. They are outside the influence of time (*kālaprabhāvamukta*), as time is not their receptacle. It is explicitly brought out that these entities co-exist, but cannot be conceived as receptacle in relation to one another.

On the other hand, production, destruction, change, etc., pertaining to the contingent, all bear the stamp of time, i.e. they are possible and conceivable only in relation to time. They are literally said to be contained (*ādheya*) in time.

On the background of this analysis it is illuminating to read the following comments from Aristotle's *Physics*:

"And it is further evident that to be in existence while time is in existence does not constitute being 'in time', just as neither is a thing constituted as in motion or in a place because a motion and place exist while it does. For if this constitutes being 'in' a thing, everything would be in any thing, and the universe in a grain of millet, because a grain of millet exists while the universe is in existence. But this latter is an incidental coincidence, whereas when a thing is said to exist in time, it follows of necessity that there should be time while this thing exists, and if it exists in motion, it follows of necessity that there should be motion while it exists.

... so we must add that for things to exist in time they must be embraced by time, just as with other cases of being 'in' something; for instance, things that are in places are embraced by place. And it will follow that they are in some respect affected by time, just as we are wont to say that time crumbles things, and that everything grows old under the power of time and is forgotten through the lapse of time ...

From all this it is clear that things which exist eternally, as such, are not in time; for they are not embraced by time, nor is their duration measured by time. This is indicated by their not suffering anything under the action of time as though they were within its scope" [79] Bk. IV, Ch. XII, 221 a – 221 b (p. 403, 405).

The idea of non-existence (*abhāva*) is equally significant for an appraisal of the different views of time. The problem has been much debated by the Indian philosophers, as to whether it is an objective category or not, whether it is apprehended by perception, inference, or non-perception (*anupalabdhi*), (the latter is accepted as a source of knowledge by such schools as Bhaṭṭa-Mīmāṃsā and Vedānta who emphasised the direct, i.e. non-inferential character of our apprehension of non-existence, but maintained that no sense-contact is possible with the non-existent).

This is not the place to go into the details of such discussions, but it requires to be stressed that the views regarding the problem are not without implications on time. In section V (iv), 'Annihilation and time – a Nyāya-Buddhist controversy', we have studied an aspect of the problem of non-existence and its significance for the views regarding time. Here it needs to be emphasised once again, that the Nyāya-Vaiśeṣika philosophers took a bold stand and attempted a thorough analysis pertaining to definition, classification, as well as to the epistemological questions regarding the problem of non-existence. The Nyāya-Vaiśeṣika classification of non-existence into four kinds is highly interesting for its bearing on the problem of time.

The non-existence that precedes the production of an entity is designated as *prāgabhāva* or the antecedent non-existence. The production of an entity is the termination of its antecedent non-existence. The idea is especially useful for the Nyaya-Vaiśeṣika theory of causality, where the effect is conceived as non-existent prior to the causal operation, which demarcates the theory from that of Sāṅkhya where the effect is said to be pre-existent potentially in the cause. The antecedent non-existence thus cannot be said to have a beginning, but has an end (*anādih sāntah*). It is indicative of time as past when the contingent entity was not.

Again, the non-existence following the destruction of an entity is termed *pradhvaṃsābhāva* or subsequent non-existence. It is conceived as having a beginning but no end, e.g. the non-existence of a jar posterior to its destruction. This non-existence can never cease as the particular jar in question cannot come into existence any more. If the antedecent non-existence points to time as past, consequent non-existence indicates future non-existence of the present contingent entity.

The temporal dimension of these two kinds of non-existence is evident. Without time as their locus the Nyāya-Vaiśeṣika philosophers could not conceive of them as objective categories of reality. On the other hand, a clear-cut formulation of the idea of contingency (*kādācitkatva*) regarding a positive entity (*bhāvapadārtha*) could not be made possible without the specific ideas of time (*kāla*) and non-existence (*abhāva*). The production of a positive entity is the termination of its antecedent non-existence implying its first conjunction with time.

The other two kinds of non-existence are, however, of absolute character. This is brought out by pointing to their beginningless and endless nature. When a connection is denied in all three times, past, present, and future, – e.g. air has no colour, we have a case of what is termed *atyantābhāva* or absolute non-existence. This kind of non-existence, as opposed to the two kinds previously mentioned, cannot be said to originate or cease in time. This holds equally true of the non-existence termed *anyonyābhāva* which covers such cases of logical negation of formal character as S is not P.[19] Thus, in these systems the classification of non-existence into contingent and absolute bears necessary reference to time.

In this connection, it is interesting to quote once more a passage from Aristotle's analysis on time in order to note his reflections pertaining to this problem:

"Clearly, then not all non-existences are in time, but only such as might exist; for instance, the commensurability of the diagonal and the side does not exist, but its non-existence is not temporal. For, as a general proposition, if time is the measure of motion on its own account and of anything else only by incidental

19 See *The Nyāya theory of Knowledge* by S. Chatterjee [31]

coincidence, obviously everything whose existence it measures must have its existence in rest or in motion. Accordingly, whatever is destructible or generable, or (more broadly) sometimes existing and sometimes not, must be embraced by time; for there must be some time great enough to exceed the time of their duration and therefore the time which measures their being. Among non-existents, on the other hand, those which are embraced by time either once were (as Homer once existed) or will be (e.g. some future event), according as they are embraced by time on one or the other side of the present moment, or, if they are embraced in both directions, they can be either past or future; whereas those which are not in any way embraced by time neither were nor are nor will be. Non-existents of this latter kind are all those things whose opposites eternally exist; for instance, the incommensurability of the diagonal eternally exists and therefore is not in time. And it follows that neither is its commensurability in time; hence it is *eternally* non-existent, in as much as it is a contradiction of what is eternally existent; whereas things of which the opposite does not exist eternally may either be or not be, and so they can come into existence and vanish from it" [79] Bk. IV, Ch. XII, 221 b – 222 a (p. 405, 407).

It is significant to put in relief that amongst the wide-ranging philosophical stands regarding time in Indian philosophy, it is only the Nyāya-Vaiśeṣika school that ascribes to time as well as space an independent, absolute, and self-existent status. They are conceived as receptacles and are themselves not contained in anything else. The conventional time-divisions and space-divisions are explained as not inherent in the absolute time and space, but as measures with reference to motion and activities and as due to relation to finite bodies, respectively.

It is interesting to observe – as we shall see shortly – that these ideas about space and time are not in the least unfamiliar in western thought, although the motivations and considerations in support of such a view might be quite different.

The Aristotelian interpretation of time continued to exert a dominating influence until the advent of the Newtonian conception. Newton's ideas on the subject were influenced by his predecessor Galileo's findings on motion. In his *Principia*, published in 1687, Newton expressed his ideas about space and time. We shall quote only briefly in order to indicate some similarities in the general pattern with the Nyāya-Vaiśeṣika view.

"Absolute, true, and mathematical time, of itself, and from its own nature, flows equably without regard to anything external, and by another name is called duration: relative, apparent, and common time is some sensible and external measure of duration by means of motion, which is commonly used instead of true time; such as an hour, a day, a month, or a year.

"Absolute space, in its own nature, without regard to anything external, remains always similar and immovable. Relative space is some movable dimension or measure of the absolute space which our senses determine by its position to bodies ..."

Again, "... times and spaces are, as it were, the places as well of themselves as of all other things. All things are placed in time as to order of succession; and in space as to order of situation" (as quoted by Whitrow [99] Ch 3 p. 56).

Note, however, that whereas in the Newtonian formulation absolute time 'flows', the Nyāya-Vaiśeṣika philosophers, on the contrary, conceived it as static (*niṣkriya*).

The influence of Newton's ideas are far-reaching in the history of Western thought. It is evident on John Locke's philosophical reflections on time. In his *Essay Concerning Human Understanding* (1690) [95] Locke discusses elaborately, amongst various other problems, the problem of motion and time. The idea of linear representation is also found. The following lines contain some of the important features of his ideas.

"... duration is but as it were the length of one straight line, extended in infinitum, not capable of multiplicity, variation, or figure, but is one common measure of all existence whatsoever, wherein all things, whilst they exist, equally partake. For this present moment is common to all things that are now in being, and equally comprehends that part of their existence, as much as if they were all but one single being; and we may truly say, they all exist in the same moment of time."[20]

However, the idea of an objective time is no permanent feature of philosophical speculations in India or in the West as the history of ideas bears witness to.

The idea is challenged in the history of Indian thought. Time as an all-pervading real per se as the Nyāya-Vaiśeṣika philosophers would have it, or the idea of a single objective moment when the whole universe undergoes change, as Yoga conceives it, are rejected by the school of Advaita Vedānta. Not only the idea of time as an independent real per se but also the idea of an objective principle of change, conceived in whatever manner, are given up in this system. Time and change are not granted ontological reality, neither are they held to be fictitious or nothing. This is precisely their indeterminable character (*anirvacanīya*). However, their empirical reality is never questioned, neither their a priori character. It is to be noted that the characterisation of the world-process as beginningless is present as much in Advaita Vedānta as in any other school of Indian philosophy.

20 *Essay Concerning Human Understanding* by J. Locke [95]. Bk. II Ch. XV § 11.

But the emphasis is shifted, in so far as the principle of becoming is denied any absolute status and is declared as phenomenal (*vyavahārika-sat*).

The rejection of an absolute time as objectively given is a philosophical event that can be traced in the history of philosophy in many versions. To take an example from western philosophy, one may refer to a highly important analysis of the problem of time, viz. that of Kant. In his famous *Critique of Pure Reason* [94], Kant focuses on the idea of time as a 'form' of inner sense, that is, of the intuition of ourselves and of our inner state. He expressly states that "time is not something which exists of itself, or which inheres in things as an objective determination ..." Kant's interpretation of time discloses a novel conceptual model. He summarises his position thus in [94], p. 78:

"What we are maintaining is, therefore, the *empirical reality* of time, that is, its objective validity in respect of all objects which allow of ever being given to our senses. ... On the other hand, we deny to time all claim to absolute reality; that is to say, we deny that it belongs to things absolutely, as their condition or property, independently of any reference to the form of our sensible intuition; properties that belong to things in themselves can never be given to us through the senses. This, then, is what constitutes the *transcendental ideality* of time."

Kant's understanding of time has been open to much philosophical debate. Criticisms against the position are advanced by philosophers and scientists alike.

Laying aside other important ideas[21] relevant for a philosophical interpretation of time, that can be found in the history of Western philosophy, let us focus on the phenomenological movement of the twentieth century.

In the reflections of Husserl, the founder of phenomenology, the problem of time comes into the forefront of philosophical investigations and receives a novel treatment. In Husserl's analysis we find a treatment of the problem of time on three levels – the objective time in which the transcendant objects have their position, the immanent time in which the immanent acts are constituted and the absolute flux of consciousness, which is the source of all temporality but is itself not in time.

Husserl's lectures on internal time-consciousness [93] are mainly concerned with the second, viz. the problem of the constitution of immanent acts as temporal unities. Each act has a temporal stretch or extension, it is analysable into a series of 'nows', each 'now' having its own retentional and protentional horizon and sinking back into the past along with its horizon. In Husserl's analysis of time-consciousness the primitive element is no doubt the now, but the now is not an isolated discrete, atomic moment, but is intentional in its structure in the

21 Such as the well-known analysis of Bergson [89].

sense that it contains within itself references to the past and the future. This is what he means by its retentional and protentional horizon. This peculiar character of the now explains how an act-continuum is possible. If each momentary datum were completely disconnected with the other, the discrete nows would never form a whole, there would always be nothing but a perishing moment. His analysis is a significant contribution towards the problem of time and consciousness.

Husserl's ideas exerted an important influence on the existentialists, such as Heidegger [92] and Sartre [98]. The problem of time, as it stands in their respective philosophical treatment, is closely connected with human existence and consciousness. The idea of an objective or physical time appears in their analysis as derived and constructed. Thus Sartre maintains that the ecstatic character of consciousness is the origin of all temporality. Temporality is only "the mode of being of a Being which is itself outside of itself".[22]

We shall not go into details of the phenomenological and existentialistic analysis of time. However, it is interesting to note with reference to Sartrean existentialism and the Vijñānavāda school of Buddhism[23] the question as to whether self-consciousness involves the idea of a subsequent moment or not – a problem already referred to in section VII (i), 'time and consciousness'.

The problem is of acute interest to both these schools, who agree in maintaining that consciousness and its awareness of itself does not involve a subsequent act, where a temporal gap can be conceived between consciousness of something and consciousness of consciousness. The philosophical stand, as worked out in their specific conceptual structures, discloses a striking similarity in their respective argumentations.

In his principal work *Being and Nothingness* Sartre discusses this problem with much ingenuity. For Sartre, intentionality is the defining character of consciousness, that is to say, all consciousness is consciousness of something. The other very important implication of the notion of intentionality, which he makes explicit, is that "the necessary and sufficient condition for a knowing consciousness to be knowledge of its object, is that it be conscious of itself as being that knowledge" [98]. In other words, Sartre maintains that knowledge would be impossible, if consciousness were not aware of itself. It is not possible for me to be conscious of the table if "my consciousness were not conscious of being conscious of the table" [98]. Thus, for Sartre, "every positional consciousness of an object is *at the same time* a non-positional consciousness of itself".[24] This is

22 *Being and Nothingness* by Sartre [98] p. 136.

23 cf. A.N. Balslev [100].

24 *Being and Nothingness* [98]. (Italics mine)

what Sartre expresses by saying that consciousness of something is consciousness (of) consciousness.

It is very important to note that the subject-object dualism, which is so typical of the knowledge situation, is said not to hold good in the case of consciousness knowing itself. If that were the case, Sartre argues, it would mean that another consciousness is required to make consciousness known to itself, and thus one cannot avoid the fallacy of infinite regress. Thus, he concludes, all reflection presupposes this non-dual awareness on the part of consciousness.

On the other hand, the Vijñānavadins maintain vehemently that consciousness' awareness of itself is not a judgmental knowledge. Consciousness does not know itself as an external object, as consciousness is not an "other" to itself. This is precisely what is expressed in the statement "that which reveals itself, being free from the subject-object dualism" (*grāhya-grāhaka vaidhuryāt svayam sa iva prakāśyate*).[25] Consciousness of consciousness does not involve any duality. It is not a relation between two terms. It is not a discursive knowledge. It is said that as light reveals and is self-revealing, so is consciousness. The cognised object and the cognition are invariably apprehended together (*sahopalambha* – co-apprehension). Thus for consciousness to be aware of its object is to be conscious of itself. "Consciousness" nd "self-consciousness", therefore, are interchangable terms.[26].

This is the very presupposition of all knowledge. It is only by means of this idea of *svasamvedana* (self-awareness), the immediate, non-cognitive awareness, that one can avoid the fallacy of infinite regress (*anavasṭhā*), as would be inevitable if consciousness required another consciousness to make itself known to itself. This is how the Vijñānavādins argue that if consciousness is not self-revealing (svayamprakāśā), knowledge is not possible. It is claimed that all cognitions, feelings are known by themselves (*sarvam cittacaittānām ātmasamvedanam*) [61].

Thus, the brief study made above with an inter-cultural perspective points out that the conclusion, that no temporal sequence can be legitimately conceived between consciousness of something and consciousness of consciousness, is arrived at by the similar philosophical argument – that the contrary idea would inevitably lead to the fallacy of infinite regress, implying the impossibility of all knowledge.

Now, to return to the analysis of time as is found in the phenomenological and existentialistic investigations, it can be noted that the source of time-experience is traced to consciousness or human existence.

25 *Yogācāra Idealism* by A. Chatterjee [59].
26 *The Buddhist Philosophy of Universal Flux* by S. Mookherji [61].

The philosophical tension between the above understanding of time and that of the positivists who assume the objective time of nature as independent of consciousness leads to further investigations.

In his recent work[27] K.E. Løgstrup, after considering the stands mentioned above, refuses to regard them as alternatives. The key point of his analysis is the idea that time is structured by consciousness or human existence, whereas the source of its origination is in annihilation and its irreversibility – which is said to be independent of consciousness.

It can be observed that a persistent problem, that appears in the forefront of a philosophical analysis of time, consists in accounting for the time-phases which form the universal and essential feature of time-experience. The actual, efficient character of the present as opposed to the absent character of the past and the future time-phases calls for an explanation. The wide variety of views that emerge in the philosophical traditions of India and the West regarding the problem of time give different accounts of this pertinent question in harmony with their respective conceptual models.

In the light of the philosophical dispute as to the subjective or objective nature of the source to which our time-experience can be traced, it is interesting to note[28] that the idea that the time-sequence is a subjective construction, whereas the objective principle of change – supporting the idea of the reality of the present moment – is independent of consciousness, finds expression in the Yoga school of Indian philosophy.

(iv) The timeless and the temporal – paradox and predicament

The theological framework of thinking discloses a challenge that involves the conceptions of the timeless and the temporal. The theological understanding of being as timeless, whether conceived as personal or not – as found in a theistic and an absolutistic structure respectively – is prevalent in the theological traditions across cultures. Equally widespread is the idea of the contingency of the temporal on the timeless. This involves a set of ideas which need to be brought into focus, as it provides an important area of study with inter-cultural perspective.

27 *Skabelse og Tilintetgørelse* [96].

28 See section II (ii).

The notion of the temporal as effect, i.e. as totally dependent on the timeless, is a theological notion which gives rise to alternative conceptual models. These could be fruitfully studied with reference to diverse theological traditions, which would contribute towards a philosophical appraisal as a necessary basis for an encounter of religions.

The idea of cause acquires a special significance with reference to being as timeless. The conventional understanding of cause as temporally preceding the effect cannot be entertained in a theological context. The conception of the timeless as cause does not involve any idea of temporal sequence, i.e. it does not precede the effect by time. Some theologians have preferred the coinage of the term 'ground' (*adhisṭhāna*, as used in Advaita Vedānta) precisely to convey this special sense, in which cause is to be understood with reference to being as timeless.

The timeless as the indispensable ground for the temporal is evidently a paradox. On the other hand, however paradoxical, it is a theological necessity. We find the philosohico-religious literature across cultural boundaries developing this theme within its own conceptual scheme.

The problem that invariably poses itself is the necessity of a conceptual device which could adequately indicate the total dependence of the temporal on the timeless. The former is caused, the latter is uncaused, *sui generis*.

Let us now note, through an analysis of such examples drawn from different traditions, the conceptual pattern that runs through the different theological structures. The theological demand, that the temporal is contingent upon the timeless, has been expressed diversely in different traditions.

A philosophical appraisal of such key expressions as 'the world has a beginning', and 'the world is an appearance' – examples stemming from the Christian and the Vedantic theological formulations – is valuable in this connection. It is to be noted that the two terms 'beginning' and 'appearance', although derived from conventional language, obtain technical significance in the respective theological frameworks. These terms perform a symbolic function, i.e. aim at expressing the theological insight which is a paradox to discursive thinking.

The Christian expression, that the world has a beginning, has a natural reference to the problem of time. The following lines enables us to understand it better.

– "Since the beginning is an existence which is preceded by a time in which the thing is not, there must have been a preceding time in which the world was not, i.e. an empty time". These lines quoted from the first antinomy formulated by Kant in his *Critique of Pure Reason* ([94] p. 397) are illuminating in a twofold way. Firstly, it indicates the meaning of the conception of 'beginning' and what it entails with reference to time in a philosophical analysis. But, again, it also helps at once to clearly distinguish the theological meaning of 'beginning' as can be found in the profound reflections of Saint Augustine in *The Confessions*. He comments on the text of Genesis: "In the Beginning Thou madest the heaven and earth". He writes, "at no time then hadst Thou not made any thing, because time itself Thou madest" [87] Bk. XI Ch. XIV (p. 262).

The theological significance lies in grasping that there is no question of any preceding empty time with reference to which 'beginning' is to be understood – "... before heaven and earth there was no time ..." [87] Bk. XI Ch. XIII.

The word 'beginning' thus can be said to acquire a technical significance of precise theological character. In other words, 'the world has a beginning in time' is the philosophical position which, when subjected to analysis, points to the conflict of transcendental ideas as an antinomy of pure reason.

The Augustinian understanding and interpretation discloses the position – that the world has a beginning – as a theological symbolism. The creation of the world is no empirical information – it is revelation.

'The world is an appearance' – despite the large spread of Vedantic thought – is still an expression liable to misinterpretation. In the Advaita Vedānta framework of thinking, to account for the total dependence of the world on Brahman, the Being *par excellence*, conceptually specified as uncancelled in all three times, i.e. timeless, is precisely the function of the doctrine of Māyā. The temporal and the timeless do not have the same ontological status.

In order to evaluate the Advaita expression of the world as appearance one has to take into account the Advaita theological terminology. Let us point out only briefly that 'the world is an appearance' is not an empirical judgement on the world. It is not an empirical illusion, it is transcendental, pointing to the reality of being as timeless, as self-existent. It is to be noted that Śaṅkara is not propounding a subjective idealism through the pronouncement of the world as appearance. He has vehemently criticised the subjective idealism of the Vijñānavāda school of Buddhism in his commentary on the *Brahma-Sūtra* 2/2/28-29. The conception of the transcendental appearance of the world has, in his thought, a foundation on epistemological realism. It is not questioning the empirical reality of the world. 'The world is an appearance' is a theological symbolism, the function is revelatory.

In the *Advaita-Siddhi* [43] appearance is characterised as that which is neither being (*sat*) nor non-being (*asat*). It is, therefore, termed also as 'indeterminable' (*anirvacanīya*). Appearance is precisely that which cannot be characterised as real per se, neither can it be said to be nothing. This is the status of the temporal as appearance in the Advaita structure of thinking. The value of the term has to be fully grasped in order to comprehend the Advaita appraisal of the status of the world.

In this connection, let us read the following lines by Saint Augustine,

"And I beheld the other things below Thee, and I perceived that they neither altoghether are, nor altogether are not, for they are, since they are from Thee, but are not, because they are not, what Thou art. For that truly is, which remains unchangeably" [87] Bk. VII Ch. XI. p. 134.

The theological structure of Advaita Vedānta operates with the three key ideas – *paramārtha, vyavahāra* and *pratibhāsa*. *Paramārtha* is being which is variously characterised as unsublatable (*abādhya*), as unchanging and unchangable (*kūtastha-nitya*), it is reality per se. *Vyavahāra* is the empirical, the realm of change and multiplicity. It is that which is transitory (*anitya*). The notion is carefully distinguished from *paramārtha* as well as *pratibhāsa*. *Pratibhāsa* is the pure nothing, the absolute naught (*tucca*). The world is an empirical reality (*vyavahāra sat*). It is not imaginary (*alīka*), not nothing (*tucca*). On the other hand, it has only epistemic status and no ontological reality.

These notions are carefully worked out in all details with all their implications. The existing literature on the subject is enormous in the form of commentaries and subcommentaries and so on and so forth. The theological appraisal of the world as appearance is precisely to focus on the idea of the reality of being as unchanging and unchangeable. Appearance is that which calls for a ground (*adhisṭhāna*). Brahman, the real per se, is the ground of the world-appearance. The problem of time is a problem of appearance in Advaita Vedānta. This is why the Vaiśeṣika conception of time as a real per se was vehemently rejected by the exponents of the system. Being as timeless is the real which knows of no duality (*ekamevādvitīyam*), no transformation (*apariṇāmī*), uncancelled by three times (*trikālabādhya*). It can be only indicated negatively (as *neti neti*).

Again, it is interesting to read the following lines of Saint Augustine from *De mor. Manich.* Ch I,

"For that is chiefly to be said to Be, which always exists in one and the same way; which is every way like itself; which can in no way be injured or changed; which is not subject to time, which cannot at one time be other than at another. For this is what is most truly said to be". (quoted in [87] in footnote to Bk. VII Ch. XI p. 134).

To round up this brief discussion, let us note that the significance of the world as created can be grasped only theologically. That the world has a beginning is not an empirical information about the world.

On the other hand, the significance of the world as an appearance comes to light within the theological frame of reference which is its own. It is not intended to question the empirical reality of the world, but intended as a challenge to any claim of the world as self-existent.

These themes could be developed at length with all their consequences and implications as a conceptual platform for a theology of encounter of religions. This is, however, not within the scope of this work. But it is to be noticed that the theological purpose of the doctrine of Māyā and the doctrine of creation as an appraisal of time and the timeless is a matter of profound and careful study. It is this alone which could enable us to extract the conceptual nucleus of theological structures, freed from all cultural clothings.

It is also interesting, in this connection, to observe the general conceptual patterns in theological frameworks. The clash of ideas is illuminating in many ways. An analysis of the Greek cosmological views of the origin of the world and the radical departure of the Judeo-Christian idea of creation out of nothing involves a set of theological ideas. The world as beginningless or everlasting – an idea recurring in Greek thought – is found inadequate, so to speak, from the theological standpoint. It grants the world a self-existent, independent status. The majesty of the conception of the Transcendent as timeless is such that no principle of material causation can be granted any self-existence. The notions of the Transcendent, creation and nothingness form a necessary sequel of ideas.

In the Brahmanical tradition itself, the Advaita Vedānta pronouncement of the world as an appearance has also this theological motive of pointing to Brahman as the non-dual reality. In other words, Advaita Vedānta cannot accept the *ārambhavāda* of the Nyāya-Vaiśeṣika or the *abhivyaktivāda* of Sāṅkhya-Yoga, which are operating with an independent principle (or principles) of material causation.

To focus on Brahman as equally the material and instrumental cause (*abhinna upādāna nimitta kāraṇa*), the system propounds *vivartavāda*, reducing the problem of creation to a problem of appearance. Advaita cosmology is epistemic. The causality of Brahman is not understood as temporally prior but as the indispensable ground for the occurrence of the effect (appearance). There is no temporal passage between Brahman and the world.

In this connection we shall also draw attention to the interesting point of opposition in the expressions of these theologies. In spite of maintaining the dependent status of the world, for the Advaita Vedānta the world (as appearance) is beginningless (*anādi*); whereas for the Christian theology, the world (as created) has a beginning. It is fruitful for an encounter of theologies to attempt to unmask such opposed expressions in order to estimate, how wide is the conceptual gulf in their philosophical understanding of such problems.

These questions immediately refer to the problem of time amongst other important theological considerations as basis for such pronouncements.

The Advaita Vedānta, like the other schools operating within the framework of Brahmanical tradition, takes the world as beginningless (*anādi*) i.e. there never was a time when the world was not. In other words, the world cannot be said to have a beginning in time, prior to which it could be taken as non-existent.

The antithesis of the position, viz. the world has a beginning in time, is not the intended meaning for those who maintain that the world has a beginning – as we have noted in Saint Augustine's discussions on the problem.

This calls for reflection – which is important for a theology of encounter – as to where the various expressions differ genuinely in their intended import and where the border is not clear-cut, despite their apparent opposition.

The Transcendent as timeless and the world as temporal confronts the theological mind across the boundaries of cultures. The conception of time and the timeless can be studied in all aspects with reference to different theological structures that operate with them.

The intellectual struggle to express and conceptualize these basic theological insights requires a linguistic medium which is naturally symbolic in character. Myths, allegories, images and a rich variety of symbols come to play an important role, as the conventional, empirical medium has to perform the significant function of pointing beyond all that is 'of this world'.

Appendix

TIME AND THE HINDU EXPERIENCE

Anindita Niyogi Balslev

An outstanding characteristic of the conceptual world, which is the abode of Hindu religious thought and philosophy, of myths and symbols, is its vast time-consciousness. Bound by a few shared convictions regarding the nature of the self and the world, the Hindu mind plays with various alternatives with regard to time. While here one breathes an atmosphere where there is no pressure of achieving uniformity of views and dogmas, there are surely a few broad and general insights that are common and which form the backdrop to the competing paradigms for interpreting time in a widely divergent manner.[1]

The richness and the enormity of the material available for exploring the many-layered meaning that the theme of time has in this complex and highly articulate tradition, calls for a gigantic scholarly enterprise.[2] In this paper my objectives will be: a) to draw the attention of the reader to the wide range of views on time that has nourished this culture by referring to some of the texts whose authenticity has been unquestionably accepted in the tradition and b) examine some cliches about the Hindu time-experience in a cross-cultural and inter-religious context. The relevant material for

---

I would like to take this occasion to thank the organizers and the audience present at the talks delivered at the Scandinavian Indological Conference, Stockholm, 1982; Ramakrishna Mission Institute of Culture, Calcutta, 1985; The Asiatic Society, Calcutta, 1985; Annual meeting of the American Academy of Religion, 1986; Institute on Religion in an Age of Science, New Hampshire, 1988; University of Kentucky, 1988; University of Virginia, 1989; Sixth East-West Philosophy Conference, University of Hawaii, 1989; the Smithsonian Institution, Washington D.C., 1989, 1990; Indian Institute of Advanced Study 1990.

[1] This essay is based on a number of my earlier publications and talks on different aspects of the theme of time in Indian thought. Publications: i) *A Study of Time in Indian Philosophy*, Otto Harrassowitz, Wiesbaden, 1983. (monograph). ii) Reflections on Time in Indian Philosophy: With Comments on So-called Cyclic Time in *The Study of Time V*, edited by J.T. Fraser and others, The University of Massachusetts Press, Amherst, 1986. iii) Time, Self and Consciousness: some conceptual patterns in the context of Indian Thought, in *Journal of Indian Council of Philosophical Research*, vol. v, no. i, sept-dec. 1987. iv) Cosmology and Hindu Thought, in Zygon, vol. 25, no. 1, march 1990.

[2] Cf. the compilation (in sanskrit), entitled *Kālasiddhāntadarśinī*, by Haran Chandra Bhattacharya, with a foreword by Gopinath Kaviraj, Calcutta, 1941.

the study of time in Hindu thought is found in the very early sources as well as in the later texts that are broadly classified as Śruti, Smṛti and the Śāstras. I will try to present some of the dominant views about time, selecting them from the vast literature of the Hindu tradition, such as the *Vedas*, the *Upaniṣads*, the *Bhagavad Gītā*, the epic *Mahābhārata* and the *Purāṇas*, from the literature of the *Saḍadarśana*, cutting across the *Āgamaśāstras* of the major denominations of the Hindus such as the Śaivas, the Śāktas, the Vaiṣṇavas etc.

In order to present an over-all picture of this complex tradition, I will draw not only on some of the basic philosophical and religious ideas, but will also focus on myths and symbols. It is hoped that the intellectual challenges and the soteriological aspirations that are embedded in all these expressions of the multi-faceted Hindu religious experience concerning time will eventually facilitate an inter-religious dialogue.

At the outset it may be mentioned that the two of the most important ideas about the self and the world that have exerted decisive influence on all Hindu thinking are: a) the idea of *anādi-saṃsāra*—that no absolute beginning can be attributed to the world-process and b) the idea that mokṣa, the soteriological goal, is not possible without 'knowledge of the self' (*ātma-vidyā*).

These ideas, as we shall see shortly, are the salient features of the Hindu ethos and are unfailingly taken into account in all reflections on time. The various configuration of ideas concerning time (*kāla*) and the self (*ātman*) present in the philosophico-religious literature makes the Hindu tradition distinctly different from the other two dominant religious traditions that originated in the Indian soil viz. the Buddhist and the Jaina, with which otherwise it shares much in common. It needs to be noticed, for example, that in the soteriological schemes of the Hindu, Buddhist and Jaina alike, the notions of Karma and rebirth play equally important roles. It is also worthy of notice that soteriology in the Indian context does not necessarily refer to a theistic frame of thinking, various other conceptual possibilities have been enthusiastically explored with intense intellectual acuity. There are many examples where within a non-theistic frame (*nirisvaravada*), the pursuit for *mokṣa/nirvāna/kaivalya* are worked out harmoniously in these traditions. However, the Upaniṣadic doctrine of *ātman* remains the central theme in the Hindu discourse.[3]

[3] Note that the terms 'Brahmanical' and 'Hindu' are used synonymously in this paper.

I. The Idea of Ātman

If the term 'self' is far from being obsolete in religious and philosophical literature across cultures, it must be emphasized that in the Hindu context the notion of *ātman* is absolutely crucial,—hence the other name of the Brahmanical tradition is *ātmavāda*. How the self is to be conceived in contrast to the not-self has been a preoccupation for centuries for the Brahmanical thinkers. As one begins to delve into the depth of Hindu religious consciousness, one captures the centrality of the idea of Ātman as that which in the midst of the flux of existence remains ever-identical, untouched by 'change'.[4] There are different approaches to the disclosure of the ātman in the Upaniṣads, such as in the Bṛhadāraṇyaka which exposes it as *svayamjyotih*—the light that invariably illuminates the fleeting states—or as in the Taittirīya which unsheathes the inner self through the idea of *koṣa*—where embodiment is explained in terms of 'sheaths', which are external to the *ātman*. In Hindu understanding of death and deathlessness, of time and timelessness, this notion of the unchanging and unchangeable self plays a role of capital importance.

Disregarding for the moment all internal differences in the tradition concerning the idea of the self, it may be noted that there is no disagreement that in the last analysis, the self (*ātman*) is seen as unsublatable (*abādhya*), as that about which it cannot be said—it was not, it is not or it will not be (*nitya*). The Bhagavad Gītā 2.20 describes it in a nutshell[5] thus:

> He is never born, nor does he die at any time, nor having (once) come to be will he again cease to be. He is unborn, eternal, permanent and primeval. He is not slain when the body is slain.

An elaboration of these shared convictions of the Hindus about the self (*ātman*) and the world, in its various versions, will involve a close examination of not only the diverse views on time, but a network of ideas disclosing the alternative perspectives about the

---

[4] Recall the famous words of Vacaspati Misra, from *Bhamati:*
Yeṣu vyāvartamānesu yad anuvartate tat tebhya bhinnam—"that which is constant in whatever is variable is different from the latter". Eng. tr. taken from T.M.P. Mahadevan, *The Philosophy of Advaita*, London 1938.

[5] Bhagavad Gita 2.20:
Na jāyate mrīyate vā kadācin
Na 'yam bhūtvā bhavita vā na bhūyah
Ajo nityah śāśvato 'yam purāṇo
Na hanyate hanyamāne śarīre
(This and english translations of Bhagavad-Gītā passages are from S. Radhakrishnan, *The Bhagavadgita*, New York, Harper 1948.)

phenomena of 'beginning' and 'end', 'change' and 'becoming' and also of the notions of eternality and timelessness.

II. On Kāla (Time)

Before going into the details of some aspects of the question of Hindu time-experience in the Indian as well as in an inter-cultural context, I will attempt briefly a general survey of some ideas that are recorded in some of the earliest sources. Some of these ideas are now part and parcel of the culture and can be said to have anticipated later theories.

Concern with time, as a distinct theme, is clearly seen in so old a document as the Atharva Veda. The Atharva Veda depicts time as the all powerful deity—as the creator, sustainer and the destroyer of the universe. Time begets all creatures, the universe is set in motion by time. The well-known hymn, called the Kāla-sukta describes time thus:

> . . . . With seven wheels does this time ride, seven naves has he, immortality is his axle. He carries hither all these beings (worlds). Time, the first god, now hastens onward. . . .[6]

A similar idea, identifying the supreme Lord with time, can be seen in the Viṣṇu Purāna as well as in the Bhagavad Gītā. Consider the following utterances of Lord Krisna in the Bhagavad Gita:

> —*Kālah kalayatām aham*—
> 'Of calculators I am Time'. x/32
> —*Kālo'smi, lokakṣayakṛt*—
> 'Time am I world-destroying'. xi/32
> —*Aham evākṣayah kālo*—
> 'I also am imperishable time'. x/33

The Upaniṣads are strewn with various allusions to time and time-divisions, which indicate the sort of notions that were then current. The *Maitrī Upaniṣad* contains allusions to time as *kāla* and *akāla*, the measurable time and that which is unmeasured and immeasurable. It is also illuminating to find a record of a view, called *kālavāda* in the *Śvetāśvatara Upaniṣad*. Reference is made to the Kālavādins, who held time to be the sole principle which regulates and controls all that there is. Not only that, the Upaniṣads are also important sources which enable us to perceive how already at an early stage of the Brahmanical tradition, the notion of self is clearly

---

[6] From Hymns of the Atharva Veda, translated by M. Bloomfield in *Sacred Books of the East*, edited by F. Maxmüller, Vol. XLII.
(The english translation is from S. Radhakrishnan, as above.)

conceived in relation to that of time. This view has influenced all subsequent Hindu formulations of these questions.

Then there is the vast religious literature of the various denominations of the Hindus such as that of the Śaivas, the Vaiṣṇavas and others which contain profound and complex deliberations on time. The ancient *Pançarātra* texts, revered by the Vaiṣnavas, contain ideas which are philosophically and theologically potent, such as the notion of subtle causal state of time (Sukṣma-kāla) or the idea that time is the power (*Kāla-śakti*) of the Lord. It is by the exercise of this power that Lord Viṣṇu brings about transformation in the world (*Jagatah samprakalanam*). Various versions of the idea of *kāla* as the dynamic energy of God runs through the literature of the theistic schools of Vaiṣṇavism and Śaivism. The Śaiva tradition, like the Vaiṣṇava, have various schools and sub-schools which have developed deep insights into these questions and their literature bears witness to the different ways in which the timeless Lord and the temporal world can be interwoven in theistic schemes. The idea of *kāla* as *kançuka* is dealt with in great detail in the *Pratyabhijñā* philosophy of Kashmir Śaivism. The importance of time for human actions and for the reaping of the consequences of these actions, is a theme which is worked out in the Śaiva-siddhānta philosophy with great care. No Karma, it is said, can fructify without the instrumentality of time. Śaiva-siddhānta also expresses the theological need to transcend time and it does so by declaring time to be an effect (*kārya*).

An account of the Brahmanical conception of time is incomplete without the profound contribution made by the grammarian philosophers such as Bhartṛhari. In his major work, *Vākyapadīya*, Bhartṛhari has bridged the concern of philosophy of grammar with that of soteriology. His reflections on time form an important section of his work, entitled *Kālasamuddesa*. A philosophy of grammar is naturally concerned with the question of time as the basis of tense-distinctions of verbs. Bhartṛhari's penetrating linguistic analysis (*Sphotovāda*), leads him further to the idea of Śabdatattva Brahman—where the word is seen to be the nature of consciousness that transcends all temporal sequence. Bhartṛhari speaks of *Śabdapūrva yoga*, a soteriological pursuit seeking union with the ultimate Word where all sequence is transcended. A detailed treatment of this complex idea of the sequenceless word (*akrama-vāk*) cannot be attempted here.

The most articulate and systematic formulations of diverse conceptions of time are to be found, of course, in the literature of the six major schools of Hindu philosophy (*Ṣaḍa-darśana*). Note that these are to be taken into consideration as these are all acknowledged as *Mokṣa-Śāstras* i.e. treatises relevant for the attainment of salvation (*mokṣa*). These positions are often incorporated in the literature of various Hindu denominations with or without much modification. These different views have slowly crystallized abandoning other possibilities along the way and bear witness to the fact that soteriology has never in the Brahmanical tradition blocked a free exploration of alternative perspectives.

Apart from the sources mentioned above, in any attempt to obtain an over-all view of the significance of time for Hindu religious consciousness it is necessary to take note of the Purāṇas, a body of literature which is a rich repository of Hindu mythology that has nourished the imagination of all stratas of Hindu society. Here one comes across a bold expression of Hindu mythic consciousness that seeks to combine human time-experience with the cosmological time. The narratives weave an intriguing pattern with threads supplied by Hindu cosmology and soteriology.[7]

It is equally important in this context, as has been mentioned above, to comprehend the meaning of some religious symbols which are profusely used in sculpture, painting and literature, such

[7] The narratives of the Purāṇas are absolutely fascinating in the manner in which these bring out the human signicance of vast stretches of cosmological time. Ideas of *karma*, rebirth (*Punar-janma*) and salvation (*moksa*) are all woven into the texture of these stories which unfold events spanning over billions of human years that make a *kalpa*.

As an example, let me recount very briefly the central theme of such a story: Indra, the king of gods, after winning a formidable victory over the titans, decides to build himself a magnificent palace, the like of which nobody has ever seen. He summons Viśvakarmā, the divine architect and orders him to construct one. Viśvakarmā builds a superb palace, but alas, it does not satisfy Indra. Many more gardens, lakes, pavillions are added in course of time to please the master but Viśvakarmā's efforts were in vain. The insatiable Indra represents the arrogant, powerful boss who is conscious of his unlimited wealth, who thinks that he is not accountable to anyone for his actions, who is even under the delusion that he is immortal. Viśvakarmā in despair seeks refuge to Lord Viṣṇu. Viṣṇu agrees to help and appears before the power-drunk king of gods in the disguise of a small boy. There are a number of plots in what follows describing in detail how Indra is gradually made aware of his finitude, of *karma* and rebirth and of the enormous expanse of time in which the universe undergoes repeated creation and dissolution. One of the dramatic aspect of the story is the appearance of a row of ants which are seen crawling along the wall during the conversation between Indra and Viṣṇu. Viṣṇu discloses to a petrified Indra that these ants were nothing but previous Indras, kings of gods of previous world-cycles. The idea that it was their immoral actions that has turned them to ants is a jolt to the pride of present Indra. As the story unfolds, Indra is shown as one who is aware of the futility of power and possession, who is conscious of his mortality and who now seeks salvation.

For a marvellous rendering in English of this Puranic story, see Parades of the Ants in Heinrich Zimmer's *Myths and Symbols of the Indian Civilization*, Washington 1946.

as the symbol of the wheel (*cakra*). Perhaps, as we shall see later in this paper, some of the stereotypes that one comes across in an inter-cultural and inter-religious context, such as the cliché that the Hindu view of time is cyclic are precisely due to not seeing the large inter-connections between philosophical concepts, religious ideas, myths and symbols.[8]

III. The Idea of Anādi-Saṁsāra

One of the basic tenets of Hindu thought is the notion that no absolute beginning can be attributed to the world-process. Whether in theological symbolism or in cosmological speculations, the Hindu mind strongly adheres to the view that 'being cannot come out of nothing' (cf. *Bhagavad-Gītā* 2/16, *Nāsato vidyate bhāvo* etc.). In many classical philosophical texts one comes across elaborate discussions about the difficulties and the absurdities that a transgression of this principle of ex nihilo nihil fit would entail. This is one of the major shared convictions that runs through the entire tradition. However, although the idea of absolute beginning i.e. creation out of nothing is rejected, the notion of repeated creation (*Punar-sṛṣṭi*) and recurrent dissolution (*Punar-pralaya*) is widespread. This is a very ancient idea and it can be traced back to the *Ṛk-veda Saṁhitā* (10-190-3): The Lord created the sun and the moon like before (*Sūrya-candra-asaudhātā-yathā-purvam-akalpayat*). These oft-quoted words suggest that prior to creation there has been a state of dissolution. This idea of cosmological cycle is widely accepted in the tradition, so much so that the idea may well be considered to be a characteristic of the Hindu conceptual world.

The question has been asked whether the *anādi* (beginningless) *saṁsāra* is also *ananta* (endless) or not. It is interesting, in this connection, to observe the intimate relation between Hindu cosmology and soteriology. There are examples of controversies amongst the different schools of Hindu thought regarding the question of dissolution (*pralaya*). Only those who accept the idea of universal salvation (*Mahā-pralaya*), such as Advaita Vedānta, admit the possibility of a state of final dissolution. The schemes

---

[8] Paul Tillich observes in his work *The Protestant Era*, Chicago. 1948:

"In every religious interpretation of history, philosophical elements are implied, first of all, a philosophy of time, and in every philosophical interpretation of history religious elements are implied—first of all an interpretation of the meaning (or meaninglessness) of existence. Whenever existence itself is to be interpreted, the difference between philosophy and theology decreases, and both meet in the realm of myth and symbol."

where no idea of universal salvation is pronounced operate with the idea of interim dissolution (*Avāntara pralaya*), i.e. there will be perpetually a fresh beginning, a re-creation (*Punar-sṛṣṭi*) after a state of cosmic rest. Cosmological speculations and soteriological ideas are worked out in harmony with each other.

IV. Time and the Cosmological Cycles

The epic Mahābhārata, the Bhagavad Gītā, the Purāṇas, all accept this notion of repeated creation and dissolution. The *Bhagavad Gītā* compares each world-cycle with a 'day of Brahma', symbolizing cosmic activity, which is followed by His 'night', the state of cosmic rest or dissolution (*pralaya*). In the *Purāṇas*, one comes across the grand cosmological model where each world-cycle is measured in astronomical figures—in one calculation a world-cycle (*kalpa*) is said to have 4320 million years. Huge time scales are used for dividing and sub-dividing a *kalpa* into *manvantara*, *mahayuga*, *yuga* etc. It is important to understand how the Hindu mind uses this idea in a soteriological framework. It should, however, be noted that although the idea of *Anādi-saṁsāra* is unanimously accepted by all schools, there are disagreements with regard to the notion of repeated creation and dissolution—a notable example is Pūrva Mīmāṁsā, a prominent Brahmanical school.

It is extremely important to make a clear conceptual distinction between the idea of 'cyclic time' and that of 'cosmological cycle'. As we shall see shortly, in an inter-cultural and inter-religious context this notion of cosmological cycle has been often misinterpreted, which has given rise to the notion that a predominant feature of Hindu thought (as well as Hellenic) is 'cyclic time'.

As we proceed, it will be evident why this appellation is to be taken as a misnomer. For this it is essential to take into consideration several ideas. Firstly, the idea of repeated creation and dissolution; secondly, what is generally understood by this designation of 'cyclic time' and its implications; thirdly, an over-all idea about the major conceptual models of time in Hindu thought and lastly, the significance of the symbol of the wheel (*cakra*) which is a pictorial imagery for conveying the Hindu view of *Saṁsāra*.

The idea of recurrent creation and dissolution has been briefly outlined above. It is important to see how the Hindu view of divine incarnation (*Avatāra-vāda*) is interwoven with it. We will then examine some of the distinct conceptual models of time that have emerged in the richly variegated tradition of the Hindus. It is illuminating to discover that there are no lack of examples of different schools holding sharply divergent views on time and yet sharing the idea of cosmological cycle (Kalpa).

V. AVATĀRAVĀDA AND THE IDEA OF FOUR YUGAS

Avatāravāda is a distinctively Hindu religious doctrine. It is widely accepted in the tradition. This is the idea of periodic divine descent in order to restore righteousness and vanquish the evil. In the *Bhagavad-Gītā*, a text revered by all denominations of the Hindus, Krișṇa says to Arjuna:

> Whenever there is a decline of righteousness and rise of unrighteousness, O Bharata (Arjuna), then I send forth (create, incarnate) Myself. For the protection of the good, for the destruction of the wicked and for the establishment of righteousness, I come into being from age to age.

The *Purāṇas* weave endless stories about Divine incarnations, assuming diverse earthly forms. The spectacular manner in which each *Avatara* accomplishes the task of crushing the evil and establishing the supremacy of goodness and righteousness form the basis of colourful legends that have fed the imagination of all stratas of Hindu society, such as the well-known stories of the ten divine incarnations—*Daśāvatāra*.

In the *Bhāgavad Purāṇa* there are detailed renderings of the various forms in which the Lord appears in each yuga. The idea of four yugas, it is interesting to observe, is very much a part of traditional Hindu ideology concerning *Dharma* or moral order of society. The epic *Mahābhārata* contains rich and elaborate descriptions of the various characteristics of the four yugas viz. *kṛta*, *tretā*, *dvāpara* and *kali*. The moral order is said to be degenerating, the standard of human conduct is seen in a state of gradual deterioration. *Kali*, the *yuga* in which we are, is the last in succession of four yugas. It is precisely the time when unrighteousness is more a predominant feature than it has been in any of the three earlier yugas. The *Avatara* who is not yet incarnated is called *Kalki*. All these form a very important part of Hindu mythology which provide an excellent document of how the Hindu mind has imbued its vast time-consciousness with religious significance.

VI. DIFFERENT TIME-MODELS: SOME EXAMPLES FROM THE *ṢAḌADARŚANA*

It is of great interest to note the divergences amongst the various Brahmanical schools of thought regarding time. It is indeed a rewarding task to perceive the implications of these contrasting views for achieving a coherent picture of the world of change and becoming as well as for comprehending the soteriological goal—variously termed as *mokṣa/nihśreyasa/kaivalya* etc. I will attempt a brief outline of four distinctly different conceptual patterns that can be found in the philosophical literature of the Vaiśeṣika (a similar position is shared by Nyāya and Mīmāṁsā), Sankhya, Yoga and Advaita Vedānta schools.

The Vaiśeṣika view of *mahākāla* is a model of absolute time. Time is a distinctly independent (*svatantra*) category of reality. It is all-pervasive (*vibhu*), ubiquitous (*niramśa*), unitary (*eka*). It is without beginning (*anādi*) and without end (*ananta*). *Mahākāla* is the substrate (*ādhāra*) of all that is contingent, but does not itself presuppose any (*anāśrita*). There is no movement or change (Nisƙriya) within time as such but no change, movement or becoming is possible or even conceivable without it. Moreover, time-divisions are not to be taken as integral to time, these are seen as nothing but conventional practices which are made possible with the help of any standard motion, usually it is the solar motion that furnishes the standard.[9]

The idea of reality of change (*pariṇāma*) is vital for the ancient school of Sānkhya but it claims that the phenomenon of change does not call for a postulation of an empty time, as a category per se (*tattva*). All that is needed is an account of the conventional use of the three time-phases, the Sānkhya idea of *visadṛśa·parināma* does exactly that. A detailed study of the system shows that it is causality which is considered the key problem for understanding change and becoming. Moreover, the fact that the Vaiśeṣika philosophers need to explain the convention of time-phases with reference to the solar motion show (as Vaçaspati has argued) that the assumption of a metaphysical entity called time (*Kāla-vastu*) is superfluous. The dynamic *Prakṛti* in Sānkhya combines space, time, matter in the same principle. Sānkhya involvement with the problem of time is therefore indirect, there is no event-in-time conception in this system.[10]

---

[9] *Vaiśeṣika Sūtra* of Kanada with Chandrakanta's *Bhasya*. Ed. by Sri Muni Jambuvijayi, Baroda, 1961.

[10] The *Tattvakaumudi*: Vacaspati Misra's commentary on *Sankhya-Karika*, text and trans. by Ganganath Jha, Poona, 1969.

Also see the excellent work by Brajendra Nath Seal: *The Positive Sciences of the Hindus*, London 1915.

For a brief discussion on the implications of the notions of *Sadṛśa* and *Visadṛśa Parinama* for Sankhya understanding of time, see K.C. Bhattacharya's Studies in Sankhya, in his *Studies in Philosophy*, Calcutta 1956.

The Yoga school joins Sānkhya in repudiating the idea of *mahākāla* á la Vaiśeṣika. It, however, has a distinct theory of discrete time. It claims the objective reality of the moment (*kṣaṇa*) but considers the notion of a collection of moments, of a time-continuum as a mental construction (*buddhi-nirmāṇa*). Since 'no two moments can be said to exist simultaneously', any idea whether that of an unitary, objective time or of an objective series of moments is seen as nothing but a subjective representation.[11]

In the literature of Advaita Vedānta, one comes across a radically different interpretation of the problems of time and change. It not only rejects the Vaiśeṣika model of absolute time but also repudiates the idea of the ontological reality of change and becoming. The approach is phenomenological, designed to reveal the absolute foundational character of consciousness. It is here that one comes across the most stringent formulation of the Upaniṣadic conception of "the-one- without- a second" (*ekamevādvitīyam*). The Advaita concern has lead to a profound understanding of the idea of being as timeless. To establish the unsublatibility of consciousness in all 'three times' (*trikālābadhyatvam*) has led to a rejection of the idea of reality of time.[12]

These four distinct stands are worked out in harmony with other basic notions such as space, causality, being and non-being, change and becoming. An in-depth study of time in the Brahmanical tradition would call for a careful examination of the polemics and exchanges not only amongst the different Brahmanical schools but also with those stemming from the Buddhist and the Jaina traditions.

In brief, for the Vaiśeṣika philosophers the idea of reality of time is indispensable for understanding creation and dissolution, bondage or salvation. The notion of absolute time is central to the entire conceptual scheme. For Advaita Vedānta, however, any such claim which fails to see the merely empirical/constituted (*vyāvahārika*) character of time is itself indicative of a state that soteriology seeks to abandon and overcome. To use the Advaita metaphor, the veil of *Māyā* covers the non-dual *Brahman* and projects the world of multiplicity and movement. Again, in Yoga literature one comes across the idea that a one-pointed concentra-

---

[11] *Yoga-Sūtra* of Patañjali with the *Bhāṣya* of Vyasa. The *Tattvavaiśāradī* of Vacaspati Misra and the *Vrtti* of Bhoja, Benares 1972. English translation by J.H. Woods, Benares 1972.

[12] For Advaita repudiation of the idea of reality of time, see Citsukha's *Tattvapradīpikā*, Benares 1974 and Sri Harsa's *Khandanakhandkhādya*. *Chowkhamba Sanskrit series*, Varanasi 1970.

tion on the *kṣaṇa* or moment is indispensable for the attainment of salvation. Yoga recommends concentration (*Saṁyama*) on the moment since discriminative knowledge (*Vivekaja jñanam*) cannot be obtained without it. The idea that the present moment alone is objective, in which the whole universe undergoes change, is also crucial for the salvatory pursuit. It is said that a one-pointed concentration on the 'moment' enables the adept to discriminate between the unchanging *Puruṣa* from the everchanging *Prakṛti*.

VII. Time, Self and Consciousness

A study of time in any intellectual tradition is inevitably related to philosophical reflections on the themes of consciousness and the self. For understanding the role that a specific view of time plays in diverse schemes of Hindu soteriology, one has to look carefully into how the view is interwoven with the notion of *ātman*, a fundamental tenet of Hindu thought. The dominant pattern is the ultimate disclosure of *ātman* as free from the influence of time (*Kālaprabhāvamukta*). Arduous spiritual practice is recommended for the attainment of this saving knowledge. The various and divergent views on time are all knitted to the one basic shared conviction, inspired by the exegetical texts of the Upanisads that the self is 'unborn' and 'indestructible' (*ajara, amara*).[13]

The idea that the world is beginningless, or that the self is unborn are based on the same philosophical insight that being cannot come out of nothing and that the human situation is incomprehensible without the idea of *karma* and rebirth.

The most familiar paradigm in theological traditions across cultures is perhaps where the self is conceived as transcending, overcoming time (the idea comes in many versions, the model of the immortal soul is only one example). The theological concern with death is intimately related to it. Time stands for death, self for immortality. Various concepts and symbols, doctrines and mythologies show this. Note that *mahākāla* in Hindu mythology is often a personification of death. A cross—cultural review of relevant literature will show that there are various ways of playing with the ideas

---

[13] It will indeed be a rather simplistic understanding of the Brahmanical view of *ātman*, if one does not take into consideration the intricacies of the analysis of I-consciousness. Cf. my papers on a) An appraisal of I-consciousness in the context of the controversies centering the No-self doctrine of Buddhism, Journal of Indian Philosophy, 16 (1988) pp. 167–175; b) The notion of kleśa and its bearing on the Yoga analysis of mind, Philosophy East-West, 1991, c) The Notion of "I" in the different schools of Vedānta: A Philosophical Appraisal, *Indologica Taurinensia*, xv–xvi (1989–90).

about death and time, about self and its overcoming of death. That consciousness is not annihilated in death is an idea which is accepted even by those who propound a no-self theory and forward a notion of 'stream of consciousness' to account for experience. Reflections on these themes have perhaps kindled human imagination more than on any other. "Lead me from death to deathlessness"—the Upaniṣadic prayer expresses a central concern of all soteriology. The Brahmanical tradition is a witness to the various ways of dealing with time and change while safeguarding the *ātman*, the notion of an abiding self which remains identical, unchanging. In some soteriological schemes, such as in Advaita Vedānta, this is achieved by denying change quâ time any ontological status.

In this connection, it is of great philosophical interest to note that the idea of *nitya vastu*—being as uncaused and indestructible/ beginningless and endless is present in every scheme of Brahmanical thought. However, there are differences in the formulations and import of this important idea. Notice that in the Vaiśeṣika, for example, it is not only the *ātman* which is considered as '*Nitya*', so are a list of other metaphysical entities such as time (*kāla*), space (*dik*) etc. In Sānkhya both *Puruṣa*, the unchanging principle of consciousness and *Prakṛti*, the principle of ever-changing matter are said to be '*Nitya*'. Thus, that which is conceived as having no beginning and end can be further specified either as constant, immutable (*kuṭastha nitya*, such as *Puruṣa*) or as that which undergoes change and mutations (*pariṇāmī nitya*, such as *Prakṛti*). In Advaita Vedānta, the idea of *nitya vastu* refers to that which is not only beginningless and endless (like in Vaiśeṣika and Sankhya) as well as unchanging and immutable (similar to the model of Sankhya *Puruṣa*, and unlike that of *Prakṛti*), but also as non-dual (unlike the Sankhya notion of *Vahu-puruṣavāda*). The Advaita idea of the non-dual Brahman is the most radical version of the idea of being as timeless.

VIII. *ĀTMAN* AND *KṢAṆABHANGAVĀDA*: AN EXAMPLE OF A PHILOSOPHICAL CONTROVERSY

A specific time-concept, it becomes evident, is so central to a given system that it cannot be isolated from other major issues or be substituted by an alternative model without seriously disturbing or even demolishing the conceptual structure. An excellent example of this can be found in the polemics of the Brahmanical and Buddhist philosophers. The Brahmanical tradition, as we have seen, has been a citadel of the idea of the immutable self. The drastic Buddhist understanding of universal flux, where the separation between time as moment and being as momentary was attributed only to an arbitrary linguistic convention, projected a world-view where nothing is exempt from change. The idea of the so-called permanent entity was shown to be fraught with logical contradictions. The implication of this view was obviously shattering for any notion of an identical and abiding self, as in this conceptual frame there can be no room for any notion of an unchanging self in the changing stream of consciousness. The Brahmanical philosophers were fully aware that the idea of *ātman* could be reinstated only if the Buddhist interpretation of time (and being) were rejected. Centuries of exchanges bear witness to the massive philosophical disputes which stimulated the Indian mind. 'That which is, is momentary' (*Yat sat tat kṣaṇikam*), the central idea implied in *Kṣaṇabhangavāda* becomes a challenge to the Ātmavādins. The Buddhist replies and Brahmanical counter-questions form elaborate documents of controversies that are results of arduous philosophical exercise on the questions of time, self and consciousness.[14]

IX. TIME-METAPHORS AND ENCOUNTER OF WORLD-RELIGIONS

One may well wonder whether in any other context the major time-metaphors have come to play such a decisive role as in the context of encounter of world-religions. Metaphors of cyclicity and linearity are used for the schematization of different cultural experiences of time, a practice which has thwarted inter-religious communication.

It is commonplace to come across the appellations of 'cyclic' and 'linear' time in the literature, wherever some attempts have been made to situate the time-experience of major traditions in a global setting. These epithets are assumed to represent radically different time-experiences. It has become almost a cliche to say, for example, that the Indo-Hellenic time is cyclic as opposed to the Judeo-Christian understanding of linear time. In order that a productive discourse may ensue in the area of inter-religious and cross-cultural studies, it seems to be specially important to examine these general and broad distinctions that are made, which are repeated endlessly and hardly ever questioned.

---

[14] see *Ātmatattvaviveka* of Udayanacarya, Chowkhamba Sanskrit Series, Benares, 1934.

In this section, I would like to examine the cliche that cyclic-time is a predominant trait of the Hindu conceptual world. It has been already observed above that like all major philosophical traditions, the Brahmanical tradition too has no unanimous view on time. In an earlier section of this paper, we have considered several distinct conceptual models of time that are well-documented in the philosophical and religious literature. This great diversity of views needs to be taken into consideration for any appraisal of Hindu conceptual experience of time. To ignore this variety of views and to reduce them under the single caption of 'cyclic time' is to distort the image of a complex and a major tradition of world-religions. It is all the more questionable, since although the appellation of 'cyclic time' features so often in the Western encounter with the Indian tradition, the idea can hardly be identified as the view of any particular school of Brahmanical philosophy or even as an issue for debate in the polemical literature. Hindu thinkers discussed and debated about such issues as whether time is discrete or continuous, real or appearance, perceived or inferred, an independent (*svatantra*) category or not, there is no record to my knowledge of any such dispute about whether time is cyclic or not. The need for probing into the significance of the appellation of 'cyclic time' arises only in the inter-cultural and inter-religious context and has little relevance seen exclusively within the frame of Hindu thought.

As an important document for understanding what is at issue reference may be made to the writings of St. Augustine, where he repudiates a Greek (pre-Christian) view of 'circular time'. An analysis of this oft-quoted passage,[15] from his City of God, makes it evident that the designation of 'circular time' carries the implication of exact mechanical recurrence not only of cosmological processes but also of individual destinies. Obviously no scheme of salvation can be worked out in harmony with such a view of time, a matter of grave theological consequence.

As I have discussed before, the idea of cosmological cycles and rebirth are common features of the Hindu world-view. The ethical and soteriological dimensions of these ideas must not be lost sight

---

[15] St. Augustine in his *City of God* polemises against a Greek view of 'circular time' in these lines: ". . . . As those others think, the same measures of time and the same events in time are repeated in circular fashion. On the basis of this cyclic theory, it is argued, for example, that just as in a certain age the philosopher Plato taught his students in the city of Athens and in the school the Academy, so during countless past ages, at very prolonged yet definite intervals, the same Plato, the same city and the same school with the same students had existed again and again. . . ." *De Civitate Dei*, trans. by P. Levine, Heinemann, Harvard University Press, 1966.

of. The idea of rebirth in the Hindu context is a necessary sequel of the doctrine of *karma*. The notion of efficacy of human actions precludes any interpretation of the human situation as simply as "an external destiny driving man to his doom, nor a blind mechanical framework from which there is no escape."[16]

The Purāṇic narratives are full of imaginative weaving of plots which point to the religious dimension of the notion of cosmological cycles. It is indeed remarkable to what extent the vast consciousness of space and time, the notion of repeated creation and dissolution and even the idea that there are many worlds have become part and parcel of Hindu religious discourse. It is not only in ancient legends and narratives, in recent times The Gospel of Sri Ramakrishna, records a conversation of this Hindu saint with a visitor where the Master compares the countless worlds to the innumerable crabs that are seen on a sandy beach in a rainy season. This is motivated by his concern to inspire a sense of humility and spiritual longing in the mind of the visitor.[17]

Yet many perceptive culture-historians like Arnold Toynbee misconstrue the Purāṇic idea. He writes in his well-known work, *A Study of History*:[18] "This philosophy of sheer recurrences, which intrigued, without ever quite captivating the Hellenic genius, came to dominate contemporary Indic minds." He refers to the Puranic idea of *kalpa* as the "cyclic theory of time" which the "Hindu thinkers had evolved".

Toynbee, unlike Mircea Eliade[19] fails to capture the significance

---

[16] T.M.P. Mahadevan, *Time and the Timeless*, Principal Miller Lectures 1953, Madras 1954.

[17] *The Gospel of Sri Ramakrishna*, tr. and intr. by Swami Nikhilananda, New York: Ramakrishna-Vivekananda Center, 1952.

[18] Toynbee, Arnold. *A Study of History*. Rev. and abridged by the author and Jane Caplan. New York. 1972.

He further writes, referring to the Puranic idea of '*kalpa*' etc: "Are these vain repititions . . . really the law of the Universe, and, therefore, incidentally the law of the histories of civilizations? If we find that the answer is in the affirmative, we can hardly escape the conclusion that we are the perpetual victims of an everlasting cosmic practical joke. which condemns us to endure our sufferings and to overcome our difficulties and to purify ourselves of our sins—only to know in advance that the automatic inevitable lapse of a certain meaningless measure of time cannot fail to stultify all our human exertions by reproducing the same situation again and again ad infinitum just as if we had never exerted ourselves at all."

These lines almost echo the same concern which was expressed by St. Augustine while polemising against the specific Greek view of exact mechanical recurrence of human destiny. His comment was: "From this whirligig they are quite unable to free their immortal soul even though it has attained wisdom, for in its own uninterrupted circular course it moves back and forth between false happiness and genuine unhappiness."

[19] Mircea Eliade in his Le temps et l'eternite dans la pensee Indienne, *Eranos*

as he does not perceive how the ideas of world-cycle and rebirth are interconnected with those of *karma* and *mokṣa* in the Hindu conceptual world. He therefore considers the idea as a 'cosmic practical joke'. Later, in the same work, he observes: "The application of the 'theory of eternal recurrence' to human affairs is a counsel of despair for humanity, since this doctrine denies, that man has any power ever to effect a permanent change in his condition, and teaches him that he is condemned to suffer the meaningless revolutions of the wheel of existence".[20]

This misconception has prevailed for a great length of time.[21] It

---

Jahrbuch, 1951, Band xx, Zurich, 1952, pp. 219–52 writes: "Il nous importe de mettre en lumiere le fait suivant: a savoir, qu'en agrandissant toujours plus audacieusement la duree at le nombre des cycles cosmiques, l'indien avait en vue un but soteriologique. Epouvante par le nombre sans fin de naissance et des renaissance des Univers, qui s'accompagnait d'un nombre aussi considerable de naissance at de renaissance humaines regies par la loi du Karma, l'indien etait en quelque sorte oblige de chercher une issue a cette roue cosmique et a ces transmigrations infinies".

[20] Toynbee, as above p. 487

[21] A pertinent example of how prevalent these cliches are (viz. that the Hindu view of time is 'cyclic' or exclusively 'mayic') and how even the best minds, keenly aware of the theological importance of bringing together the major views concerning time and history in a global framework, fall prey to these misconceptions can be seen in the writings of Paul Tillich. In his work entitled, The Protestant Era, Chicago, 1948, he attempts to classify the major views by making a sharp distinction between the 'historical' and the non-historical types of interpreting history'. From his summary of the characteristics of 'the non-historical type' which comprises Indian thought amongst other similar world-views, let me examine a few points. One main point, Tillich notes is that " . . Time is considered to be circular or repeating itself infinitely". I have already commented on the designation of time as 'circular' earlier in this paper.

The other two characteristics which Tillich notes are that the temporal world has lesser reality and no ultimate value, and that the true being and the ultimate good are eternal, immovable, above becoming, genesis and decay. Tillich refers to "The Indian Brahman doctrine" and the notion of *Māyā*, which according to him, "Deprives all things in time and space . . . of their ultimate reality and meaning. They have reality—but from the point of view of *Māyā*; they are not simply products of imagination . . ."

Tillich obviously has the philosophy of Advaita Vedānta in mind, which is one of the variety of stands that has fed Indian imagination with regard to these questions. The idea of reality of time has also played a predominant role in Indian thought. The inner divergences of a tradition must not be overlooked. Moreover, a greater appreciation of theological attitudes is an essential prerequisite in a cross-cultural setting. Advaita Vedānta makes use of three key concepts of *paramārtha*, *vyāvahāra* and *pratibhāsa*. Vyāvahāra is the empirical which is distinguished on the one hand from the *paramārtha*, as that which is unsublatable in all three times (*trikālābādhya*) as unchanging and unchangeable (*kutasthanitya*) and the pratibhāsa which is purely imaginary (*alīka*) or nothing (*tuccha*).

No matter how different philosophico-religious traditions otherwise are, parallels to awareness of this kind is perhaps not difficult to find in traditions which Tillich will not consider to be non-historical type. Consider, in this connection, the following lines by none other than Saint Augustine:

is evident from the past records[22] that studies pertaining to inter-religious and cross-cultural issues cannot accomplish what it seeks to attain if there is a built-in theoretical bias at the very starting-point.[23] Cycles and arrows are major metaphors for representing the two fundamental poles of human experience of recurrence and irreversibility. However, the implications of these time-metaphors become a pressing issue for anyone involved in cross-cultural studies, as one cannot but take note of how cycles and arrows gradually cease to be simple time-metaphors and come to get associated with such concepts as history, progress, and salvation.[24] One of the major tasks before the scholars, who wish to explore the cross-cultural dimension of the varied human perceptions in the treatment of the issues of time and history, is to identify and dismantle some of the stereotyped devices and strategies that have blocked inter-religious communication.

In this context it is also essential to carefully examine the familiar image of the wheel that pervades the Hindu-Buddhist world and comprehend the notion of recurrence that it represents.

"And I beheld the other things below Thee, and I perceived that they neither altogether are, nor altogether are not, for they are, since they are from Thee, but are not, because they are not, what Thou art. For that truly is, which remains unchangeably." (*De Civitate Dei*, Bk. vii Ch. xi p. 134).

It seems to me that more caution needs to be exercised in setting traditions as 'diagramatically opposed' to one another.

[22] Arnaldo Momigliano in his essay Time in Ancient Historiography, in *Quarto Contributo*, Rome 1969 made the following observation:

"Many students of historiography and especially the theologically minded among them, appear to assume that there are neat and mutually exclusive views about time, the Jews had one, the Greeks another. To judge from experience, this is not so; and one would suspect that philosophers would have an easier task if it were so."

[23] This 'bias towards overthematization' also draws the attention of anthropologists. P. Kay observes in the preview of *Culture Theory*, Ed. by R. Shweder and R. Levine, Cambridge University Press, 1984, that "Time is perhaps the favourite thing that anthropologists point to so as to exaggerate the exoticness of other people, they love to say things like 'time is this' for us but it is like that for the folks that I studied."

I take this important observation as a specimen of self-criticism of a discipline regarding how it ascribes a sense of otherness to the culture which is the object of its study. A keen awareness of conceptual distinctions in the different interpretations of time-experience is indeed rewarding but caution must be exercised lest the zeal for finding differences in the area of cross-cultural studies tantamounts to projecting a distorted image of the 'otherness' of the other culture.

[24] In his *Time's Arrow Time's Cycle*, Cambridge, 1987, Stephen Jay Gould, while recognising the arrow as the major metaphor of the Western culture, reclaims the place of time's cycles. Cycles and arrows, he says, are "so central to intellectual (and practical) life that Western people who hope to understand history must wrestle intimately with both" (p. 16). He quotes from the Book of the Ecclesiastes to confirm that time's cycles is an idea which has a religious foundation.

X. SAṀSĀRA-CAKRA: THE METAPHOR OF THE WHEEL

One of the most profound metaphors of the Hindu (as well as the Buddhist[25]) conceptual world is the *cakra* or the wheel. It pervades the literature and the arts, the life and culture in a variety of ways. Consider, for instance, the idea of *Saṁsāra-cakra* which is profusely used in Hindu religious and philosophical literature. One authentic example of the function of the symbol can be seen in the Yoga literature. The commentary by Vyasa on the *Yoga-Sutra* 4/11 describes the idea of *Sadadam saṁsara-cakram* (six-spoked wheel of existence) by pointing to how from 'virtue arises happiness, from impiety pain, from happiness attachment, from pain aversion; attachment and aversion both lead to efforts, resulting in actions, which in turn again give rise to virtue or impiety, happiness or pain, attachment or aversion. Thus, it is said, revolves 'the six-spoked wheel of existence'. To the participants of this culture, the wheel captures the pole of experience which allows to arrive at a notion of a law, focusing on the recurrent generic pattern. The metaphor conveys a message which is to be deciphered in the specific context where it is used.

[25] The Buddhist tradition makes the symbol of wheel a vehicle of Buddhist thought. *Bhava-cakra* or the wheel of becoming, for example, is the pictorial image representing the twelve links (nidānas) in the chain of rebirth.

One also comes across this metaphor in the Buddhist literature, describing the Buddha's 'setting in motion the wheel of law' (*Dharmacakra-pravarttana*).

Philosophers discussed in this work and their approximate dates

Indian philosophers discussed in this work and their approximate dates (Century A.D)

It is well known, that there is much uncertainty about the chronology of Indian authors. The present list is based on the works referred to in the bibliography as [7], [111] and [116]

Appaya Dīkṣita	16th
Bhartṛhari	5th-6th
Candrakīrti	7th
Citsukha	13th
Dharmakīrti	7th
Dignāga	5th–6th
Īśvarakṛṣṇa	3rd–4th
Jayanta Bhaṭṭa	9th
Kamalaśīla	8th
Kumārila Bhaṭṭa	7th-8th
Mādhavāchārya	14th
Madhusūdana Sarasvatī	16th
Nāgārjuna	2nd–3rd
Nārāyaṇa	16tn-17tn
Nemichandra	12th
Pārthasārathi Miśra	11th
Patañjali	3rd-4th
Prabhāchandrāchārya	9th-10th
Ragunātha Śiromani	15th-16th
Śālikanātha Miśra	8th-9th
Śaṅkarachārya	8th–9th
Śaṅkara Miśra	15th
Śāntarakṣita	7th–8th
Śrīdhara	10th
Śrī Harṣa	12th
Uddyotakara	7th
Udyanāchārya	10th–11th
Umāsvati	1st–2nd
Vācaspati Miśra	9th
Vallabhāchārya	12th
Vasubandhu	4th
Vātsyāyana	4th
Vidyāraṇya (identical with Mādhavācarya)	
Vijñānabhikṣu	16th
Viśvanātha	17th
Vyāsa	5th

Approximate dates of Greek philosophers B.C.:

Anaxagoras	500-428	Haraclitus	535-475
Anaximander	611-547	Parmenides	515-
Aristotle	384-322	Plato	429-347
Democritus	460-370	Pythagoras	582-506
Empedocles	495-435	Zeno	489-

Approximate dates of

Philo of Alexandria	30 B.C.–40 A.D.	St. Augustine	354-430 A.D.

Bibliography

Indian Philosophy, general

[1] Atharvaveda Saṃhitā with the commentary of Sāyanācārya, Bombay, 1895.

[2] Bhagavadgītā, text and transl. by S. Radhakrishnan, Blackie & Son, (India), 4th reprint, 1976.

[3] The Principal Upaniṣads, Ed. with introduction, text, transl. and notes by S. Radhakrishnan, The Muirhead Library of Philosophy, London, 1953.

[4] The Cultural Heritage of India I-V, Calcutta 1937, Reprint 1969.

[5] The Sarvadarśanasaṃgraha of Mādhavāchārya, a) Gaekwood Oriental Series, 1924, b) Transl. by E.F. Cowell & E.E. Gough, London, Kegan Paul, Trench, Trübner & Co., 1904.

[6] Haran Chandra Bhattacharya, Kālasiddhāntadarśinī, Calcutta, 1941.

[7] S.N. Dasgupta, A History of Indian Philosophy I-V, Cambridge University Press, 1969.

[8] S. Radhakrishnan, Indian Philosophy I-II, Allen & Unwin, London-New York, 7th impr., 1962.

[9] H. Zimmer, Myths and Symbols in Indian Art and Civilization, Washington, 1946.

Saṅkhya-Yoga

[10] Yoga-Sūtra of Patañjali with the Bhāṣya of Vyāsa, the Tattvavaiśāradī of Vācaspati Miśra and the Vṛtti of Bhoja, a) Benares 1972, b) transl. by J.H. Woods, Motilal Banarsidass, Delhi, 1914, reprint, 1972.

[11] The Tattvakaumudī. Vācaspati Miśra's commentary on Sāṅkhya-Kārikā, text and transl. by Ganganath Jha, Poona, 1965.

[12] Sāṃkhyadarśanam, with the Sāṃkhyapravacana Bhāṣya of Vijñānabhikṣu, Kashi Sanskrit Series No. 67, 1928.

[13] Yuktidīpikā, ed. by R.C. Pandeya, Motilal Banarsidass, Delhi 1967.

[14] S.N. Dasgupta, Yoga Philosophy, Motilal Banarsidass, Calcutta, 1930, Reprint Delhi, 1974.

Nyāya-Vaiśeṣika

[15] Nyāya-Sūtra of Gotama, ed. by B.D. Basu, transl. by S.C. Vidyabhusana, Sacred books of the Hindus 8, Allahabad, 1913, cf. also [30].

[16] Nyāya-Bhāṣya of Vātsyayana, with extracts from Uddyotakara's Vārttika and Vācaspati Miśra's Tātparyaṭīkā, ed. by G.S. Tailanga, Vizianagram Sanskrit Series 9, Benares 1896 (cf. also [30]).

[17] a) Vaiśeṣika Sūtra of Kaṇāda, with Chandrakānta's Bhāṣya, ed. by Muni Śri Jambuvijayi, Gaekwood Oriental Series no. 136, Baroda 1961. b) Vaiśeṣika Sūtra of Kaṇāda, Upaskāra of Śaṅkara

Miśra, extracts from Jayanārāyana's Vivṛti and notes from Candrakānta's Bhāṣya, transl. by Nandalal Sinha, Sacred books of the Hindus 6, 2nd ed., Allahabad 1923.
[18] The Padārthatattvamirupaṇam of Ragunātha Śiromaṇi (A demonstration of the true nature of things to which words refer), Text, transl. and ed. by K. Potter, Harvard-Yenching Institute Studies XVII, Cambridge, Massachusetts, 1957.
[19] Praśastapādabhāṣya with commentary Nyāyakandalī of Śrīdharabhaṭṭa, Varanasī 1963.
[20] Praśastapādabhāṣyam, with the commentary Kiranāvalī of Udayanāchārya, ed. by J.S. Jetly, Oriental Institute, Baroda, 1971.
[21] Nyāyavārttikatātparyaṭīkā of Vācaspati Miśra, ed. by Rajeshwara Shastri Dravida, Kashi Sanskrit Series 24, 1925.
[22] Bhāṣā-Pariccheda with the Siddhāntamuktāvalī of Viśvanātha and the commentaries of Dinakara and Rāmarudra, Kashi Sanskrit Series 6, Benares, 1951.
[23] Ātmatattvaviveka of Udayanācārya, Chowkhamba Sanskrit Series, Benares, 1940.
[24] Nyāyakusumāñjali of Udayanācārya, Kashi Sanskrit Series 30, Varanasi, 1957.
[25] Tarkabhāṣā of Keśava Miśra, Bombay Sanskrit and Prakrit Series, 1937.
[26] Nyāyalīlāvatī of Vallabhāchārya, Chowkhamba Sanskrit Series, 1934.
[27] Nyāya-Mañjarī of Jayanta Bhaṭṭa, Kashi Sanskrit Series, 1936.
[28] S. Bhaduri, Studies in the Nyāya-Vaiśeṣika Metaphysics, Bhandarkar Oriental Research Institute Series 5, Poona, 1947.
[29] B. Faddegon, The Vaiśeṣika System, Amsterdam, 1918.
[30] Phanibhusana Tarkavagisa, Nyāyadarśana (in Bengali), vol. 1-5, Calcutta 1917-29.
[31] S.C. Chatterjee, The Nyāya Theory of Knowledge, Calcutta, 1939.

Pūrva Mīmāṃsā

[32] Ślokavārttika of Kumārila Bhaṭṭa, edit. by Rama Sastri, Chowkhamba Sanskrit Series 11, Benares 1898-99.
[33] Śāstradīpikā of Pārthasarāthi Miśra, Nirnaya Sagar Press, Bombay, 1915.
[34] Prakaraṇa Pañcikā of Śālikānātha Miśra, Benares Hindu University, 1961.
[35] Mānameyodaya of Nārāyaṇa, ed. and transl,. by C. Kunhan Raja and S. Suryanarayana Sastri, Theosophical Publishing House, Adyar, Madras, 1933.
[36] Ganganath Jha, Pūrva Mīmāṃsā, Benares Hindu University, 1942.
[37] Mīmāṃsā Sūtra of Jaimini, text and transl. by Ganganath Jha, Panini Office, Allahabad

Vedānta

[38] Saṅkara's Bhāṣya on Aitareya, Bṛhadāraṇyaka, Chāndogya, Īśā, Kaṭha, Kena, Māṇḍūkya, Muṇḍaka and Praśna Upaniṣad, ed. and transl. into Bengali, with Gauḍapāda's Māṇḍūkyakārikās, by Durgacarana Saṃkhyavedantatirtha and Anilacandra Datta, vol. 1-9, Calcutta 1911-21.
[39] Brahmasūtrabhāṣya of Śaṅkara, ed. with Vācaspati Miśra's Bhāmatī, Amalānanda's Kalpataru and Appaya Dīkṣita's Parimala, by N.S. Anantakrishna Sastri and V.L.S. Pansikar, Bombay 1948.
[40] Brahma Sūtra with Śaṅkara's commentary, transl. by G. Thibaut, Sacred books of the East, vol. XXXIV, Oxford, 1890.
[41] Tattvapradīpikā of Citsukha, Benares, 1974.

[42] Pañcadaśī of Vidyāraṇya Swami, text and transl. by Swami Swahananda, Sri Ramakrishna Math., Madras, 1967.

[43] Advaitasiddhi of Madhusūdana Sarasvatī, with Gauda Brahmānandi, 2nd ed., Bombay, 1937.

[44] Vedāntaparibhāṣa of Dharmaraja Dikṣita, text and transl. by Swami Madhavananda, Advaita Ashram, Calcutta, 1963.

[45] Khaṇḍaṇakhaṇḍakhādya of Śrī Harṣa, Chowkhamba Sanskrit Series, 1970.

[46] Asutosh Bhattacharya, Vedāntadarśan-advaitavād (in Bengali). Three volumes, Calcutta. n.d.

[47] T.M.P. Mahadevan, The Philosophy of Advaita, Luzac & Co., 1938.

[48] K.S. Murty, Revelation and Reason in Advaita Vedānta, Motilal Banarsidass, Reprint 1974.

[49] T.R.V. Murti, The two definitions of Brahman in the Advaita, in K.C. Bhattacharya Memorial Volume, Indian Institute of Philosophy, Amalner, 1958.

[50] A.G. Warrier, The concept of Mukti in Advaita Vedanta, University of Madras, 1961.

Buddhism

[51] Abhidharmakośa and Bhaṣya of Vasubandhu with Sphutārthā commentary of Ācārya Yasomitra I-II, ed. by Swami Dwarikadas Shastri, Bauddha Bharati, Varanasi, 1971.

[52] Vijñaptimātratāsiddhi par Vasubandhu, Viṃśatikā et Triṃśikā, Publiés et traduits par Sylvain Lévi, Champion, Paris, 1925-32.

[53] Pramāṇavārttika of Dharmakirti, Edited by Rahula Sankrityāyana, Kitāb Mahal, Allahabad, 1943.

[54] Tattvasaṃgraha of Śāntarakṣita, with the commentary Pañjikā of Kamalaśīla, ed. by Swami Dwarikadas Shastri, Bauddha Bharati, Varanasi, 1968.

[55] Milinda Pañha, Les questions de Milinda, traduit de Pali par Louis Finot, Paris-Bossard, 1923.

[56] Mādhyamika Kārikā of Nāgārjuna, ed. by L. de la Vallée Poussin, St. Petersborg, 1907.

[57] Madhyamakśāstra of Nāgārjuna, with the commentary Prasannapadā by Chandrakirti, ed. by P.L. Vaidya, Dharbanga, 1960.

[58] Bu-Ston, History of Buddhism 1-2, transl. from Tibetan by E. Obermiller, Heidelberg, 1931.

[59] A. Chatterjee, Yogacara Idealism, Varanasi, 1962.

[60] A.K. Bhattacharya, Vaibhāṣika Darśana, Calcutta, 1955.

[61] S. Mookherjee, The Buddhist Philosophy of Universal Flux, Delhi, 1935, reprinted, 1975.

[62] T.R.V. Murti, The Central Philosophy of Buddhism, Allen & Unwin, London, 1955.

[63] Th. Stcherbatsky, Buddhist Logic Vol. I, Dover publications, New York, first published 1962.

[64] Th. Stcherbatsky, The Conception of Buddhist Nirvāṇa, Leningrad, 1927.

[65] Th. Stcherbatsky, The Soul Theory of the Buddhists, Bulletin de L'Academie des Sciences de Russie. Petrograd 1919.

Jainism

[66] Dravya-Saṃgraha of Nemichandra Siddhanta, ed. and transl. with Brahmadeva's Vṛtti and editor's commentary, by Sarat Chandra Ghoshal, Sacred books of the Jainas 1, 1917.

[67] Tattvārthādhigama Sūtra of Umāsvati Acharya, The Sacred books of the Jainas vol. 2, A.M.S. Press, New York, 1974.

[68] Pañcāstikāyasāra of Kundakundāchārya, The Sacred Books of the Jainas vol. 3, Arrah, 1920, Reprint New York, 1974.

[69] Prameyakamalamārtaṇḍa of Prabhāchandrāchārya, Bombay, 1912.
[70] Jaina Sūtras, Sacred books of the East vol. 22, 45, transl. from Prākrit by Hermann Jacobi, Delhi 1964.
[71] Syad-Vāda-Mañjarī of Sri Mallisenasuri, transl. and annotated by F.W. Thomas, Delhi, 1968.

Indian Philosophy of Language

[72] Vyākaraṇa-Mahābhāṣya of Patañjali, University of Poona, 1968-75.
[73] Vaiākaraṇabhuṣaṇasāra of Kunda Bhaṭṭa, Benares, 1947
[74] The Kālasamuddeśa of Bhartṛhari's Vākyapadīya, transl. by Peri Sarveswara Sharma, Motilal Banarsidass, Delhi, 1972.
[75] The Vākyapadīya of Bhartṛhari, transl. with exegetical notes by K.A. Subramania Iyer, a) Ch. I 1965, Ch. III pt. i 1971, Poona, Deccan College, b) Ch. III pt. (ii) Motilal Banarsidass, Delhi, 1972.
[76] K.A. Subramania Iyer, Bhartṛhari, A study of the Vākyapadīya in the light of the ancient commentaries, Poona, 1969.
[77] G.N. Sastri, Philosophy of word and meaning 1, Calcutta Sanskrit College Research Series No. 5, 1959.

Greek Philosophy

[78] Plato, Timaeus, transl. by R.D. Archer, MacMillan, London, 1888.
[79] Aristotle, The Physics, with an English transl. by Philip H. Wicksteed and Francis M. Cornford, London, Heinemann, Cambridge, Mass., Harvard Univ. Press, 1957-60.
[80] Aristotle, Metaphysics, transl. by Kirwan, Oxford, 1971.
[81] Aristotle, On the Heavens, with an English transl. by W.K.C. Guthrie, London, Heinemann, Cambridge, Mass., Harvard Univ. Press, 1960.
[82] Aristotle, Problems, with an English transl. by W.S. Hett, London, Heinemann, Cambridge, Mass., Harvard Univ. Press, 1957-61.
[83] J. Burnet, Early Greek Philosophy, 3rd ed., 1920.
[84] W.T. Stace, A critical History of Greek Philosophy, London, MacMillan, Niew York, St. Martin, 1960.
[85] E. Zeller, Outlines of the History of Greek Philosophy, 13th ed., Routledge & Keagan, London, 1969.

Western Philosophy and Theology

[86] Philo I, transl. by F.H. Colson and G.H. Whittaker, London, first printed 1929.
[87] Augustine, The Confessions, transl. by E.B. Pusey, New York 1957.
[88] Augustine, De Civitate Dei, transl. by P. Levine, Heinemann, London, Harvard Univ. Press, Camb. Mass., 1966.
[89] H. Bergson, L'essai sur les données immédiates de la Conscience, Paris, 1889.

[90] G. Florovsky, Creation and Redemption, Collected works vol. 3, Belmont, Mass. Nordland, 1976.
[91] Erich Frank, Philosophical Understanding and Religious Truth, Oxford 1945.
[92] Martin Heidegger, Sein und Zeit, Jahrbuch für Philosophie und Phänomenologische Forschung Band 8, Halle 1927.
[93] Edmund Husserl, The Phenomenology of Internal Time-Consciousness, Indiana University Press, 1964.
[94] Immanuel Kant, Critique of Pure Reason, transl. by Kemp-Smith, London, 1970.
[95] John Locke, Essay concerning Human Understanding, London, 1965.
[96] K.E. Løgstrup, Skabelse og tilintetgørelse, Metafysik IV, Gyldendal, 1978.
[97] Isaac Newton, Philosophiae naturalis Principia Mathematica, London, 1687.
[98] J.-P. Sartre, L'Etre et le Néant, Bibliothéque des Idées, Paris, Gallimard, 1943. English transl. "Being and Nothingness", Philosophical Library, New York, 1956.
[99] J.G. Whitrow, The Structure and Evolution of the Universe, New York, 1959.

General and Comparative Philosophy

[100] A.N. Balslev, Une étude comparée de quelques thémes philosophiques proposés par l'Existentialisme et le Bouddhisme, Thése, Paris, 1968.
[101] K.C. Bhattacharya, Studies in Philosophy, Calcutta, 1956.
[102] J.T. Fraser, F.C. Haber, G.H. Müller, eds., The Study of Time I-IV, Berlin-Heidelberg 1972-81.
[103] A. Toynbee, A Study of History, revised and abridged by the author and Jane Caplan, Oxford University Press, New York 1972.
[104] Sanskrit-English Dictionary by Monier Williams, 1st ed., Oxford University Press, 4th reprint, Motilal Banarsidass, 1974.
[105] The Encyclopedia of Philosophy, Editor in Chief Paul Edwards, the McMillan Company and the Free Press, New York, 1967.

Indian Philosophy. Supplementary Bibliography

[106] A.N. Balslev, An over-all view of the Problem of Time in Indian Philosophy, Indologica Taurinensia 1983, to appear.
[107] André Bareau, The notion of time in early Buddhism, East and West 7, 1957, 353-364.
[108] J.A.B. Van Buitenen, Studies in Sāṃkhya, J. Amer. Oriental Soc. 76, 1956, 153-157; 77, 1957, 15-25, 88-107.
[109] Edward Conze, Buddhist Thought in India, London 1962.
[110] Mircea Eliade, Le temps et l'éternité dans la pensée Indienne, Eranos Jahrbuch 1951, Band xx, Zürich 1952, p. 219-259.
[111] Erich Frauwallner, Geschichte der Indischen Philosophie, Two volumes, Salzburg 1953, 1956.
[112] A.B. Keith, The Saṃkhya System, Calcutta 1924, 1949.
[113] Étienne Lamotte, Histoire du Bouddhisme Indien, Louvain 1958.
[114] T.M.P. Mahadevan, Time and the Timeless, Principal Miller Lectures 1953, Madras 1954.
[115] K.K. Mandal, A Comparative Study of the Concepts of Time and Space in Indian Thought, Varanasi, 1968.

[116] Karl H. Potter, Editor, The Encyclopedia of Indian Philosophies, Vol. I-II, Motilal Banarsidass 1970.

[117] S. Schayer, Contributions to the Problem of Time in Indian Philosophy. Mémoires de la commission orientaliste no. 31, p. 1-76, Polish Academy Krakow 1938.

[118] Shri Mahavir Jaina Vidyalaya Golden Jubilee Volume Part I, Bombay 1968.

[119] Lilian Silburn, Instant et Cause. Le Discontinu dans la pensée philosophique de l'Inde. Paris 1955.

[120] E.J. Thomas, History of Buddhist Thought, London 1933.

Index